ENDORSEMENTS

"Moving. Emotional. Inspirational. Smith paints a real-life master-piece with words that causes us to grasp for breath one moment, then imparts hope to take our breath away the next. A must read."

Erin Campbell,
Water through the Word Ministries

"I really enjoyed reading *Whispered Truth*, a mother's heart came through very powerfully. *Whispered Truth* actually shouts truth to the reader—a truth that assures one of God's incredible love, forgiveness and healing in one of the most difficult situations in life.

While the names have been changed, this is a real account of one woman's journey out of domestic abuse and the additional horror of sexual abuse and the devastating effects that followed. You will be deeply touched by God's faithfulness to gently and powerfully bring miraculous restoration."

Dianne Leman, Senior Pastor
The Vineyard Church of Central Illinois, Urbana IL
Executive Team Vineyard Churches of America

"Cindy L. Smith has done a wonderful job of describing the trauma of abuse. Through this compelling story, she highlights the signs and symptoms of abuse of women and children.

Sadly, she also paints a realistic picture as to how difficult it can be to be heard and to receive the appropriate help. I hope and pray that through this book, victims of abuse will feel understood and find hope. *Whispered Truth* is a reminder to those like me who offer help, the importance of believing and acting when our clients attempt to tell us about abuse.

I so appreciate Cindy's courage and passion to make a real difference for women and children. She reminds us that there is always hope!"

Barbara Steffens PhD,
Licensed Professional Clinical Counselor (Ohio)

Whispered Truth

"Your story could be the key that unlocks someone else's prison. Don't be afraid to share it."
Unknown

Cindy L. Smith

Whispered Truth is the 1st book
in the Truth, Trust, Treasure series

Whispered Truth

© 2019 by Cindy L. Smith

Publisher: Living Hope for Today
www.livinghopefortoday.org

Cover Design: Alicia Redmond, www.thecovergirlsdesigns.com
Artwork: Kay Worz and Cami Bradford
Editor: Deborah A. Gaston, www.deborahgaston.com
Interior Design: Donna Amos, Solopreneur Solutions

ISBN: 978-1-7324634-1-7 (paperback)
Library of Congress Cataloging-in-Publication Data: 2018949387

1) Fiction based on a true story   2) Abuse Prevention   3) Spirituality
4) Miracles   5) Empowerment   6) Forgiveness 6) Hope

Book may also be purchased in bulk from Living Hope for Today, PO Box 11545, Cincinnati, Ohio 45211, www.whisperedtruth.com

Printed in the United States of America

Dedication

To Jesus who healed me through His shed blood, the Holy Spirit who gave me understanding and led me to the truth and to God my perfect Father.

To my children, someday I hope you can appreciate my younger self and the story that needed to be told. I love all of you beyond measure; only God loves you more!

To the love of my life, my husband, who has been my best friend for over thirty years. Your love truly lifted me out of the pit! Life hasn't always been a fairytale, but you are my knight in shining armor who carried me through it all!

To the women and children who once resided at Living Hope Transitional Homes.

To Jordan, I believed you and fought hard to protect you. Maybe in the future *they* will listen and keep children safe.

To all women who have walked through the valley of abuse and found victory in healing on the other side of the mountain. My hope in sharing my story is that you too will find a God of unconditional love and healing in your own story.

"Be strong and courageous. Don't be fearful or discouraged, because the Lord your God is with you wherever you go."

~ Joshua 1:9 NLT

CHAPTER 1

October 1984

Breathe, Denise! Stop being so paranoid! I told myself as I ducked behind the truck at the sight of a slow-approaching car. *Pull it together. After all, you have the car and Doyle has no reason to come home before his work-day ends. Breathe!! This is going to work.*

I hoisted the huge box of clothes into the truck of my friend and closest confidante, MariLu Short. Sweat crept down my forehead, stinging my eyes. I squinted at the bright sun, trying to determine how much daylight was left. I knew I had to leave before dark or I'd never find my way through the back roads that led to MariLu's house.

I swept back a wisp of blonde hair that refused to stay in my ponytail. A jolting vision flashed before me: Doyle storming through the front door. I could almost hear him scream, "Denise, what the hell are you doing with all *our* stuff packed in that truck in the driveway?"

Breathe!! It's just your imagination!

I trudged back into our brick ranch, dry autumn leaves crunching under my feet. In the family room, I picked up a stuffed Minnie Mouse that belonged to our three-year-old daughter. The moment Jaime discovered it under the Christmas tree last year, she'd given Minnie a tight hug, then danced around the room and sang the cartoon's theme song. A giggling Samantha, our sixteen month old, had waddled up to Jaime to see what all the commotion was about. Just the image warmed me inside for a moment.

I looked around the big family room and a wave of sorrow hit me. The girls would no longer play here or romp in the backyard. We had looked for a home with a huge yard for the girls to play in. We'd spent so many hours of laughter, jumping rope, playing hide and seek. I looked down at my arm and was jolted back to reality. The sight of the black and blue marks trailing down my arms and the ache in my muscles strengthened my resolve. I had to leave.

I looked through the kitchen, deciding what I needed to take. The bakeware and dishes were wedding gifts from my family, so rightfully they were mine. There wasn't much time left to get the rest of the things we needed. The sun would be setting soon.

After filling a cardboard box, I went into the family room to finish packing toys. A loud ring pierced the quiet, sending a rubber ball flying out of my hand. It came crashing down on top of a single red rose in a crystal vase, leaving shards of glass and red velvet petals on the table and floor. A shiver ran down my spine. The rose had been Doyle's sorry attempt to convince me to "forget" his latest eruption, and the vase was a present from his mom. The irony did not escape me. It was the perfect depiction of our marriage.

I clutched my chest to calm my pounding heart. The phone rang again. *What if Doyle's calling?* He would expect me to be home. But he never called from work.

Breathe! It could be anyone.

I picked up the receiver. "Hello," I said, with forced cheerfulness.

"Hey, honey. What are you doing?" Doyle inquired in a syrupy voice.

The receiver nearly slid out of my sweaty palm. Doyle *never* called me honey. Did he know what I was doing? How could he?

"Nothing. Why?"

"I just wanted to know if you'd do me a favor. Could you bring me the stash of money that I put away for Christmas gifts? There's a sale today at Maupin's and I want to get a new suit during my dinner break."

Relief washed over me. "Of course. Be there in a few."

I felt the room spin and fade as I hung up the phone. Flecks of light shot at me from my peripheral vision and I slid down the wall. I put my head between my legs, determined not to faint. When the spinning stopped, I lifted my head. My stomach rumbled, reminding me I hadn't eaten all day. I'd lost thirty pounds in the last three months and now, where there once had been curves, my clothes loosely draped my twig-like frame. For the sake of my girls, I had to take better care of myself. But I didn't have time to think about that now. I had to get to Doyle's office before he suspected something.

I fought to get up, then tugged at the drawstring on my pants to tighten it. I found the granola I'd stuffed into my purse that morning and nibbled on it while walking down the hall to our bedroom. Doyle was a bit OCD – everything was neatly in its proper place, which made packing my things easy. The dark, four-poster wooden bed and the matching dresser and desk had been his when we got married. I'd be happy to leave them behind, along with the ugly rust-and-brown-plaid couch.

Every item I packed brought back a chilling memory. I vividly recalled the day he stormed off into our bedroom and, in one fell swoop, knocked everything off my dresser. When I walked in after him to find out why he was so upset, he picked up a perfume bottle and threw it at me, yelling, "Dinner should be ready to eat by 6 … every night!" I shook my head to release the memory so I could focus on the task at hand. The desk drawer rattled and shook as I got the money out. I shoved the money in my pocket, glanced at my Timex and hurried down the hall.

Searching frantically around the living room for my windbreaker, something caught my eye. I walked over to the end table and gingerly picked up a shard of glass that had pierced the middle of a rose petal. I gasped as I viewed the haunting image from every angle. It was my wounded heart, stabbed so many times by his angry words. I freed the velvet rose petal and rubbed it between my forefinger and thumb, then threw the tiny weapon to the ground. A boldness grew in me as I spied my windbreaker behind the lazy boy chair. I had to cover up the massive bruising or risk interrogation from Doyle's employees.

I pulled it on, put the rose petal in my pocket, grabbed my purse, and walked out the door.

MariLu and her brother, Jerry, would be here in less than thirty minutes to drive the truck to my parents' house and unload it for me. Shifting the gear of my silver Fiesta into drive, I took deep breaths to try and calm my nerves. Then I headed to Nobel's Jewelry Store at nearly breakneck speed. I'd learned it wasn't wise to keep Doyle waiting. Not that he'd physically harm me in front of his employees. No, he'd never risk his good-guy image. But I also knew that behind closed doors, I'd endure a verbal lashing and a reminder of my incompetence. I didn't want to hear it.

I zoomed into the nearest parking space, slammed the car door and made my way inside. The store wasn't crowded. It rarely was this time of day. Zigzagging through the store, I ignored the sideway glances and a wave from a sales person as I headed to the back towards Doyle's office. He almost plowed into me when he came around the corner. "Whoa. You're in a hurry!" He beamed at me.

"Couldn't wait to see me, huh? Thanks for bringing up the money. Where are the girls?"

Oh crap. It never entered my mind that he would ask where the girls were!

Panic set in. Doyle knew my mom never kept the girls because she was always so busy with golf, bowling or her bridge club, and I was not a good liar. Suppressing the urge to run, I said the first thing that came to mind. "Oh, my mom stopped by just before you called to drop off a book I'd left at her house. She offered to stay with them while I ran up here."

Now I am a liar! I held my breath.

"Oh, OK. Well, have fun with your mom. Remember, I'm closing the store tonight. So, you'll need to pick me up at 10."

"Got it."

He doesn't suspect a thing I thought as I exited the store as composed as possible.

I sat in the car, gripping the steering wheel tightly for a few seconds. I rolled down the windows, and as I drove off, I peered through the rearview mirror to see the Nobel's Jewelry Store sign fading from view. The familiar fear that had lurked like a lion waiting to pounce, controlling my every move, was gone! A fresh, delightful breeze wafted through the car, my pulse slowed, the black grip of fear released me, and I sailed away free from his fierce control. Now all I had to do was quickly gather the last few things at the house.

A tear trickled down my cheek. There would be no happy-ever-after for us.

*"Everyone is a moon and has a dark side
which he never shows to anyone."*

~ Mark Twain

CHAPTER 2

A Week Earlier

"Couldn't you keep them quiet for another hour?" scowled a bedraggled Doyle, shuffling out of our bedroom. "My tee time isn't until ten."

"I'm sorry. I was trying," I apologized, my voice feigning strength.

"Really? You could have fooled me!" he snorted as he stomped into the bathroom.

My stomach tightened. I scampered into the kitchen and pulled out the coffee maker. Maybe breakfast would make him happy. All of a sudden, I heard screeching and then, out the corner of my eye, I saw Doyle bouncing into the family room acting like a crazed gorilla, growling at the girls, making them shriek with laughter. I poured batter into the waffle maker, my mood lifted from the antics I heard coming from the family room. Doyle really was a kid at heart and loved playing with the girls.

I had been a very naïve, impressionable nineteen-year-old when I met this man who was eight years my senior. Doyle Boese managed Nobel's Jewelry Store, where I'd landed a job just days after moving to Missouri from Texas. We'd moved because my father's job had transferred him. From the moment I witnessed Doyle work his magic, seducing a customer into buying just about every piece of expensive jewelry in the store, I was infatuated. Oozing confidence, he would lean into the customer, joking, "This newly created design will get you noticed from across the room at your next party." Eyebrow raised, he'd wink. "It's sure to compel any admirer to come over and explore your beauty." Falling for the lure, hook, line and sinker, the customer giggled like a school girl, admired herself wearing the piece he had fastened around her neck, then add coyly, "How can I pass up on such a stunning charm that will help me cast spells on unsuspecting admirers? I'll take it!" The magnificent piece now adorned her chest as she walked out of the store minutes later.

"Hmmmm," MariLu, better known as Loui, my fellow customer service rep, had chortled one afternoon. "I do believe that man is a bit smitten with you. He seems to find any excuse to make his way to the diamond counter, and I'm pretty sure he is not drawn by *my* dazzling beauty. My dear, he has his eyes on you!"

"No, he's just being nice," I replied, hoping Loui hadn't notice that I was, in fact, the smitten one. Each time he sauntered our way, my heart pounded, my stomach fluttered, my face flushed. He'd lean his tall, muscular frame on the counter, sweeping his hand through his jet-black wavy hair, and bore through my soul with his piercing sky-blue eyes which were magnified by his pale complexion. And he had the most intoxicating baritone voice! A simple "hello" in that deep, sensual voice made my knees weak and everything in me melted. He was the most handsome, mesmeric man my nineteen-year-old eyes had ever seen, and I was drawn to him. I just couldn't imagine that he could really be interested in me. I never imagined we'd ever become more than co-workers.

And then it happened. He asked me out. Doyle's charming smile captivated me on that first date, and his sense of humor made me laugh until my side hurt. He was a perfect gentleman; opening car doors for me, pulling out my chair, even ordering my dinner for me. He made me feel safe and significant, something I'd never really felt before. He lavished me with compliments and was so focused on me that even in the crowded five-star restaurant, I felt as if I were not only the most beautiful woman in the room, but also the *only* woman in the room. We talked about everything. He was so intelligent, so sophisticated, so knowledgeable on a multitude of topics, and he seemed to genuinely care about the things that interested me. He got me to talk about my family, my dreams and desires. But when I asked about his family, emptiness filled his eyes.

"I prefer not to talk about my family. Let's just say I witnessed some bad things growing up. My parents didn't have the most loving relationship. I hated the way my dad controlled my mother – even picking out her clothes, never wanting to let her out of his sight. I hated even more that she let him." He seemed to drift into some deep hole as he spoke. Then suddenly, he chuckled, "Aaahh! No more talk of the past. What matters most is you and this moment."

We began seeing one another on a regular basis. He wined and dined me. Doyle was so gentle with me -- his hand on the small of my back, directing my steps around the dance floor, whispering compliments in my ear – all the things a girl likes to hear, wants to hear to make her feel beautiful and desirable. And the candlelit dinners while being serenaded by romantic tunes on a piano. He'd even attempted to sing to me, "You are the sunshine of my life." Who could resist such attention?

But it all came to an abrupt end three months later.

"NO! I will not have an abortion!" I protested after I'd told Doyle I was pregnant. When he proposed marriage a week later, I convinced myself he really did love me and had only suggested terminating the pregnancy out of a moment of fear.

We'd only been newlyweds for three weeks when the anger that had been simmering just below the surface finally erupted. He'd arrived at the mall early to pick me up from work and saw me laughing with my boss and co-worker. The moment I got in the car, before I had time to fasten my seatbelt, he'd jammed his foot on the gas pedal with such force that I was propelled into the dashboard. I'd seen him angry before, but this was something foreign to me. This was pure, unfiltered rage. The out-of-control vehicle spun across the parking lot that was blanketed with snow, while Doyle voiced his displeasure at what he had witnessed. I'd chalked it up to unfounded jealousy and tried to be optimistic that as our marriage progressed, it would become less turbulent and more peaceful. Then two years later, I found out I was pregnant with Samantha and his control tightened.

I had recently coerced him into going to counseling by threatening to leave him after one of his especially abusive tirades, but he found a way during the session to make everything my fault.

Sandy Sawyer, our counselor, made small talk to help us feel comfortable, and then she asked us about our marriage and how we handled conflict. I was too scared to bring up the abuse and he made jokes to divert the conversation to unimportant things - - everyday things, like how I didn't keep the house clean enough and that I was always tired and in bed when he got home from work at 11:00. He admitted that he only came to counseling to appease me.

She then asked about our communication. When I brought up my frustration that he didn't share his feelings about anything going on in our life, he brushed it off, saying I made too big a deal out of everything. He skated around every issue that came up and deflected the attention onto things he perceived to be wrong with me. We'd quit going after three sessions. Maybe he was right.

Maybe I needed to try harder to fix our marriage. Maybe the problem was all me.

I decided to continue seeing Sandy by myself. In our first session she probed, "You have shared that you and your twin sister Diane were adopted at five days old. How does that make you feel?"

"Rejected. I don't fit into my parents' world. They tell me I wear my emotions on my sleeve and it makes me think something is wrong with me. And I feel abandoned by my birth mom who just gave us away to strangers."

"How did having an identical twin sister make you feel?"

"The adoption attorney told my parents they didn't have to take both of us." My eyes filled with tears. "I would have been lost without Diane. We did everything together and having each other filled a vast void in my life and made the abuse we suffered through bearable."

Sandy helped me understand that I craved love at any cost. I believed that the mother that gave me life couldn't give me the deep abiding love I so desperately needed. And I didn't receive from my alcoholic parents the unconditional love that erases rejection. Once I was able to accept that, the healing process started.

During one session Sandy asked, "How does Doyle's dad treat his mom?" Our first date and Doyle's moment of vulnerability flashed through my mind. "Doyle doesn't talk much about his parents. I can only remember one time he opened up a little about how controlling his father was. I never met his father. He died when Doyle was nineteen. His mother is great with the girls and kind to me, almost . . . well, almost sympathetic. I think she knows how he treats me. But we never talk about it. She loves her son and . . . I don't think she'd ever expose him."

"Most people," Sandy explained, "learn how to treat each other from their family of origin. Doyle is most likely repeating with you the pattern he witnessed in his parents' relationship. Do you think that's what you have been experiencing?"

It was as if a bright light bulb had just been turned on and for the first time I was starting to realize I wasn't the cause of our disastrous marriage! No matter how much I'd try to change, things wouldn't get better if he didn't change. But he was a good dad. He loved the girls and was good with them. That had to count for something.

The ready light from the waffle maker brought me back into the present. "Are there any hungry chimpanzees? Breakfast is served!"

The girls came bouncing over to the table, still playing their roles as they devoured their waffles. "Now, let's eat like human girls. Then you can go back to playing in the jungle." Doyle poured a cup of coffee and sat down.

"What time do I need to drop you off at the golf course?" I asked. He shot me a stern look.

"I'm sorry. I wanted to get some things at the grocery store." My heart started to pound. *Why had I assumed? Why had I even asked?*

"Never mind," I quickly added. "No big deal. I can find something here to fix for dinner. You go and have fun. Play 18 holes. Go to dinner with the guys afterward."

Lord, please let that appease him and please don't let him drink too much on the course.

His unblinking eyes bore into me. "That's what I was planning on doing," he snapped in a tight, monotone voice. He leaned back in his chair, hands clasped behind his head, challenging me. "Besides, don't you have a lot of cleaning and laundry to do around here? That should keep you plenty busy." He smirked and added, "And having the car would only be a distraction from what you really need to be doing on 'the list'."

The List. The mere thought paralyzed me. Just last week when he arrived home from work, he had verbally outlined cleaning chores he assumed I would have completed by that time. He put on white gloves and proceeded to wipe down the tops of the door casings while he yelled obscenities at the top of his lungs as the dust flew. He then stomped to the bathroom and ripped the toilet paper holder off the wall because the paper was hung in the wrong direction. I cowered in the family room, waiting for the tirade to end, praying the girls would not wake up.

Forcing the memory from my mind, I silently cleared the table. I felt Doyle's eyes follow me as I moved to the sink. Any response in this moment could prove dangerous. So, I just nodded and went back to washing the dishes. I anxiously listened for his footsteps as he walked away. A sigh escaped from my lips when I heard him tramp down the hall to get dressed.

A few minutes later, Doyle appeared from behind, causing me to shriek. He bent down, kissed my neck, sending goose bumps down my spine. "You'll have my undivided attention when I get home. Have a great day," he hissed seductively, before turning to leave. The door closed behind him and I felt free to expel the deep breath I was holding.

I was determined to push his comment from my mind and focus on my precious time alone with the girls. We would get some fresh air at the park before lunch. Experiencing the world through their eyes while they played was a wonderful escape. Samantha loved to chase ducks while Jaime swung, pumping her little legs so hard she'd reach the sky! This was my salve for the physical and emotional wounds inflicted by Doyle. Then I would put them down for naps and clean, do laundry and pray that I would miss nothing on *the list*.

Peering out the bathroom window as the light grew dim, I witnessed the end of a spectacular pink and purple sunset. I held onto the calming picture in my mind and tested the bath water to make sure it was just right. "Jaime! Samantha! Time to play with your toys in the tub," I called. Dinner dishes and one last load of laundry had been completed. Last on the agenda for the night: a bedtime story and prayers.

Once the girls were tucked in and sound asleep, I got cozy in bed to read my latest novel before Doyle got home. It wasn't long before I felt the book slip from my hand as I dozed off. I was slipping, slipping more deeply into a place of sweet reverie, a dream world where all was peaceful, bright, full of hope. I could see the girls running through a meadow of sunflowers, giggling as they attempted to hide from me. They were so free and filled with joy, and I was light and at ease. I ran after them and finally catching them, we all roll in the grass with uproarious laughter. This is what I wanted for them always. Happiness, laughter, wonder and delight, not the trepidation and pain that had become my life. I would do everything in my power to protect them and assure that their lives would be so different from mine.

I was jolted from my dream by the thud of the front door and footsteps galumphing down the dimly lit hallway. Just as I sat up, Doyle tripped through the doorway and landed on the floor. I jumped out of bed to help him and gagged from the stench of alcohol that seemed to cover him like a shroud. He made no effort to get up. He just lay there with his eyes shut and an idiotic grin on his face while he belted out a poor rendition of Kool and the Gang—both loud and off key. "Celebrate Good Times. Come on!" he wailed, getting louder and louder as I pleaded with him to stop.

Please, Lord, don't let the girls wake up. I stood over him grabbing his hands trying to pull him into a sitting position; he was nothing but dead weight. If he slept on the floor the rest of the night, it would be my fault and I'd bear the bruises for it.

I turned to glance at the clock. 3:00 a.m. He'd been wailing for over thirty minutes and I was exhausted. This foolishness had to stop.

I went to the bathroom and filled a glass with water. Then I stood over my inebriated husband, slowly pouring it on his face, hoping to sober him up so he could get to bed in his own power. He sobered up, all right. Immediately. A storm brewed in his eyes, and his contorted face flushed red.

I ran out of the room and down the hall to escape his ire. No longer in a full drunken state, Doyle moved like a panther after its prey. He caught up with me and grabbed my t-shirt with so much force that it ripped. Before I knew it, the panther pounced on top of me, his hands around my neck, choking me. One of his thumbs was close to my mouth, so I bit it, and he released me.

"You piece of trash!" he hollered, sucking his injured thumb. Then in a calm, calculated voice he hissed, "I will kill you. Do you understand me? *I... will... kill... you!*"

I started crying hysterically, barely able to breathe. He finally let go of me and turned to go into the bathroom to tend to his wound. I darted to the front door, grabbing my purse on the way out.

I've left my precious girls with a monster, I thought as I sat in our car. *Lord, please just let him go to bed and pass out! He's never physically hurt the girls before. But what if his ranting wakes them? What if Jaime ventures into our bedroom! Who knows what he might do in his drunken rage?*

Why hadn't I pay attention to the warning signs before we got married? Was I that taken in by his smile, his sweet promises that he would never hurt me like he did that first time?

The vivid memory flooded my mind. I was in the kitchen browning the rice so I could put it in the oven to finish cooking when he came in and put his arms around my waist. He started gently kissing the nape of my neck, suggesting we continue this in the other room.

I laughingly responded, "I've got to get this done before it burns, or dinner will be ruined. Can't you wait?" The rage inside burst. He went to the closet, picked up my night shirt and started ripping it to sheds. Then he came back into the kitchen ranting at me that he was more important than dinner!

Was I that blinded by love or. . . Why did I stay? How could I continue to endanger my life and my daughters' lives?

A ray of sunlight came through the windshield, causing me squint and blink. *Where was I?* My aching muscles screamed as I tried to sit up. Scenes of the nightmare flashed through my mind, jarring me awake. I had to go inside to make sure the girls were all right. I got out of the car, stretching my cramped, sore body into an upright position. I gently closed the car door and headed to the house. When I peeked around the front door, I saw Jaime sitting at the table. The minute she saw me, she left her half-eaten waffle and ran to me to give me a big hug. "Where were you, Mommy?"

"I... I had to go to the store, but silly Mommy went too early and they weren't open," I explained, pulling at my collar to hide the marks on my neck. I walked toward the kitchen table, gave Samantha a kiss on her forehead, and silently thanked God that they were unharmed.

Doyle sat there grinning like a Cheshire cat as if nothing had happened. He joked and laughed with the girls. And yet one stealthy glance from the piercing darkness in his eyes told me I had crossed him, and if I did it again, he would make good on his promise. I forced a smile, breathing deeply, then turned to go down the hall. Just as I closed the bathroom door, the deluge of tears erupted before I could stop them.

I've lived through enough terror. What damage am I doing to my precious ones by exposing them to such abusive behavior? But what could I do with only a high school education? The income from a retail job would never be enough support us.

So many times, I'd thought of leaving him, but every time all I envisioned was my babies living in deplorable conditions – maybe even in a shack. Now I realized even that shack looked like heaven compared to what I was living through. I needed a plan, a way of escape.

I had even turned to God a few weeks after he hit me for the first time by starting to go to church. I had confided in the pastor who had counseled us before we got married. I told him about Doyle's anger, but I got the impression that either he wasn't experienced in dealing with such situations or he just didn't want to get involved. He offered some religious platitudes that meant little to me. "It's probably nothing but anxiety that comes just before marriage and a child. But I suggest you go ahead with your plans to marry. Your baby needs both parents. Pray, Denise! Just pray and God will work it all out!" he'd said. I'd thought, *Why would God rescue me anyway? After all, I had gotten pregnant out of wedlock. I had made the bad decision to marry Doyle. I felt like I was on my own.*

Later that morning, I played the devoted wife and drove Doyle to work. I even gave him a peck on the cheek as he got out of the car. Then I stopped by the bank to make a withdrawal. I left Doyle enough money to live on and to cover the outstanding checks I had written to pay the bills that were due. During Jaime and Samantha's nap, I started making phone calls to put my plan in motion. I would make my escape the next day while Doyle worked a twelve-hour shift.

I dialed my mother's number. She answered on the first ring as if she'd been anticipating a call.

"Hello," she chirped.

"Hi, Mom. How are you? I need to ask you a big favor."

"Denise? Is that you?"

"Yes, Mom."

"You know you and Diane sound exactly alike on the phone, and I was expecting a call from your twin sister this morning," she added, a bit irritated.

"Sorry I didn't identify myself, Mom. I'm under a lot of stress... It's a long story, but I am leaving Doyle. Can you watch the girls tomorrow while I pack up some of our things?"

There was a long pause. "I know you and Doyle have had your differences, but do you really want to leave? You just got settled in that nice house ten months ago. And bought furniture and appliances!" she insisted.

"Yes, Mom, I know. But I've made up my mind. And right now, I could care less about that stuff," I retorted.

Another pause. "You aren't coming here, are you?"

"No. I wouldn't put you and Dad in that position. I know Doyle may try to find us and I don't want that to happen until his anger blows over. I am sure Loui will let us stay with her over the weekend. Then I would like to come to your house on Monday. Can I store our things in a corner of your garage?"

"Sure," she answered with a hint of reluctance.

"Thanks. I think we'll only need to stay with you for a month until I can get a job and find an apartment." I explained.

"Then you have decided to get a divorce?"

"Yes, Mom. You know how long I have tried to make it work, but what options do I have? I can't take the way he treats me one more day! I met with an attorney a month ago who advised me to have papers drawn up, just in case it ever got this bad. She's filing them tomorrow."

"Oh, really? I had no idea it was that serious."

"The attorney says that I should be able to get child support right away, and I already have enough money for a security deposit on an apartment along with the first month's rent."

"Sounds like you have thought this through. Well, if you're really sure you won't change your mind about all of this, bring the girls over in the morning after you drop off Doyle."

"I won't be changing my mind, Mom. Thanks for all your help."

ᕙᕙᕙᕙᕙᕙᕙᕙᕙᕙᕙ

As soon as Loui picked up the phone the dam burst. I cried so hard I couldn't breathe. "Who is this?" she asked.

I coughed a couple of times and said, "I'm sorry Loui; it's me... I'm leaving Doyle!"

"Good! He is never going to change," she calmly said. "He's proved that when he comes home drunk and beats you up. You have lived through the Dr. Jekyll/Mr. Hyde terror long enough. You've tried to make it work, Denise. Now you need to do what is best for the girls by staying away from that monster!" She paused, then asked, "What do you need?"

"Can we stay with you over the weekend? I am afraid he will come looking for us."

"Sure, Roger is out of town. So, we can plan some fun things with the kids. Denise, I am so glad you made this choice. I have been worried about you and the girls."

"Loui, I couldn't do this without you."

"One of the happiest moments in life is when you find the courage to let go of what you can't change."

~ Unknown

CHAPTER 3

A peace surrounded me as I went into the bathroom and tossed the last of my toiletries into a box. I did one last walk through the house and prayed I wasn't forgetting anything. The cat eyes on the whimsical face of the ticking kitty clock in the kitchen followed my every move, insisting I was out of time.

I pulled into my parents' driveway to pick up the girls. I spotted my boxes stacked high through the garage window, confirming Loui and her brother had had no trouble finding the place. Andy, my younger brother, came strolling down the driveway. He was my parents' miracle baby, he arrived six years after they were told they couldn't have children – the reason they had adopted Diane and me. I rolled down my window. "Hey, thanks for being here to help Loui unload," I said.

Andy nodded. "No problem. Just happy you finally made the decision to leave Doyle! Dad is getting wound up. You might want to get in there before the girls start crying."

I got out of the car. "Thanks for warning me!" I said and hugged him. Fierce barking greeted me, and I could see black and white spots bouncing in the front window as I passed by and opened the door. There was Penny, my parents' Dalmatian and protector of the house.

I cringed knowing that the girls would be covered in dog hair and dust from the unkempt house. My mom was an escape artist, too busy with social obligations. So, cleaning the house was last on her list. I stepped into the foyer; the dark wood floor was covered in a fine layer of black and white hair. Penny's tail thumped wildly against the wall. She jumped on me, sending a trail of her saliva down my cheek. My attempts to fend her off were futile.

Just as I gave Penny a hard shove and commanded her to sit, I heard tormented shrieks coming from the family room. *Dad's happy hour must have started early today.* Teasing the girls was his entertainment.

The distressing cries quickly became joyful when I walked into the room. Dad sat on his throne, a tan leather recliner with dark, worn spots on the arms. He was holding a Pabst Blue Ribbon in one hand. With his other hand he rubbed his bald head, feeling for any traces of hair that might be left. A rubber ball sat on his swollen beer belly. I bent down and Samantha toddled into my arms, Jaime trailed behind. Without warning a ball flew through the air and bounced off the back of Jaime's head. Jaime rubbed the spot and scowled back at her grandpa, which only made him laugh harder. "The Mess and The Whiner aren't happy because they don't like playing keep away," he roared in delight.

"Really, Dad? Do you have to tease them and call them names like that? It's mean!"

"Ahh, it will put hair on their chests!" he cackled. I turned to pick up the diaper bag, heat flushing up my face. I brushed the dog's hair from Samantha's pants, and took the girls into the kitchen so I could talk to my mom.

The enticing smell of browned beef with caramelized potatoes hit me when I walked into the kitchen, making my stomach growl. Mom pulled the roast out of the oven and set it on the stove. "Hi honey. Did you want to stay for dinner?"

"Unfortunately, we can't stay that late. Mom, can't you do something about Dad unmercifully teasing the girls the way he does? They are going to be traumatized living here until I find an apartment."

"Oh, you know your father. If he wasn't teasing someone about something he would be miserable!"

She was right. I remembered when my twin sister, Diane, and I were nine. We had been tricked into eating a Jalapeno pepper because Dad had convinced us it was a pickle. The tormenting burns it left in my mouth were forever seared into my mind, and to this day I hate spicy food of any kind! His teasing during our childhood left a multitude of scars.

"But it's OK for Dad to make us miserable?" I snapped back in disgust. She shot me the *look* which told me I had crossed a line. That shut down any further pleas from me.

Children are to be seen, not heard. The all-too-familiar saying that I had grown up with, now chorused in my ears. And that meant even adult children. I was resigned to the status quo and was certainly not going to hang around for an argument. "Thanks for watching the girls. We'll be back some time on Monday."

My mother suddenly realized what I had been doing all day. "Oh, how did it go?"

"Fine. I got what we needed. When I was done, I was surprised by how much peace I felt. But we have to go now. I'm gonna have enough trouble finding Loui's driveway off Holler Hills with no daylight." I was relieved to be staying at Loui's—even if it was only for a few days.

I got Samantha in her car seat before turning my attention to Jaime. "Jaime, I am so sorry Grandpa hit you with that ball. Grandpa can play rough sometimes." A smile spread across her face. She made a throwing motion with her arm and said, "I wanna throw that ball back at him!"

I would love to help you smack him right in the face with it!

I pulled out of the driveway and decided to take Jaime's mind off the incident by asking, "Are you both ready to go on an adventure?"

Jaime growled, "To the dark forest? To find... lions and tigers and bears?" Then she gasped, "Oh my! Oh my!"

I chuckled. That was our favorite line from *The Wizard of Oz*. Jaime always made me laugh; she had such a vivid imagination.

"Well, not exactly," I replied, "but as we near the edge of the city, you will want to keep a close look out for the mysterious old house on a hill where enchanted fun and dinner with the Prince await you!" Jaime giggled and peered out the window, excited to play along.

Loui had become my closest confidant when we worked together behind the diamond counter at Nobel's. She was a tell-it-like-it-is ray of sunshine on a gray day. She knew everything I had been through with Doyle.

The sun was casting its last shadow of the day as I searched for Loui's driveway. "Are we there yet?" Jaime asked, squirming in her seat.

"Yes!" I turned into the long gravel driveway. Jaime clapped her hands and shouted with delight when the white shiplap-sided 1700s farmhouse on the hill came into view.

"We get to stay at Loui's and play with Chad and Ben!"

I'd done it. I'd left Doyle and I was at such peace with my decision. I no longer had to endure his angry tirades. Still a storm churned in the pit of my stomach when I thought about the call to him I still had to make.

I got Samantha out of her car seat. Jaime hopped out of the car and ran up to the house. Bruno, the family's tan and white

Rottweiler bounced out the door with a grinning Loui trailing behind. She reached down and tussled Jaime's hair. "The boys are waiting for you inside," she announced.

The Jaime went in the house to play and I held Samantha while Loui helped me get my things out of the car. We sat down at the oak table in the cozy red and white kitchen. The window overlooked an ancient stone wall that held up the hillside. The smell of freshly baked chocolate chip cookies wafted through the room, reminiscent of Grandma's kitchen and her warm embrace. I began to share the day's events with her.

Loui noticed me glancing at the colorful rooster clock on the wall several times. She cajoled me, "Just call Attila-the-Hun. He can't yell at you while he's at work. I'll put the kids to bed."

"Thanks, Loui. I don't know what I would do without you!" I gave her a hug and watched her go up the stairs.

I picked up the phone on the kitchen counter. *Maybe I don't need to call him. If I didn't show up, he'd walk home from work. When he arrived at an empty house, he'd figure out I was gone.*

No, calling him was the right thing to do. My hand trembled so badly as I dialed, I had to hang up. It took three tries.

The store operator answered on the first ring. I could tell from the Southern accent it was May.

"Is Doyle there?" my voice cracked.

"Well, hi Denise. I haven't talked to you for a while! How are ya'll?"

Ugh, the last thing I needed was small talk!

"Just fine, May. I'm in a hurry to catch Doyle. Can you put me through to him?"

"Why sure, sweetie. Wait just a sec while I get him on the line."

I tried to compose myself while I waited for him to come to the phone.

"Denise?"

"Yes, it's me."

"Oh. Why aren't you here?"

"I won't be picking you up tonight," barely able to get the words out I continued in a murmur. "I've taken the girls, along with our things and the car. I won't be coming back. It's over."

After a long pause, he barked, "Do you know how much a divorce is going to cost me?"

His first concern was not his children or me—just money, further confirmation that I had made the right decision.

Anger rose, and I spoke loudly, "I'm not concerned with money right now. I only care about the well-being of my children and being away from you so I can have peace." I hung up the phone before he could respond. It felt like I had walked out of a dark forest into sunshine, warming my soul, the weight of the nerve-racking day lifted. I was free.

Loui came downstairs, and we sat at the kitchen table.

"I did it!"

She put her hand on my shoulder and smiled, "You sure did!"

"Now I know I made the right decision. That bastard is only concerned about money! Why didn't I make this decision sooner?"

She comforted me. "Don't beat yourself up. It took a lot of courage and strength to leave him." She stood and gave me a big hug. "I'm going to make you some Chamomile tea to calm your nerves and you can tell me all about the phone call."

"Doyle's going to try and find us. And you know, he'll figure out I came here. He could easily borrow a car from one of his co-workers and come after me."

Loui chuckled. "You know how hard my driveway is to find after dark!" Then her smile faded. "If he comes anywhere near here, I will call the police." She patted the Rottweiler's huge head. "And Bruno will tear apart anyone who tries to get in the house!"

Loui was right. I smiled at her enthusiasm. "Bruno's ability to protect us and the fact that the driveway is so hard to find certainly gives me comfort. Loui, I think we need more protection than Bruno can give. This may seem strange, but lately I have had a deep desire to know if God is real, does He intervene in our personal lives. It started after the girls and I were baptized. And today I had a strange peace that I could not explain when I left the house to get the girls. It could only have come from God. I believe that peace was letting me know that I was making the right decision. I really think we should pray for God's protection."

She thought for a moment. "Well, it couldn't hurt to ask God to help Bruno rip Doyle to pieces if he shows up!"

I shook my head and laughed. "A better prayer might be that He hides us from Doyle and gives us peace."

Loui and I held hands and asked God to be our protector throughout the night. Immediately we felt a calm presence. Loui still thought it would be wise to keep a look out for any suspicious activity.

"You look exhausted," she said. "Why don't you try and get some sleep. I'll keep watch." And she planted herself on the couch by the living room window.

"I doubt I will fall asleep. Come and get me in a few hours so we can trade places and you can get some rest."

She agreed and then got up to get sheets and blankets out of the closet. "Why don't you sleep in the family room on the futon. Since it's at the back of the house, you won't be disturbed." I nodded, and with sheets and blankets in hand, and headed to the family room.

ভ ভ ভ ভ ভ ভ ভ ভ ভ ভ ভ

"I've never seen so many headlights appear and then disappear down my little country road," Loui said when she woke me a few hours later. "I am really worried Doyle's been trying to find my driveway."

I stretched and yawned, "He won't find it."

Loui looked astonished, "What do you mean?"

"I have a peaceful feeling that we are being protected. He might as well stop hunting me down because he won't find me. I'm trusting God to keep us safe." Loui admitted that she would rather go to sleep than stay up the rest of the night fearfully watching the road. We both settled in and I slept better than I had in a very long time.

I felt revived as the sun broke through the darkness. God had answered our prayer.

The kids woke up at dawn. Loui offered to make a humongous breakfast with all the fixin's which delighted all of us. After stuffing ourselves, I told the girls they would get to stay with Ben and Chad one more night. They jumped up and down with excitement. "Then we will need to stay with Grandma and Grandpa for a while."

Jaime stopped jumping and looked at me in bewilderment. "Mommy, why aren't we going home?" she asked.

I took Jaime by the hand, led her into the living room and I sat down on the blue and grey plaid Early American couch with wooden arms that perfectly accented the Colonial Era room with its built-in closets and high ceilings. I pulled Jaime into my lap.

I investigated her confused face and tried hard to convince myself that I had an answer she would accept. "Remember that day when Daddy got really angry and started knocking things off the table and shelves? Then you went behind him picking the things up and putting them back?" She nodded. "It scares Mommy when Daddy gets that angry. Does it scare you?" Again, she nodded. "Well, I think the best way to help Daddy is to stay with your grandparents for a little while until Daddy can get help."

Jaime was sympathetic. "But I want to help Daddy."

"I know how you feel. I wish we could help Daddy, but Mommy has tried and for now I think we are helping him by staying with your grandparents."

"Can I go upstairs and play now?"

"Of course, you can!"

I went into the kitchen. I could tell from the look on Loui's face she had overheard our conversation. "Wow! You explained that in a brilliant, sensitive way. I would have been tempted to use some not-so-nice words!"

"Thanks. I surprised myself! I'm not sure why I remembered that awful day. I totally forgot that Jaime witnessed the whole thing. It was so sad to watch her go around picking up the things he had knocked off the table, like she was trying to fix what he had done. Remember? During his rampage, I had to shield Samantha in my arms. He was wearing wingtip dress shoes and kept kicking me in the back of my legs! I was afraid if I put her down he would turn his rage on her."

"Yes, I do. You were a wreck when I got to your apartment. Your legs were a mass of grotesque bruises. It hurt just to look at them! I'm so glad you no longer have to put up with that temperamental, over-critical, pompous . . .you- know-what!"

I took Samantha from Loui and planted kisses all over her cheeks, then held her close. "I know by leaving him, I have protected my precious girls."

I held her up in the air, swinging her around and I asked, "So, what do think Samantha? Should we all go on a hike and explore the woods today?" She looked down, and babbled away, in some unknown language, her total agreement.

Loui added, "I would not want to waste this unseasonably warm day by being inside. Besides, they will love raking the leaves!"

"I think you mean jumping in the piles we rake!" I said.

Loui chuckled.

The kids didn't fight getting baths that night. They were worn out from a day in the woods and went to bed without hesitation.

I lay down on the couch and quickly slipped into a sound sleep. There was fog all around me as I strolled on the moonlit path, when suddenly Doyle appeared with a crazed, dark look in his eyes. In an instant, he turned into a vicious wolf with razor-sharp teeth, snarling at me. Then he chased me into the woods. The wolf pounced. He was mid-air, ready to devour my flesh when the nightmare jarred me awake. My whole body went into convulsions. I tried to convince myself for the next few hours that I did not hear Doyle's car tires crunching up the gravel driveway. Dim rays from the sun had made their way through the trees when I finally fell back to sleep.

I woke up to the sound of the kids in the kitchen and to the smell of Loui's delectable homemade cinnamon rolls baking in the oven, soon to be iced with cream cheese frosting. Forcing my weary body to get up, I slowly shuffled, exhausted, across the room. I felt a pang in my stomach and my mouth watered when I entered the kitchen.

Yawning and stretching my hands above my head, I mused, "I guess my begging worked. I can't believe you made those just for me! You must have been up for hours."

Loui stood up from the table and gave me a hug. "Yes, of course, I made them just for you! And I must confess the roosters woke me before dawn. So, I thought I'd put the time to good use."

"After the miserable night I had, I can't believe their crowing didn't wake me!"

"Yep, you were dead to the world when I walked through the room. You can tell me why you slept so poorly while we taste my amazing creations."

After a filling breakfast, the kids played hide-and-seek outside. In the afternoon, I gathered our things together and packed up the car. I thanked Loui again for her hospitality and gave her one last wave as we turned out of the long driveway.

I dreaded going to my parents' house. I didn't know if it was the way my dad teased the girls or my mom's emotional distance that made me extremely uncomfortable. I couldn't quite put my finger on it. It really didn't matter; this was our only option.

"Well, girls we're here. It will be fun to spend some time with Grandma and Grandpa, won't it?"

Jaime climbed out of the car, looked at the ground and whined, "I don't want to stay here. I wanna to go home."

"I know. I wish we could. After Mommy gets everything out of the car, we will go for a walk and play in the park. We can even feed the ducks!" She smiled slightly and nodded. I carried Samantha in through the garage and held Jaime's hand going into the family room. A startled Penny barked fiercely until she recognized us and then covered Jaime with wet kisses. Samantha giggled with excitement.

Mom came into the room wearing fuchsia skorts and a floral polo, her futile attempt to look the part of a professional golfer. She greeted the girls with pats on the head. "How was golf today?" I asked.

"Frustrating. I didn't par once, and my ball found its way into several sand traps! I'd hoped you and the girls would come later. I just made myself a drink and wanted to sit down so I could unwind for a few minutes before I start dinner."

"You don't have to worry about entertaining us. I promised to take the girls for a walk to Sunset Park."

I held Jaime up and she climbed onto the jungle gym. Then I picked Samantha up and walked over to the swings and placed her in the baby seat. Jaime pretended to be king of the park and climbed to the highest point to view her domain. A few minutes later Jaime saw the ducks coming out of the nearby pond. She pointed to them and proclaimed, "I have to feed the pets in my kingdom!" I was glad I'd remembered the bread. Jaime tossed the last few crumbs at the squawking ducks, who proceeded to fight over them till the last morsel was gone.

I heard a familiar voice behind me playfully ask, "Hey, what are you doing making all that commotion?"

Jaime quickly recognized her aunt and ran into Diane's arms; Samantha looked quizzically back and forth between us. I got her out of the swing and explained, "Honey that is Mommy's sister. We look alike because we are twins." The closer Diane came, the more confused Samantha got, and it didn't help that she was going through a shy phase. To escape Diane's attention, she buried her face in my shoulder. "It's OK honey," I cooed into her ear while swaying back and forth. I was overjoyed to see Diane standing there. "Hey! What are you doing here?"

"I stopped by Mom and Dad's to get something and Mom told me you were here."

"I thought coming to the park would burn up some of their energy, so bedtime wouldn't be a fight. And Mom had a bad day at the course. I knew she would have no patience with two rambunctious girls during 'happy hour.'"

Diane laughed, "Of course, it is always better to get out of Dodge when they're drinking. I hope your stay with them is as short as possible." She was the only one who understood what the neglect and abuse from two alcoholic parents had done to our childhood.

"Anyway, I think I can help."

"Let me guess. You bought us tickets to fly to a deserted island, so we can disappear forever?"

"Sorry, nothing that dramatic. My boss -- you remember him -- Barry Schumer? Well, he just lost his secretary and I think you would be perfect for the job!"

"Wow, really? A 9-to-5 job in an office would be a dream. Do you really think I could do the job?"

"Sure. The secretary leaving will have to train anyone he hires. So why not you? I am going to have Barry call you tomorrow."

I gave Diane a hug. A tear trickled down my face.

"It will all work out," Diane assured me. "I'll help you with the girls and just think about it -- we might be working together!" We smiled at each other and walked back to the house. I thanked Diane for the job lead and we waved good bye as her car disappeared down the street.

My parents didn't eat dinner until eight o'clock, so I made sandwiches and veggie sticks to feed the girls. I had just put Samantha in the highchair when I heard a loud knock at the front door that sent Penny into a frenzy. "Don't open the door!" I yelled to Mom and Dad. My heart started to pound and my chest got tight. I peeked out the front window.

It was Doyle. Hands trembling, I cracked open the door. He looked forlorn, furrows of worry lined his forehead, his shoulders slumped, his lips were pursed. I almost felt sorry for him. Then I reminded myself that I had fallen for this act before. He had mastered the art of manipulation and proved it too many times in our marriage. He could not be trusted.

"I need to talk to you," he muttered.

I stepped out onto the front porch, keeping my hand on the door knob in case I had to make a quick getaway.

He continued, "I really want you and the girls to come home. We can work this out."

"Doyle, we have already tried counseling. Body slamming and choking me isn't the way to work on our marriage."

"I am so sorry for doing that. Things will change if you come home and give me a chance."

"I have heard way too many apologies, and nothing has changed. Your words mean nothing. If I came home, I know you would continue to hurt me. I don't want the girls growing up thinking it's OK to be hit by a man!"

"I know with your love I can change. I need you, sweetheart. You need to come home, so you can ... take care of me and the girls. I can't cook all the meals, clean the house and keep track of the bills."

"Oh. So, the only reason you want me to come home is to be your slave? I've made up my mind; we won't be coming back." I paused. "And you won't need to bother with the current bills. I paid all the ones that were due and mailed them on Friday." His face instantly turned ashen and I thought he would faint. I opened the door and backed into the house. Doyle just stood on the porch, flabbergasted.

The next morning the bank called. Doyle had withdrawn two thousand dollars from our account the day after I'd left. *So that explains his reaction*, I thought. Every check I had written to cover those bills had bounced! "It's a good thing Mrs. Boese that you had your name taken off the joint account. You aren't liable for having insufficient funds to cover the check that was written by your husband," the bank manager said.

I hung up the phone and cackled out loud. It all made sense now. He had no one to blame but himself when he got hit with all those bank fees!

Occasionally the planets do align and there is justice in the world.

"From the end spring new beginnings."

~ Pliny the Elder

CHAPTER 4

November 1984

I wriggled my toes in the cool, soft sand, and dug deeper until my feet were concealed by the white powdery sugar. The sun peeked out behind a puffy cloud, instantly warming my back. Waves intermittently crashed over the calm turquoise water while seagulls screeched overhead. Tiny yellow crabs, stuck their heads out of the sand, taking cover after any perceived disturbance.

I longed to stay on this serene, deserted beach forever.

A faraway scream interrupted the tranquility. Jarring shrieks grew louder and forced me into consciousness. I opened my eyes to see a figure running at me. Jaime took a flying leap, and landed, petrified, in my bed. "A big hairy monster is chasing me!" she cried.

I pulled her trembling body close to mine. "Oh, honey, I will never let anyone, or anything hurt you," I assured, gently stroking her hair.

Strangled emotions formed a giant knot in my stomach. This must stop! I couldn't stand one more night of Jaime being tormented by nightmares. They'd started sporadically six months ago, shortly after I left Doyle. Now they occurred almost nightly. I softly hummed "Jesus Loves Me" until we both fell asleep.

A stab shot through my thigh. I was being kicked by a warm body sleeping next to me. I fought to remember why Jaime was in bed with me. I rolled over, stretched, and squinted as a bright beam of sunlight warmed my face. I pulled my aching body out from under the covers and let my feet dangle over the edge of the bed. My gaze landed on a laundry basket piled high with clothes. I'd washed them over the weekend but had run out of steam before putting them away. I dug out a multi-colored sweater from the basket then found a blouse and a black skirt in my closet and got dressed.

I sat on the bed, looked at Jaime's peaceful face, and stroked her hair. I mulled over the thoughts that kept bombarding me. *Why is she having these nightmares?* Something had to be extremely wrong. I wished I could help her and make the nightmares stop. But a glance at the clock told me figuring that out would have to wait. My time belonged to my employer now.

I gently jostled Jaime awake. She peeked at me through one eye, then gave me a smile that lit up her whole face. I gave her a bear hug. "Come on, sleepy head. Let's go get your baby sister up."

We peeked around the corner and I saw Samantha playing in her crib. She babbled with delight when she saw us. My heart ached for the past when I could stay home and play with them all day. But now, if I had any hope of keeping my new job, we had to hustle to get out the door to daycare. I could not be late again.

I had been hired as a secretary at Shumer's Land Surveying Company by the owner, Barry. My skills fell short of qualifying me to do secretarial work. I had flunked typing class in high school, and the talents I'd developed as a stay-at-home mom were deemed useless by employers. Diane's call to her boss helped me land the job. She'd studied drafting in high school and had co-oped at area businesses, giving her a viable career after graduation. She got paid three times what I made interpreting the work of the land surveyors at $5.50 an hour. With the child support I received from Doyle, I barely paid the bills.

I arrived at the office without a minute to spare. The fifteen-foot Christmas tree in the lobby greeted me with its decorative plaid ribbon bows, shining ornaments, and bright lights. An angel in a flowing white gown was perched atop, reminding me of what was important during this season. At home our pine was a three foot "Charlie Brown" twig masquerading as a Christmas tree. At such a young age, the girls would not remember that tree nor the stuffed doll and book they'd each receive. But the presents from the rest of my family would make up for what I could not give them.

It was a blessing to have a job as a diversion from the pain of the abuse I had suffered. And yet, as my work became more familiar and less mentally demanding, my thoughts often wandered. I berated myself for not recognizing the signs of abuse during our dating and then in our marriage. If I'd been a better wife, maybe this wouldn't have happened. Maybe I should have stuck things out—for the sake of the girls. Then maybe Jaime wouldn't be having nightmares.

"God is our refuge and strength,
a very present help in trouble."

~ Psalm 46:1 NLT

CHAPTER 5

January 1984

J walked past the surveyor's huge drafting tables, then headed into Barry's office to give him the latest land document that I had completed.

"Thanks, Denise. I was just going to ask you for this. I thought we could go to Beck's for lunch today." He stood and reached across the desk. His short stature contrasted his bigger than life personality.

"Sure, I would love to go. I wanted to thank you for being so understanding about the calls from my attorney. I am expecting him to call again today."

"No problem. You are doing a good job keeping up with your work. I know how consuming going through a divorce can be. I am so glad mine is over! Close the door on your way out."

"Ok. Let me know when you are ready to go to lunch," I replied. *Had Diane overheard his invitation?*

I looked straight ahead when I passed Diane's desk. I could see her in my peripheral vision. *Please..., don't... stop... me.*

"Oh, Deniiiiiise. Don't think you can walk by here without talking to me about what just happened."

I cringed and took two steps back. Innocently, I replied, "What are you talking about?"

"I heard Barry ask you to go to Beck's."

"So? I'm sure he will be inviting you and the guys along also."

"Nooo, he won't. We are leaving at lunch time to go out of town to set up a surveying job. We won't return until tomorrow after work. Remember?"

Ugh! I had forgotten all about that. My snarky reply slipped out before I could stop myself. "Forgive me. I didn't know I was supposed to keep track of your schedules."

"Denise, do you think it is a good idea to have lunch alone with the boss?"

I whispered, "Do you really think we should be discussing this right now?"

She whispered back, "Just think about what you're doing before you get yourself in another mess." I shot her a look of defiance and walked back to my desk, which sat behind a wall several feet away.

I knew in my heart she was right. I loved the attention Barry gave me. He understood everything I was going through, but that was not a good basis for a relationship. I knew dating the boss could be dangerous. I kept questioning my motives. Were we really dating or just hanging out?

The ringing phone startled me. I recognized my attorney Joe Schwartz's number. Hopefully he had good news. I hated his calls; they upset me and then I'd find myself typing the rest of the day with blurred vision. Doyle had a pit bull for an attorney, so I never knew what trick they would try to pull next.

"Hello. Schumer Surveying. Denise Boese."

"Hi Denise. It's Joe Schwartz. I'm sorry I had to leave a message on your home phone about calling you at work today, but it's important," he said somberly.

Diane's sanctimonious opinion had already frazzled my nerves. *Now what?*

"Doyle has relayed a bizarre story to me through his attorney about your babysitter's husband. He is saying that the babysitter's husband has touched Jaime inappropriately. Supposedly, he put medicine on her vagina."

I tried to absorb what he was telling me. Thoughts bombarded me. *What happened? Why wouldn't Doyle tell me? Why did he tell his attorney?* My world stopped. I tried to process the words he'd just spoken and could hardly focus on what his steady voice continued to share.

"Your husband is adamantly requesting you change daycare providers. Immediately!" he emphasized.

Alarmed, I peppered him with questions. "Are you telling me I have to change providers based on Doyle's word only? He has never met my babysitter, Suzie, or her husband. How can he say Tony touched Jaime? Doesn't there have to be some evidence or an investigation? The YMCA covers most of the cost for the girls' daycare; I am only paying a small amount. How am I going to move the girls anywhere else?"

Joe's response was unsympathetic. "I don't know where Doyle got the information. But I do know you have no choice but to move them to another daycare before the next court hearing, or Doyle's attorney will make allegations that you have allowed them to stay in a harmful environment."

I hung up. My mind reeled. Is Doyle telling the truth? At his core, he is cunning and full of deceit. But he would never lie about something like this, not even to control me.

What if Jaime has been sexually abused? Does this have anything to do with the monsters in Jaime's bed? My heart broke and panic took over. I had to see Jaime and make sure she was alright.

Through tears, I told Diane what Joe had called about, then headed into Barry's office. I shared the details of the call and Barry immediately agreed I should leave and pick up the girls. Diane stopped me, came around her desk and hugged me, "I'm so sorry you're going through this!"

During the thirty-minute drive to Suzie's, I thought back to the first time I'd met her. Suzie kneeled down by Jaime, looked into her eyes and said, "You are just the most adorable thing I've ever seen! I've got all kinds of toys for you to play with right over there." Then she turned and made a fuss over Samantha. I had interviewed three possible sitters and Suzie was referred to me by a trusted friend with glowing references from past clients. Suzie's tender, loving heart towards children was displayed each time the girls were with her, and it gave me the assurance that they were in good hands.

I was so conflicted. I wondered when Suzie's husband had been around the girls. He was never there in the morning when I dropped them off nor in the afternoon. I decided the best thing to do was question Suzie. By end of the conversation, I would know the truth.

Jaime was sitting on the floor in the playroom decorated with Disney characters. She was bent over a coloring book, meticulously coloring Cinderella. She heard footsteps, glanced my way and a smile spread across her face. Jaime leapt into my arms and hugged me. I swayed back and forth, squeezing her tightly.

In a casual manner, still holding Jaime, I turned towards Suzie. "Does your husband ever get to play with the girls? Is he ever here during the day?"

Bewildered, Suzie said, "No. But Tony loves children, and I know he would enjoy these precious angels! He enjoys helping me with the kids in my Sunday school class. They all have a blast when he is there. Why are you asking?"

Jaime squirmed out of my arms and started to chant, "I love Miss Suzie! I love Miss Suzie!" and hugged her legs.

Jaime's fondness for her tugged at my heart. *She didn't seem to be traumatized.*

"I hate to tell you, Suzie, but the girls' father has made a horrible allegation against your husband." I explained the call from my attorney.

Suzie became indignant. "I cannot believe anyone would accuse Tony of such a thing. I am with the girls all the time and he is never home when they are here."

Between Jaime's display of affection for Suzie and the fact that I'd never seen Tony here, I believed her.

"I'm sorry. I'm starting to think Doyle made this whole story up. I just don't know why!" Suzie looked relieved.

"The worst part," I continued, "is my attorney is telling me I have to change daycare providers. He is convinced they will use it against me at the next hearing."

"I totally understand. I love these two sweethearts and would never leave the girls alone with anyone. I'm just relieved and grateful that you believe me. I want what's best for the girls."

The anger started to build at the realization of what Doyle had done. "*You* are what's best for the girls!" Tears glistened in Suzie's eyes. She hugged me. Then she kneeled and hugged Samantha and Jaime, and we said goodbye.

The girls climbed in their car seats and played with their Cabbage Patch dolls, blissfully unaware that they would not be going back to Suzie's. I was puzzled. I had been so fearful that Doyle would show up at the sitter's and take the girls that I never told him where Suzie lived. They'd never met and now this bizarre story! And if he really believed something this horrendous had happened to Jaime, why didn't he call me?

I pulled into our apartment complex. Jaime helped me carry the extra diapers and clothes from Suzie's house up the steps to our door. Samantha trailed behind cradling her doll in one arm and dragged Jaime's doll up the steps by its hand. Once we were all inside, Jaime dropped what she was holding and picked her doll, rubbing the Cabbage Patch's bald head. "Samantha, that wasn't nice to hurt my doll!"

"I sorry, I sorry," Samantha replied.

I watched the girls hug and smiled at their love. They were adorable together and I was so grateful they had each other.

The Jaime ran to their room with Samantha following behind to play while I laid down on the couch. I closed my eyes, so I could concentrate on finding a new daycare. Instantly, a picture of my new church where I had been a member for the past six months, came to my mind. Then it hit me—my church has a daycare!

Jaime danced into the room just as I placed the call to June Andrews, the daycare director at Kirkwood United Methodist Church.

"Hello. My name is Denise Boese. I'm a member of the church. I wanted to know if you had any spots open for a toddler and a three-and-a-half-year-old."

Jaime got up on the couch and snuggled next to me.

"I believe we do have two openings. When would you need them to start?"

I looked at Jaime's face, the allegations echoed in my mind. "Right away. But..." I hesitated. "I'm not sure I can afford what you charge," I whispered. Tears came without warning.

June was very kind and understanding. I explained my situation between sniffles.

"I need to talk to the Daycare Board over the weekend," she said, "but I have an idea that might work. I will call you on Monday."

I hung up, wrapped my arm around Jaime, and planted a kiss on the top of her head.

I called Loui next to fill her in and to ask her to babysit the girls on Monday. "Denise, you know I picked up the girls from Suzie on several occasions. I never saw her husband there. And if there was any abuse going on, the girls wouldn't have loved being there. My gut tells me that Doyle is doing what Doyle does best... lying!"

I thought about the girls' overnight visit with their father the next day and, for the first time, the thought of them being with him caused anxiety to engulf me like a consuming black cloud.

"O Lord of Heaven's Armies,
what joy for those who trust you."

~ Psalm 84:12 NLT

CHAPTER 6

*M*y stomach was in knots on the drive over to Doyle's to drop the girls off for their visit. I was tempted to ask him about the call from my attorney but decided against it.

Doyle answered the door, that same old Cheshire cat grin that always made me feel uneasy, pasted on his face. He leaned down to tickle Samantha. She giggled and pushed his hand away. He lovingly scooped them both up in his arms and kissed their cheeks. He confirmed the time he would bring them home and closed the door. I was glad the girls were happy to spend time with their father.

But after the "Mr. Wonderful" act Doyle just put on, my mind was in over-drive during the trip back home. One nagging question continued to rise to the surface: How could he tell his attorney that Suzie's husband had inappropriately touched Jaime and then act like everything was perfect in his world? He didn't know anything about Suzie or her husband. Suzie had no reason to lie. Nothing was adding up.

The only thing I knew to do was ask Jaime directly if she had been around Suzie's husband. I marveled at my three-and-a-half-year-old; she was intelligent and perceptive. I knew I would discern the truth in her eyes when I asked her about Suzie's husband.

That night I went out to dinner with some friends. It was always therapeutic to go out and commiserate with other divorced women. Sunday morning, I went to church, then spent the afternoon doing laundry. I was putting the last load away when there was a knock at the door. The children were home.

Doyle stood there holding Samantha as she slept in his arms; Jaime pushed past him and ran into the living room. I took the slumbering angel, confirmed with him the next visit and shut the door. I avoided any unnecessary conversations with Doyle to keep my emotions from boiling over.

I walked down the hall into the girls' room, which was decorated with one of my latest projects. A stuffed swinging clown, dressed in bright polka dots and ruffles, hung from the ceiling at the end of Samantha's crib. My creation brightened the room. I smiled, and gently placed her into bed.

When I walked back into the living room, Jaime couldn't contain her excitement. She was dancing in circles chanting, "Bice lives with Daddy now. Bice lives with Daddy."

"Shh, shh. Samantha is sleeping. Please whisper. Bice?... Bice?" I repeated.

"Who is that?"

"Daddy's friend"

Oh, that must have been Bice's car I saw in Doyle's driveway.

"Do you like him?"

She giggled and shrieked, "Bice is a girl!"

She quickly turned her attention back to the Mickey Mouse cartoon. Then it hit me, Jaime had some difficulties saying her R's. Maybe she meant Brice.

"Jaime?" I asked, "Do you mean 'Brice'?"

Brice was Doyle's new employee. Loui had filled me in on Brice, who was ten years younger than Doyle, describing her as a provocative flirt who strutted like a runaway model through the store in her tight miniskirts and low-cut sweaters. Brice provoked stares from the customers, and every time she bent down to retrieve a piece of jewelry out of the display case it became a show. Loui had been the one assigned to train Brice on sale procedures which took hours. Brice kept trying on every diamond ring in the store, admiring each one from every angle as she held out her left hand. Just then I remembered what Loui said: "It's obvious that she is on the hunt for a man and can't wait to use her discount at Nobel's!" I walked over, blocking Jaime's view of the TV and asked again, "Is the person staying with your dad named Brice?" She nodded her head, too engrossed in the cartoon to verbally answer me.

Doyle has a girlfriend? Reality smacked me in the face. He has a girlfriend! I couldn't believe it and felt my heart sink. Another woman in his life was an inevitability I knew I would have to face someday, but not before we were divorced. The thought of another woman taking care of the girls made me see green and feel nauseated. How dare he bring another woman into the girls' lives so soon! And he's living with her! What kind of example does that set for my impressionable young girls?

With every breathe I took my chest felt like a boa constrictor was tightening its grip. To relax, I took some deep cleansing breathes. Once I was calm I had a revelation: I never had any control over Doyle while we were married, and I had no control over who he saw or lived with now! So, I decided to be grateful that the girls spent the majority of their time with me.

Jaime had disappeared into the bathroom. "Mommy, Mommy..." she called.

"Ok, I'm coming!" I was curious when I saw her sitting on the bathroom floor, rubbing herself between her legs.

"Mommy, it hurts."

"Ok, let me take a look." I smiled and tickled her, so she wouldn't notice my growing concern. "You are swollen and red. How long has it hurt?" I placed a cold wash cloth on the area to soothe her. She shrugged her shoulders. I figured she was probably just irritated from the new laundry detergent I was using. Or could Doyle be right? Had Suzie's husband been inappropriately touching my daughter? No, I believed Suzie, or at least I *wanted* to believe her.

"Do you feel better?"

She nodded her head. I decided this was the perfect time to ask Jaime a few questions to get to the bottom of Doyle's accusations.

"Jaime, do you like staying with Suzie when I'm at work?"

"Yes."

"Do you like Suzie's husband?"

Jaime looked puzzled. "I don't know him," she said.

I knew she was telling the truth, but I asked again. "Has Suzie's husband ever been there when you're at her house?"

She sat up and answered, "No. Can I go watch cartoons now?"

I smiled at how fast she could change directions. "Yes, of course." I helped her pull her pants up. She went running into the living room and planted herself back in front of the TV.

Her genitals are really red. She has got to be uncomfortable. Could she be irritated from rubbing herself? Or is something else going on? Suzie's husband was never around the girls! I knew Doyle had to be lying! Why would Doyle tell his attorney that lie? Did his new girlfriend have anything to do with this? Every time I figured one thing out more questions kept mounting! At least now I knew Tony had nothing to do with all of this.

Dinner had to be started soon so baths and bedtime would happen on schedule, or we would be dragging in the morning.

While doing the dishes, I sent up a silent prayer that the monsters would give us a break tonight. I was sleep deprived and couldn't remember the last time I had dreamed. I was desperate to revisit that deserted, white powdered beach with balmy breezes and turquoise water so I could escape reality, if only for a little while.

The next morning, I woke up rested for the first time in weeks. Maybe God was listening to my sporadic prayers? I had just put my purse away in the desk drawer after arriving at work when the phone rang.

"Hello, Schumer's Surveying. Denise Boese speaking."

"Hi Denise. It's June Andrews from Kirkwood United Methodist Daycare. I have good news! I think you will qualify for a sliding fee based on your income. I just need to get some financial information from you."

"Thank you for getting back to me so quickly. It would be such a relief knowing my daughters were in a good daycare!" I quickly faxed her the information she requested.

June called me back within the hour. "I think you will be happy! The fee for five days a week will be one hundred dollars a month. Is that doable?"

"Yes, I can afford that! Thank you so much."

I hung up and called Loui, explaining the last saga in my life.

"I can't believe because of Doyle you have to switch daycare providers!" Loui exclaimed.

"I know it stinks but maybe being at a daycare will be better for the girls. I need to ask a big favor...The girls can't start daycare for two weeks; can you watch them?"

"Of course, I can!"

"Thanks Loui! I don't know what I would do without you!" My anxiety was gone, and an overwhelming peace gave me the assurance that someone was working this out for us!

☙☙☙☙☙☙☙☙☙☙

Being at Loui's for two weeks was like a vacation for the girls, and they loved every minute they got to play with their buddies Chad and Ben. Jaime and Samantha adjusted quickly to the nurturing environment of their new daycare. My exhaustion from another rough night with the monsters, caused me not to hear the alarm that morning. We arrived at daycare without a minute to spare.

Jaime started to pout and whine when I got her out of the car. "Don't *leeeaaaave* me. I wanna go with you!" she cried. I tried to divert her attention by pointing to her friend from church walking in behind us.

"Look who is here! You get to play with Holly today on the playground."

My ploy didn't work; she just stood there. I grabbed Samantha's hand and picked Jaime up, carrying her into the building. Inside the classroom door she wiggled out of my arms and fell to the floor.

She started to kick and screamed at me, "Don't leave me!"

A curious Samantha peeked out from behind my leg, "Sissy, it's OK I here, I here," she comforted.

Jaime's teacher came up and put her arm around me. "She is acting out because of separation anxiety. Go ahead and leave. She will calm down the minute you're out of sight," she assured.

A huge knot formed in my throat from fighting back the waterworks. *How could I leave her like this?* I leaned down and blocked her legs from kicking me, kissed the top of her head, then walked out the door. I drove to work through a blur of tears.

*"You're allowed to scream, you're allowed to cry,
but never give up."*

~ Unknown

CHAPTER 7

The girls had been asleep for an hour when the mounting tension I could no longer ignore, erupted. It had been building since Jaime's meltdown at daycare that morning. I paced around the living room, hoping to gain a clearer perspective. But after each lap, I came to the same conclusion. Jaime's escalating separation anxiety, nightmares, and inflamed genitals were all the clues I needed. Without words, in the only way she knows how, Jaime is crying out for help. My intuition told me someone was abusing her.

The only thing I knew to do was call the police. I wiped my clammy hands on my sweatpants and placed the call to the police, barely able to breathe. I felt relieved when I shared the details and they took me seriously. They asked for Suzie's address and phone number, so they could question her and her husband, but I knew that was a dead end.

The officer I spoke with wanted me to take Jaime to Children's Hospital immediately. She would be examined by a doctor in the child abuse clinic to determine if there was any physical evidence. I made the appointment for the next day right after work.

Jaime was close to her father, a daddy's girl. The thought of taking her to this appointment without him made me nervous. She would be calm if he went with us. I decided to call Doyle.

"Hi. We need to talk," I sternly announced.

"Ok. What's up?" he answered, guarded.

In the background, I heard a female voice and got the impression I was interrupting something. A spark of rage ignited.

Aggravated, I challenged, "Why did you tell your attorney that Suzie's husband put medicine on Jaime's genitals?" He didn't answer me.

"Obviously, you know I had to switch daycare providers on the advice of my lawyer. Why didn't you come to me with that information?" I queried.

There was a long pause. Then he coolly answered, "Because of how you are acting right now."

"Really? I have good reason to be upset." I hesitated. "Jaime's genitals have been red and swollen! Almost every night she is having nightmares about monsters in her bed. I am afraid someone has molested her!"

"Denise," Doyle said, "I'm sure there is a reasonable explanation for all of this. You're the one that took her out of a stable home and caused all her stress. Have you thought about that?" He was chiding me, practically accusing me.

Oh yeah, blame me. I'm not falling into this trap because you want to provoke a fight. "I wanted you to know I called the police tonight and they are starting an investigation. I have to take her to Children's for an exam after work tomorrow."

Silence. "Did you hear me? I called you because you really need to go with us."

"I can't go. I have to work." His voice was taut.

I was adamant. "For Jaime's sake, you need to ask someone else to close the store and come with us. She needs her dad!"

"I can't!" he shouted.

My stomach churned as I slammed down the phone.

His response baffled me, and I could feel my blood pressure rise. I dropped on the couch, convulsing sobs poured out of me as I pommeled the flowered chintz pillow until exhaustion set in.

I just told Doyle our daughter may have been molested and she must be seen by a doctor! And he doesn't care? Nothing makes sense!

The next day I couldn't concentrate at work; five o'clock couldn't come soon enough. On the way home, I tried to decide how I could prepare Jaime. I envisioned her fighting me, not wanting to get in the car. I made the decision not to tell her until we were there. Loui was watching Samantha, so I would have no moral support.

I pulled up to the hospital and the parking staff gave me directions to the clinic. We walked into the lobby, then down a long, winding claustrophobic tunnel to the clinic. I had an ominous feeling I just couldn't shake.

I knelt and looked Jaime reassuringly in the eyes. "Jaime, a doctor is going to exam you to find out why you are red and irritated in your private area. Mommy wants to make sure you are OK." She just nodded her head.

When we checked in, the receptionist handed me paperwork to fill out. Jaime's attention was drawn to a huge aquarium across the room. She watched with fascination as fish chased each other around a neon colored chest. She pointed and smiled when bubbles escaped from its lid. I handed the paperwork back to the receptionist. Jaime stood at the tank, mesmerized. For a minute, I almost forget why we were there. Then a nurse appeared.

"Jaime Boese," she called. My heart skipped a beat. She took us back to a bland examination room with stark white walls. "The doctor will be right in," she droned and left.

I lifted Jaime onto the table. "What fun things did you do at daycare today?" Before she could answer, a broad-chested, six-foot four-inch, white-haired male in a lab coat entered the room. This stranger held a clipboard detailing the intimate questions I had answered on Jaime's behalf.

He wore a stern, steely look and nodded his head towards me. "Hello," he grunted. Then he rapidly flipped through the paperwork. He gave no introduction. He didn't even try to engage Jaime. He walked over to us and, with no warning or explanation, pulled down her pants and started to examine her.

Jaime's eyes grew wide and she struggled to push his hands away. Then she kicked at him and became agitated when he didn't stop touching her. He ignored her emotional distress and continued with the exam.

"You need to stand by her head and help me hold her down," he ordered.

I tenderly whispered in her ear, "It's OK. I'm here. How about we get some ice cream when we leave?"

I turned my head, so Jaime couldn't see the uncontrollable tears rolling down my face. The doctor had almost finished when she became hysterical. She couldn't catch her breath. I gathered her up in my arms and tightly hugged her. I did not let her go until she quit shaking and I had calmed down.

He flatly pronounced, "I see no physical evidence of abuse." Then he turned and left the room.

I despised myself for allowing Jaime to be violated further by this so-called 'professional'! I was more determined than ever to figure out what was happening to my daughter, so I could get her the help she needed.

*"Live for what tomorrow can bring,
not what yesterday has taken away."*

~ Unknown

CHAPTER 8

"Mrs. Boese, we were forced to end our investigation. Tony Flanagan denied ever being around the girls, and there was no physical evidence of abuse from the exam," the apologetic police detective informed me.

"I knew the girls had never been around Tony. Jaime's private area no longer looks inflamed like it did weeks ago, so I didn't think the doctor at Children's would find anything. How will I ever find out the truth? I need to know if Jaime has been hurt so I can help her," my voice quivered.

"There is a child therapist we can refer you to who has good luck using anatomically correct dolls to question children who have been abused," the detective suggested.

A few days later, we walked into a brightly decorated waiting room full of toucans, parrots and monkeys hanging from palm trees, for the appointment. They led Jaime back to a dimly lit room that immediately had a calming effect on us both. The therapist, Kim, was short, her dark hair was pulled back in a ponytail and she wore an Izod polo shirt and tan pants. She looked like a college student. Her soft, flowing voice engaged Jaime. She asked her what toys and games she liked to play. Then she brought out dolls to use as visual aids, and asked Jaime to show her different body parts. She explained what a good and bad touch is and then asked if anyone had touched her inappropriately. Jaime, who sat on the floor, looked down and held her knees while rocking back and forth. She seemed to withdraw into her own world and shook her head.

Kim said, "Jaime, I know it's hard to talk to someone you don't know but I'm glad you came to see me today. Thank you for listening to me. You are such a beautiful girl!" Then she led her back into the waiting room.

"Jaime has been having recurring nightmares and separation anxiety every time I leave her. I know something is wrong!" I insisted.

"I agree. I can tell by the way she withdrew during the session something has happened that she feels she can't talk about. Children that have the behaviors Jaime is exhibiting need therapy. The session we just did is a starting point to bring criminal charges if evidence of abuse is found. Since Jaime didn't share anything, I would suggest you take her to Child Advocacy. They will do in-depth therapy to help her cope with what is triggering her behavior."

I called Child Advocacy the minute I got home. They conducted a phone interview to assess what therapy Jaime might need and set up an appointment for the middle of March. *How am I going to deal with Jaime's monsters and tantrums by myself for another four weeks?* Panic set in and a vise tightened around my chest.

I had to talk to someone. Maybe Pastor Whitcomb could help. It was late afternoon, so I was surprised when he answered the phone. He showed concern and graciously agreed to meet with me before church. The girls and I spent Saturday with Loui and the boys, which helped to take my mind off the dismal things that were happening.

Sunday morning, I stretched and looked out my bedroom window. The wind whistled through the pane of glass and trees swayed. Dark clouds were forming overhead; the weatherman had called for blustery weather with some snowfall. *How fitting*! Despite my gloomy mood, I was hopeful that my meeting with Pastor Whitcomb and the worship service would lift my spirits. My thoughts transported me back to my first church experience.

The Dallas I had grown up in and knew was called the 'Bible Belt', full of people known as 'Bibles Thumpers' -- to my parents anyway. The 'Bible Thumpers' main goal was to get you 'saved'. I had no idea what that meant when I was younger, but my dad warned my sister and me to stay away from the crazy neighbors next door. "We'd love ya'll to come to church with us. Jesus loves you and died for your sins," they'd say every week. And every week my parents emphatically declined their invitation. My parents considered themselves to be intellectually evolved and totally self-reliant, which meant they had no need for God, Jesus or anyone else. And they certainly didn't want our sins broadcast with a megaphone to the entire neighborhood.

Diane and I became curious about God when we were twelve and asked to go to Sunday school. We pestered our parents for several weeks until one morning they relented and dropped us off at the nearest church. We walked into the building, the stares of curious adults following us down the hallway. We found the classroom by ourselves. We were embarrassed during the lesson because we had never heard the story of Jesus' birth and could not answer any of the questions being asked. We looked on, bewildered. We were outsiders who didn't fit in, but who were anxious to learn.

The following week, Dad dropped us off and told us he would be back in an hour. We walked up and yanked on the door several times, to no avail. Diane and I quickly realized why the door was locked and the parking lot was empty. The time had changed, and our parents hadn't set the clocks back. We sat on the sidewalk and waited. Dad returned just as families were arriving for Sunday school. We could feel their eyes follow us as we climbed into the car and drove off. The disappointment and humiliation were too much. We never asked to go to church again.

After I had separated from Doyle, I had a growing desire to know God even though attending church made the voice in my head taunt me repeatedly. *You don't need church; those people can't help you...you aren't worthy of their time...you should be ashamed to step foot through the front door! And what will your parents think? You've lost your mind trusting those Bible Thumpers!* It was a fight to ignore that voice every time I went to church and to play catch up to learn all the Bible stories I missed as a child, but I had to know if this God loved me for any reason at all.

I tossed the two Cabbage Patch dolls I'd almost tripped over on the bed as I went to the closet. My tan wool pants and burgundy turtle neck would be just the outfit to keep me warm. I applied makeup to my ruddy complexion, squirted mousse into my hand, then ran it through my perm, scrunching my wet hair until the curls came back to life. My beauty routine was complete.

The girls' conversation drifted into the hall. I popped my head into their room. "Boo!" I hollered. They laughed with delight. "We've got to get to church early today. So, cereal is on the menu this morning!" We were ready to go in record time and headed out the door.

I put the girls in the nursery and went to the pastor's office. The door was open, so I peeked around it. Pastor Whitcomb motioned for me to come in. "Hi there. Have a seat," he invited and closed his worn Bible.

He had a meticulously trimmed, salt-and-pepper beard and mustache, and a full head of white hair framed his face. Pastor Whitcomb was a perfect portrayal of a trusted father figure, in his wire-rimmed glasses. His desk was strewn with piles of papers and books on Biblical topics.

"Good morning, Pastor Whitcomb. Thanks for meeting with me."

His bright emerald eyes smiled at me. "Just call me Pastor Whit; everyone else does. How are the girls adjusting to daycare?"

"Oh, I really want to thank you again for making it possible for the girls to come here. They are doing well." Jaime's daily morning tantrums flashed through my mind. *How am I ever going to explain what is going on to a pastor?*

In a reassuring tone, he asked, "What did you want to talk to me about? Maybe I can help."

I glanced around the small room full of bookshelves. Then my eyes landed on a picture of a smiling Jesus. *Surely, I can trust this pastor. He's not at all like the one who married Doyle and me.*

I began hesitantly, "I'm not sure anyone can help. I don't even know how to explain what has been going on, but I'll try."

I started by telling him about the tantrums in the morning, praising the teachers for their understanding and compassion for Jaime. Then through choking sobs, I told him about her nightmares and Doyle's lie. "I know Jaime's behavior is a cry for help. Something has happened to her!" He sat there in silence while I blew my nose.

Pastor Whit came around the desk, sat in the chair next to me and put his hand on my shoulder. "You have certainly been through a lot and I can't say I understand what you and Jaime are going through, but I know the One who does. Jesus walked this earth and was mistreated and abused. He understands all your pain and heartache, so I'd like to pray for His strength to get you through all of this."

I felt a peace that was beyond understanding while he prayed. I left his office with an assurance that I was not alone. Pastor Whit's sermon, "Put Your Problems in God's Hands," greatly encouraged me that morning.

"Hidden truths are unspoken lies."

~ Unknown

CHAPTER 9

luebirds chirped, flying from tree to tree when I walked into Child Advocacy. Nature's music and warmth of the spring day filled me with hope that I would find some help for Jaime. They had a cancellation that moved my appointment up by two weeks. The vibrant wall in the waiting room had an impressive mural of kids jumping rope and playing games. Some children sat at tables coloring and others raced trucks around the floor, toys were scattered everywhere. The scene set my mind at ease. It was a welcoming place that made children feel safe and comfortable.

A woman dressed in a flowered sweater and black skirt came out. "Hi. I'm Lisa Miller. I will be the therapist working with Jaime. Thanks for meeting with me so I can get some background from you." Her kind, amber eyes, framed in designer glasses, enhanced her short curly hair. Lisa led me into a room with two over-stuffed recliners and a side table with Kleenex on it.

"I understand from the intake information, your daughter, Jaime... Is that her name?"

"Yes."

"Jaime has been exhibiting a lot of behavior that you believe may point to abuse. Is that right?"

"Yes. She has separation anxiety and nightmares. Since the girls and I have been on our own, I have seen Jaime's personality change dramatically. She went from being a happy, talkative child, full of life, and not afraid to express herself to a child who is withdrawn, scared and confused."

"I can see why you are concerned. Today I would like to start by getting some background information on your relationship with your husband. I want to understand what was going on in the home before we talk more about Jaime. Does that sound like a good starting point?"

"Sounds like a good place to start to me. After all, it was my soon-to be ex, Doyle, that accused my babysitter's husband of inappropriately touching Jaime."

"Good. Tell me about how you met your soon-to-be ex and what it was like being married to him."

I filled her in on the details of our short romance. Then choked out the details of our turbulent, abusive marriage. I blew my nose and composed myself. "I can tell you Doyle loves playing with the girls, especially Jaime. I know parents aren't supposed to have favorites, but he spends most of his time with her. There is a special bond between him and Jaime, although, he is a good father to both. I just don't understand what possessed him to tell his attorney that lie."

"Why are you so sure it was a lie?" Lisa probed.

"Because I know Suzie and her husband. They were telling the truth about Tony never being around when the girls were there. And Jaime told me she never met Tony. Jaime also told the first therapist she didn't know him, and he never touched her," I insisted.

"Well, Mrs. Boese, thank you for sharing all of this with me today. Let's make an appointment for next week and continue where we left off."

"Should I bring Jaime with me?" I anxiously asked.

"No, not just yet."

I saw Lisa once a week for the next three weeks. Her compassion and insight gave me understanding about the abuse I had suffered at Doyle's hands. She explained that abuse comes out of another person's need to control someone. She then assured me the abuse I suffered from Doyle was not my fault. I had done all I could to save our marriage.

I was becoming restless and frustrated as Jaime's behavior deteriorated. Lisa's endless questions about my marriage and abuse were not helping Jaime. Finally, Lisa agreed to have Jaime come in the following week.

I was relieved Lisa was meeting with Jaime and relaxed during the drive to daycare. From the church parking lot, I could see the children on the playground. I looked between the darting kids in the middle of a game of keep-away and found Samantha. She sat on her teacher's lap and intently babbled away while Sheila shook her head in agreement.

"I am glad you don't understand her yet. I bet she has filled you in on all my secrets!" I said.

Sheila played along. "You're too late. I caught some of the words and have figured out the code for the rest. So, who's the mysterious cute guy she's been telling me about?"

"Ha, right! Even if I knew one, I wouldn't be interested. I am happy being single."

"Don't blame ya there. I need to let you know she fell asleep during lunch again today, so she only ate her snack."

"Oh, Samantha, what am I going to do with you? Thanks for letting me know. See you tomorrow." Sheila put Samantha down and I grabbed her hand. "Let's go find your sister," I said. Jaime ran right into us trying to escape a boy who tagged her out. "Hey there. You almost knocked down your sister!"

"Ahh, she was in the way and I got tagged!" Jaime stomped her foot.

"You still have to watch where you are going, honey. Let's go."

On the way home, thoughts about Jaime's upcoming appointment crept in my mind and the "what ifs" started to make me anxious.

What if she doesn't talk to Lisa? What if she does and she has been abused? Then what will happen? The unimaginable questions bombarded me and nearly drove me crazy! I had to stop, and I forced myself to think only about positive things.

The girls were tucked into bed and I had plopped down on the couch ready for a break when the phone rang. It was an old friend I had worked with at Nobel's Jewelry Store. I had not talked to Betty since I left the store, so my guard was up. The rumor mill at Nobel's was always churning out whoppers. I wondered if she was calling out of concern or just to be nosy.

She reminded me of the drama queen, Scarlett O'Hara, from *Gone with the Wind.* Her black wavy hair complemented her short thin stature and her flare for pulling off the latest styles. Betty's spunky personality had made every shift we worked together an adventure.

After some small talk, my curiosity was piqued when Betty started telling me about a conversation she overheard weeks earlier between Doyle and one of his employees. "I was in the stock room when I heard John tell Doyle that his neighbor, Suzie Flanagan, was babysitting your girls. Doyle seemed surprised, like he didn't know Suzie. It seemed odd when Doyle started to ask John a lot of questions."

In a barbed voice I replied, "I didn't want him to know where my babysitter lived because I didn't want him to be able to pick the girls up."

"Well, he knows now. John gave Doyle detail after detail about Suzie and Tony, answering all of Doyle's questions. John told him where they lived and that he loved hanging out with Tony because he was so much fun."

I cut her off. "It doesn't matter now. Suzie isn't watching them anymore."

Betty, who loved to gossip, was going on a fishing expedition, and I wasn't about to let her reel in any juicy details from me.

Then my heart started to race. "Tell me again, how long ago you overheard that conversation."

"I think two months ago. Why?"

"What made you call me about it now?

"Quite frankly, I had forgotten all about it until I saw John and Doyle having lunch in the break room today. The strange conversation from the stockroom wouldn't leave my mind, so I thought you should know. Do you know why Doyle was asking John so many questions about your babysitter?"

"I have no idea why he wanted that information. Hey, let's go to lunch next Tuesday at La Casa's. Does that work for you?" I wanted to wrap up the conversation quickly.

"Sure does. See you then!"

My mind was in overdrive when I got off the phone. What else had she heard? Now I knew that Doyle had found out who my babysitter was and that she was married! But why would he tell his attorney that Tony had touched Jaime inappropriately?

I know he made the whole thing up. But why would he do that? Something has happened to my daughter; her behavior screams "HELP ME!" Yet I don't know how. I'm so frustrated. Nothing is adding up.

I turned on the TV to distract myself from the all the questions I couldn't answer. It had been a generous present from my parents who were convinced the girls needed one. I had to buy a dining table, couch and chair when I moved into my apartment, so having a TV was the least of my concerns.

Struggling a few minutes later to keep my eyes open during *Miami Vice,* I decided to wash my face and go to sleep. Just as I slipped into bed a blood-curdling scream made my heart skip a beat.

Jaime ran into my room. Terrified, she whimpered, "Monsters are in my bed!" I pulled her under the covers and looked down at her tear-filled baby blue eyes. We cuddled.

"Well, they will not come in here," I exclaimed. "If they try, I will chase them out!" I looked down at Jaime and stroked her light blonde hair, amazed at her beauty. The turmoil created by the monsters had exhausted her, but now serenity took over and she was fast asleep in my arms.

I mentally vowed, "IF IT'S THE LAST THING I DO, I WILL PROTECT YOU!"

Then a nagging thought plagued me: *What if it's too late?*

"The trust of the innocent is the liar's most useful tool."

~ Stephen King

CHAPTER 10

April 1985

My foot kept time with the tick of the clock and I stared at the document in front of me. I resisted the urge to check the time again. Jaime's first appointment with Lisa was this afternoon and I had to leave work early to drop Samantha off at my parents' house. The "what ifs" were back, and I strained to make myself breathe deeply. I pushed away every negative thought about the truth that might come out. *Whatever the truth is, Jaime will get the help she needs. This is no time to fall apart! The truth about what is causing her behavior has got to be better than not knowing.* I raced out the door the minute the clock struck 4 to beat the afternoon rush.

Lisa greeted us warmly in the waiting room, but Jaime stared at the floor and hid behind me walking down the hall to Lisa's office. The therapist picked up a doll with long blonde hair and a sparkly dress. She told Jaime she wanted to ask the doll some questions. "Hi, Julie," she said. "Can you tell Jaime what you like about this place?"

Then Lisa's voice became squeaky. "I love all the children who come to play with me. It's such a fun place to live." Lisa handed the doll to Jaime. "Would you like to play with Julie?" Without saying a word, Jaime took the doll and sat down on a bean bag chair.

Lisa pulled me aside and explained, "I will ask Jaime some basic questions about her likes and dislikes. I want to take my time doing this to build a rapport. Then I will ask her about what happens during her visits at her dad's house."

I was astonished. "But, why would you ask Jaime about visits with her dad?"

Lisa was genuinely sympathetic and put her hand on my shoulder. "With the behavior Jaime is exhibiting and the abuse Doyle has put you through, we have to consider that he could be the one abusing Jaime."

Everything went silent, the room started to spin, my thoughts went wild.

But he is a good father. She loves going to his house. Jaime is a daddy's girl! She's his favorite.

A picture of the hospital room and Doyle holding Jaime for the first time came to life in my mind. He was so nurturing and gentle with her. Jaime felt special because she had all of Doyle's attention, especially after Samantha came along.

The overload of emotions sent me into shock. I could hear my pulse thumping in my ears. Lisa led her out of her office and motioned for me to follow.

"Jaime, what is your favorite color?" Lisa nonchalantly inquired as she led Jaime into a small, cozy room.

"Blue," she whispered sheepishly.

Then Jaime went over to a child's table that had a coloring book and crayons on it and sat down in one of the small chairs;

Lisa sat in the other. I walked over to a love seat across the room and sat down.

"I love that color too! Can you tell me what toys you like to play with the most?"

I zoned out and didn't hear Jaime's next reply. I spontaneously snapped out of it when Lisa opened the manila file she had brought with her and showed Jaime the drawing I had made of her father's house.

"Can you point to the rooms you like to spend time in when you visit your dad?" The picture showed the floor plan of the ranch house we had rented, and where Doyle still lived.

Jaime started to giggle as she pointed to the main room. "We play games and watch movies in that room. It's fun. And in the kitchen, we eat waffles with syrup."

Lisa continued, "What about this bedroom? Do you and your sister sleep here?"

Jaime's smiled faded; she withdrew.

"It's OK. Tell us anything you want to that happens in your bedroom," Lisa coaxed.

In a barely audible voice Jaime said, "I sleep in Daddy's bedroom, not in Samantha's."

Lisa dug deeper. "Thank you so much for sharing what you do at Daddy's house with me. Can you tell me what happens when you are in Daddy's bed?"

Jaime hesitated, then she looked away and mumbled, "Daddy says it's a secret.... I... I can't tell you."

"You look sad. Can I give you a hug?" Compassion filled every word. Timidly, Jaime nodded her head. Lisa warmly embraced Jaime and then gazed into her eyes. "I just want you to know you can tell me anything you want to. I'm a good listener."

Jaime slid to the floor, taking a pink crayon and the coloring book with her. She continued to color in Strawberry Shortcake's dress; a Lemon Meringue doll sat on the floor next to her.

Lisa continued. "What else happens when you stay at your father's house?"

Jaime dropped the crayon and laid down, rolled on her side and put her hands over her face. "He wets the bed." Then she whispered, "He touches me."

Lisa showed no emotion, only interest. "Can you show me where he touches you?"

Jaime reached up under her skirt touched her underwear and pushed her fingers up inside of her.

What? No, this can't . . . No! I couldn't process what I heard and saw. *How could this be? Doyle? His daughter?* I couldn't comprehend the mortifying truth Jaime had just disclosed!

Lisa hugged Jaime. "I know the secret your dad asked you to keep was hard to share. Thank you for telling me. Would you like to take Lemon Meringue home with you for a visit?" Jaime smiled, hugged the doll, and nodded her head. Lisa called in her assistant and asked her to take Jaime into the waiting room. We went back to her office, Lisa shut the door, and pointed to a chair in front of her desk. "Have a seat. Do you understand what Jaime shared and what has happened to her?"

I sat there staring at the bright colored pens in a pencil holder in front of me, dumbfounded.

"Well, from what Jaime shared... Doyle has exposed himself in front of Jaime and has molested her," she delicately explained.

My mind went numb. Then I blurted out, "I don't understand what Jaime meant by 'he wets the bed.'"

"He's ejaculating in front of her," Lisa bluntly stated. The horrified expression on my face gave my innocence away and made Lisa come around from behind the desk. She held my hand. "I know it's hard to process all of this, but we've got to talk about what needs to happen next."

Reality sank in. My heart raced. I frantically replied, "Oh No! She cannot go to his house again!" Then I kept repeating, "She can't be alone with him, she can't be alone with him," while crying hysterically and gasping for air. *It was too late to keep my promise to her. I would never be able to keep her safe.*

Then, in an excruciating panic, I asked, "How am I going to protect her from her own father?"

"We will get a court order to stop visitation."

"But he's supposed to have them this weekend! There is no way..."

"We can get an emergency order to stop his visitation tomorrow," Lisa assured me.

I breathed deeply to calm myself as I gave Lisa my attorney's number. She felt confident that Joe would call the judge in Juvenile Court the next morning to put the order in place.

I hugged Jaime tightly as we walked to the car, wishing I could hold her close forever and never let her out of my sight. I thought of all the sleepless nights a terrified Jaime came running into my room, trying to escape the monsters in her bed. Now I knew Doyle was the cause of these nefarious nightmares! He was the monster! She had no words to tell me what was happening to her, and I hated myself for not knowing the right questions to ask.

On the drive home, I imagined being in Jaime's shoes, trying to understand what she had been going through. A dreadful childhood memory darted through my mind. My father's business partner was in the room with me, pulling me into his lap, my sister was across the room on my dad's lap. Every time he came over, he made me feel so uncomfortable, the way he would slip his hand under my shirt and touch my back and then . . . *Oh, no!! Had I been sexually abused?*

I shooed the thought from my mind like it was a pesky fly. The more pressing matter was Jaime. My precious baby has been violated by her own father! The unanswerable questions swirled like a raging sea at high tide crashing into rocks. *How could he do this? And to his own daughter? His flesh and blood? How could he do this to any little girl? Did he do this to Samantha?*

When I got to my parents' house, Jaime had fallen asleep in the back seat of the car, and I was no longer traumatized by the truth. Anger had taken its place. I gripped the steering wheel until my knuckles turned white, then violently shook the immoveable object back and forth without letting a sound escape from my lips. Every muscle tense, exhaustion overtook me, and my head drooped against the steering wheel. A consuming black cloud of explosive rage filled me again, making me feel like a huge, vicious Tasmanian Devil, the tornadic character from Looney Tunes. I imagined this wild, long-fanged beast racing to catch a wide eyed whimpering Doyle, ferociously ripping him apart, limb by limb until there was nothing left. He had to be destroyed. I shook my head loose of the image and feigned composure as I got Jaime out of the back seat and we went into the house.

"Jaime, honey, please go play dolls with Samantha in the living room while I talk to your grandparents," I said.

"So how did it go with the rug rat?" my dad asked.

"Really bad. And from ...now...on, I would appreciate it, Dad, if you would never refer to my child as a 'rat' again!" My parents were speechless. Never had I stood up to my dad and been so bold.

They sat there and stared at me.

"Jaime told the therapist that she sleeps with Doyle during her visits." I took a cleansing breath and I tried to get the words out. "She said... he touches her... she showed us! The S.O.B. told Jaime it was a secret and she was not to tell anyone!" I fumed. Just speaking the words out loud made the hatred grow.

"Are you sure this really happened?" my mom challenged. Dad sat there motionless, expressionless, silent.

No emotions, no sympathy, no hugs, no comfort. Not even anger, which surprised me. That was the one emotion they were good at expressing. I expected some reaction. After all, this is their three-year-old grandchild. *Aren't they angry about this? Don't they care or have any compassion for Jaime?* I had never felt so alone.

"Do you really think Jaime could make something like that up...especially at her age? That's all you have to say? Well, I guess I'll let you get back to your precious happy hour!" I stuffed down my frustration before it got me in trouble, gathered up the girls and made a beeline for the door.

"Darkness cannot drive out darkness;
only light can do that."

~ Martin Luther King Jr.

CHAPTER 11

I called Loui as soon as the girls were asleep. I was in a frenzy and paced back and forth. "That sinister, psycho Doyle has molested Jaime! We are asking for an order to stop his visits immediately!" I shrilled, then filled her in on what Jaime said during the session.

"No, that can't be! I'm so sorry, Denise. I knew Doyle was deceitful and cruel to you!" Loui let a string of obscenities fly and yelled, "He should be drawn and quartered!"

The next day, while I was at work, Joe called to tell me Doyle had been notified of the judge's order to stop visitation.

When I got home my thoughts were a jumbled mess... *he's going to have a fit that the visits have been stopped and he's gonna show up and kill me!* The swirling thoughts were like a whirlpool going around and around threatening to drown me. Then fear took over and my heart started to race as if I'd just run a twenty-mile marathon in ten minutes. I got out the 7-Up and Seagram's Seven and stirred the two together with a shaky hand. I promised myself that it would be my only drink. The continual stress day after day tempted me to drink. *One more couldn't hurt. Just one more... one more drink will erase the pain.* I'd seen too many go down that dangerous road, so I had made the decision to control the alcohol before it could control me. One drink took the edge off and stopped the *what if*'s from consuming me. The three doctors I sought out for a different solution had said no to any prescriptions that may have helped, so I was forced to come up with my own solution.

An hour later, I hesitantly picked up the phone when it rang. Before I could even say hello, I heard, "You can't do this. I have a right to see my kids! You can't keep them from me... You will burn in hell for this!" Doyle raged at the top of his lungs.

I wanted to scream, "*You have done the vilest, most destructive, detestable thing imaginable to my daughter, and you should never be allowed to see her again!!*" But I refrained and just slammed down the receiver. He continued to call, but each time I bit my tongue and hung up. The persecution finally stopped when my attorney threatened to file harassment charges.

Judge Waters agreed on Monday to an emergency order to stop visitation. A date was set in Juvenile Court for two months later to hear the evidence against Doyle. Lisa would meet with Jaime several times before the first hearing. Our ongoing divorce proceedings in Domestic Court were taxing. There seemed to be no end in sight, and now there would be more court dates.

෬෬෬෬෬෬෬෬෬෬෬

I was glad for a diversion and looked forward to lunch with Betty at the Tex-Mex diner, La Casa. It was a cheerful place with pictures of agave plants and parrots adorning the walls. The tables were embellished with orange and yellow Mexican tile. Betty strutted in wearing a vibrant color block silk blouse which complemented the décor of La Casa. She saw me, frantically waved, and raced over to my table. I got the impression she was about to burst with some juicy tidbit she had received on the sly.

"You won't believe what I found out today!" she exclaimed.

"No, I won't cause I'm not good at guessing. So out with it!"

"Doyle is remarried! He got married last weekend in Mississippi."

I paused, then tried to digest this ludicrous information. "Really! Who would want him? Why Mississippi? Nice joke, Betty. Couldn't come up with a better one than that?" I snarled.

"No, really. He married some floozy named Brice who works at Nobel's. No idea why they went to Mississippi," she said adamantly.

Brice? My heart sank. She was the new employee at Nobel's that Loui had told me about and she told me all I needed to know! Loui was convinced Brice was hunting for a man and now I knew the prey she took down was Doyle. My skin crawled to think that the girls now had a stepmom that flaunted everything she had and was so self-absorbed. Loui mentioned that she was a single mom, so I hoped there might be some redeeming qualities about this Brice I had never met.

"Jaime just told me a few weeks ago that a Brice was living with her dad. But that's insane...he is still married to me!" I said.

Betty crowed, "He's committed bigamy!"

"He certainly has because our divorce is nowhere near being finalized!"

"Since Doyle and Brice were announcing it all over the store, I just assumed your divorce was over by now," she admitted.

"He sure thinks he is above the law," I muttered.

Betty got a glimmer in her eye. "You know what you should do?" She leaned in close. "Press bigamy charges against him!"

"Bigamy? Just what I want to do—be in court every week instead of twice a month!" I moaned. "Well...maybe it would show him he can't push me around. Could make the divorce proceedings go quicker."

And help protect Jaime. But I was not about to share my soap-opera life with this queen of gossip. I would call my attorney as soon as I got back from this kooky lunch.

All the puzzle pieces had fallen into place. Doyle had found out through his co-worker that Suzie was my babysitter. Her husband was an easy scapegoat to cover the fact that he had molested Jaime, and now Brice and Doyle were married! I was more determined than ever to protect Jaime and stand up to Doyle.

I called Joe after work and told him Doyle was remarried. Joe felt charges should be filed, but he wasn't sure the state would be interested in prosecuting Doyle. He would get back to me when he knew something.

After I put the girls to bed that night, I sat on the couch and flipped from one channel to the next. I froze when I heard the upcoming news: *"Mothers Forced to Disappear with Children. Find out why in this On Your Side investigative report coming up next. A story you won't want to miss!"* My eyes were glued to the TV a close-up of a reporter and a young, attractive woman with no makeup and with her hair pulled back, came on the screen.

The news anchor gave details of the mother and child's disappearance six weeks earlier, then asked, "Can you share what made you so desperate that you would vanish with your four-year-old daughter?"

The mother dissolved in tears. "My daughter came home from a visit with her father one night. She became hysterical when I took off her shirt to give her a bath. I was shocked and appalled to see red welts and cigarette burns all over her back. Visitation was stopped, but when the court gave him back joint custody a few months later, we went into hiding so I could protect her from her sadistic father! My daughter became so scared she would have to see him again, she started wetting the bed and having nightmares. I was willing to do anything to protect her!" The camera panned to a wide shot. I was sickened to see this compassionate, loving mom in an orange jumpsuit!

"My ex-husband hired a detective to track us down. I was thrown in jail for violating the court order; my daughter is now living with him. My appeal won't be heard for six months." She gasped to catch her breath between sobs.

I couldn't believe my ears! This mother had done the right thing and was thrown in jail for protecting her child. *What will happen if the court fails to protect Jaime in the same way? How many more moms are facing this agonizing choice?*

My stomach churned. Her poor daughter continued to be abused by her father. The daydreams I had of taking off with the girls to protect them completely evaporated. Doyle would only have them every other weekend if he got visitation back. They would be with me the rest of the time. I hated to think this way and was grateful the abuse had come to light only six months after our separation. If Doyle had not made up the story accusing Suzie's husband, the abuse might have gone on for years!

I had a drink to calm my nerves before bed, hoping sleep would overcome my heavy thoughts. To no avail, they continued to swirl in my head. I tossed and turned for hours. Rolling over, I glanced at the clock; it was 5:30. My alarm was due to go off in thirty minutes. I stared at the ceiling and once more I envisioned the image of Doyle and his overdue consequence as it replayed in my mind:

Doyle ogled a woman standing on the street corner in a scandalous red dress that hugged every curve. He kept his eyes planted on her as he crossed the busy street, not realizing he was in the path of a speeding bus. The bus morphed into a steam roller like the one in the cartoon movie, Who Framed Roger Rabbit, smashing him flat. Now his pulverized body would have to be peeled off the pavement. I smiled.

My entertainment all night was to watch his demise play out on the screen of my imagination over and over again. If only this concocted fantasy could become reality.

The constant yawning from a night without sleep didn't stop until after lunch. I was surprised when caller ID showed my attorney's number. It had only been a week since I called him with Betty's information.

"Denise, the state prosecutor believes there is enough evidence against Doyle to press bigamy charges. But to make the investigation go more quickly, they need to know what city they got married in—not just the state. Can you find out?"

"I think so. Let me call my friend."

I called Betty that night. She was happy to play detective and ask some questions at work.

ప్ర ప్ర ప్ర ప్ర ప్ర ప్ర ప్ర ప్ర ప్ర ప్ర

The next afternoon Betty called all revved up. "Brice was more than happy to spill the beans! They had an intimate ceremony on the beach. Afterwards, they went on a romantic dinner cruise and saw..."

"Ok, already! I don't need all those details!" I said impatiently. "I just need to know what city they got married in."

"Oh, I'm sorry I wasn't being very sensitive, was I? They got married in Gulfport, Mississippi."

Suddenly regret devoured me, my whole body was on fire. *When we were married he rarely took me out or made me feel special!*

I took a second, composed myself and responded, "Thanks for the info, Betty. I owe you."

I was done with the espionage business and decided to call Joe right away with the information I had gathered. I needed to stop the slow burn from consuming me.

Joe picked up on the first ring. "Thanks for getting the information so quickly. I know the prosecutor will be able to look up the marriage records today and charges will be filed tomorrow. Doyle will be picked up in the next few days, fingerprinted and booked. I wanted to make sure you knew the timing, in case he figures out that you helped us."

Oh great! He will make my life a living hell if he finds out I had anything to do with these charges! Then a confidence overrode the constant fear. Doyle could not control me any longer. I found relief in that truth, and I assumed the information could be used in our favor at the visitation hearing. Everything hinged on proof that Doyle had abused Jaime. If Joe couldn't accomplish that, he would get visitation back. There was no physical evidence to prosecute him in a criminal trial.

The judge's decision was my only hope of protecting Jaime. Surely the judge would decide Doyle was unfit to get visitation back.

*"A comfort zone is a beautiful place,
but nothing ever grows there."*

~ Unknown

CHAPTER 12

I tried to read the book *Motherhood* in hopes that Erma Bombeck's wit and humor would distract me from my present reality, but the attempt was futile. The constant ringing of the phone and a child pulling at his mother's pant leg, whining to go to the vending machine and demanding M&Ms, consumed my attention in the waiting room. This was the last appointment Jaime would have with Lisa before our first court hearing. Jaime came out of her Art Therapy session and colored at a table while Lisa and I went into the office.

"I wanted to show you a picture Jaime just drew. These sessions help her express emotions that have surfaced and enable her to communicate through pictures about the abuse," Lisa pointed out.

She handed me a huge folded piece of paper. When I opened it and I saw what Jaime had created, I became confused. "Is this what I think it is?" I asked. The life-like depiction took up the whole 24-by-24-inch piece of white paper.

"If you think it is a penis, then yes."

The penis was outlined in black and colored in like a rainbow with bright stripes of red, yellow, green and blue. It didn't make sense to me.

"Why is it rainbow colored? I thought she was traumatized by the abuse. Shouldn't the whole thing be colored black?"

"Doyle manipulated her into believing what he did was OK ... even normal. But when he told her '*It's our secret... don't tell anyone,*' she was given mixed signals. We all have a conscience, and even children instinctively know when something is extremely wrong. Her subconscious has been trying to make sense of what has happened, and it comes out in the nightmares. I will be using this drawing as evidence when I testify at the visitation hearing."

"I really appreciate your work with Jaime. That picture gives me a lot of hope and should prove Doyle exposed himself in front of Jaime."

Lisa added, as she walked me out, "You never know how the judge will view it, but that is my hope also."

Joe Schwartz and Lisa met to plan her testimony. They said I had nothing to worry about, but one question gnawed at my mind: *How long could they really keep Doyle from seeing the girls?*

I felt nauseated every time I thought about going to court and could barely breathe when the panic set in. I would force myself to recognize the negative thoughts that came right before the rope tightened around my chest. Then I would redirect my mind to positive thoughts. *I have two wonderful, healthy girls that go to a great daycare. I have a job I love, a great apartment. Court will get me one step closer to protecting Jaime and having to see Doyle will not kill me. This will not continue forever.* The positive self-talk made the rope loosen and the symptoms of panic would subside.

That Monday was a typical summer day, sunny and humid. I shielded my eyes with my hand as I stood on the courthouse steps, gazing up at the huge monstrosity. Nervousness overwhelmed me, my mouth felt like I had eaten cotton balls for breakfast and my throat constricted. I took a cleansing breath and tried to imagine staying calm when I saw Doyle.

Joe Schwartz came around the corner. "Hi. Are you ready for today?"

I sputtered, "As ready as I will ever be." Then I added, "What do you think will happen?"

"The judge will hear our evidence, that is, if they let Lisa testify as an expert witness. Then, most likely, he will set another court date," Joe replied.

My mind raced with questions that I was too scared to ask. *Wasn't she automatically an expert witness? What if they didn't let her testify? Another court date? Why would they prolong this when a child's safety was at stake? And if it was prolonged, what was my recourse to protect Jaime?* Ugh! My heart sank.

Joe noticed my facial expression and added confidently, "Nothing to worry about. We've got it covered!" Then he patted me on the back.

We proceeded into the courthouse where Lisa was waiting. Before I could even say hi, Joe took her aside to discuss her testimony. I looked down the hall, apprehensive that Doyle would appear. I didn't want to face him before the proceedings began. I didn't want my anger to cause me to say or do something I'd regret.

The courtroom door opened. Doyle, dressed in a dark suit, was already seated next to his attorney. He turned and looked my way. I felt his cold piercing eyes follow me across the room as the clerk ushered us to the opposite side.

"All rise," I heard the bailiff say. "The Honorable Robert Waters, presiding."

Judge Waters was an intimidating figure. He had a massive chest and he towered well above the other men in the courtroom.

He had to be close to seven feet tall, and the scowl on his face made him seem all the more menacing. Hyper-aware of my surroundings, I felt like a spectator in the courtroom, observing my own life. My heart rate slowed when I reminded myself I didn't have to say a word during the proceedings. Judge Waters explained this was a preliminary hearing. Then he asked Joe to have the first witness come up and testify. Joe introduced Lisa Miller and read through her qualifications.

"I would like this witness, Lisa Miller, to be qualified as an expert."

Doyle's attorney jumped up and said, "I object, Your Honor. The information she has is biased to her client."

"Lisa Miller will not be seen as an expert witness during this hearing," Judge Waters said, "but I will allow her testimony."

My palms started to sweat. This was not going the way we had planned. If Lisa wasn't considered an expert, who was? Lisa testified to what Jaime had confided in her during their first session that led her to request an emergency order be filed to stop visitation with Doyle. She went on to explain the art therapy she was doing with Jaime, and why it helps children through the trauma of abuse. The judge thanked Lisa for her testimony as she stepped down from the stand. Lisa sat down next to me. Judge Waters asked the attorneys to approach to the bench.

Shaken, I whispered to Lisa, "Why didn't you show the picture Jaime drew last week?"

"We thought it best to save that piece of evidence, if they didn't qualify me as an expert witness, until we get further into the case against Doyle."

The attorneys walked back from the bench. I turned my attention back to the judge.

"I am ordering monitored visitation. The same schedule stands until the next court hearing." Looking directly at Doyle, the judge asked, "Who will be on record as monitoring your visits, Mr. Boese?"

"My wife, Brice, Your Honor."

"Is there a reason your mother, the children's grandmother, can't monitor the visits? We find it works better if the grandparents can be involved."

"She lives two hours away."

"OK, I will allow your wife to monitor the visits. The next court hearing is set for September 10th. Everyone is dismissed."

My attorney stood, then escorted me out into the hallway.

"Why would Doyle get any visitation back, even monitored visitation, after Lisa testified to what Doyle did?" I asked, stunned and confused.

Joe led me around the corner. "This was an initial hearing to provide evidence showing why we stopped visitation," he explained. "They rarely deny visits altogether. This was the best we could hope for. It should keep the girls safe until the next hearing."

"But I don't think you understand. Brice works when Doyle is off work. There is no way she will be able to monitor the visits. I doubt Doyle will even tell her the visits have to be monitored."

"If you find Doyle alone with the girls, call me and we will stop the visits. I'm sorry. All we can do is bring that up at the next court hearing."

I was disgusted that no one understood how deceitful Doyle could be. I started to wonder how far he would take his lies.

෪෪෪෪෪෪෪෪෪෪

During a session with Lisa a few weeks later, Jaime created another masterpiece. It was like the first, but showed the organ in action, depicting black outlined drops of color coming out of the top of the penis. I was encouraged; we now had two pictures to show the judge and, as the therapy continued, the nightmares slowly began to wane. But, the separation anxiety only grew worse.

*"Forgiveness is a funny thing it warms
the heart and cools the sting."*

~ Arthur Ward

CHAPTER 13

I could no longer leave Jaime with a babysitter if I had a night out with my friends or went on a date. The minute I tried to leave, she would lay on the floor, kicking, screaming and begging me not to go. It broke my heart to watch the emotional toll life had put her through. Overnight my social life came to a screeching halt. I tended to go out only when the girls were at Doyle's house. Everything we were going through infuriated me. Doyle was to blame for making our lives miserable.

It was Sunday. After the morning Bible study, I decided to ask Pastor Whit if he could pray with me before the service. I put the girls in the church nursery. Jaime sat down at a table to play a game with the other girls. This seemed to be the only place I could leave Jaime without her throwing a tantrum. My mind wandered during the Bible study as they debated scripture and man's role in

it. By the time it was over, I had chickened out on sharing my horrific story with Pastor Whit. *What was I thinking? No one understood what I was going through, and how could I explain what
had happened without melting into a puddle of tears?* I felt so
alone.

I went into the service. Everyone had smiles on their faces, and
were chitchatting about life, unaware that mine was coming apart
at the seams. I thought about making a quick exit. After all, my
heart wasn't in the mood to worship a God who would let Jaime be
abused. I couldn't wrap my mind around such injustice in a world
this God of love had created. But, not wanting to draw attention to
myself, I decided I should stay. My mind was a continuous loop of
negative thoughts, reliving Jaime's words of what Doyle had done
and Lisa's testimony at the trial. I didn't hear one word of the songs
and totally tuned out the announcements. Pastor Whit began his
sermon, titled: GOD LOVES EVERYONE AND FORGIVES ALL

What? Wait. I don't think I heard that correctly.

"GOD LOVES EVERYONE AND FORGIVES ALL," he repeated.

*That can't be true! What about murderers, rapists, molesters?
Doyle?*

He began. "God's Word says in 1 John 4:8 that God is love ...
Love is not something God has; it's Who He is and everything He
does flows from that love. And He does not withhold His Love from
anyone – even those we deem unlovable, even those who have
committed the most heinous acts. Out of His love, He forgives. He
forgave Moses, a murderer; He forgave David, an adulterer; He
forgave Peter who betrayed Him. He has forgiven me and He has
forgiven you through His greatest demonstration of love – the sacrifice of His own Son. As we read in John 3:16; 'God so loved the
world' – that means *everyone.*

"And He wants us to love others as He loves us and to forgive
others as a demonstration of His love. Matthew 6:14-15 reads: 'For
if you forgive other people when they sin against you, your heavenly Father will also forgive you. But if you do not forgive others

their sins, your Father will not forgive your sins.' We are even to forgive those who commit revolting, hideous crimes such as murder, rape and child abuse!" Pastor Whit boldly preached.

I nearly jumped out of my skin when I heard him repeat my thoughts. I was very tempted to bolt out of the service, not caring if every eye in the place followed me out the door. I weighed my options and planned the easiest escape route as Pastor Whit continued.

"Even our beloved King David set up Bathsheba's husband, Uriah, to be murdered in battle by sending him to the frontline so he could have Bathsheba all to himself. David was an adulterer *and* murderer. David asked for forgiveness and God forgave him because He loved him. Holding grudges creates bitterness and hate. And don't think it's OK to visualize in your mind harm coming to someone who has sinned against you! You know, we have all done that! Unforgiveness is unhealthy. We need to take these emotions and thoughts to the Lord and let Him heal us," Pastor Whit passionately declared.

OK, now that's just creepy. How in the world could Pastor Whit know about my fantasy?

My fabrication of Doyle being killed by a bus barreling down on him seemed harmless enough. It wasn't like I pictured Doyle being skinned alive and boiled in oil. I felt God understood my delusion. It helped release my pent-up anger. Surely, He was OK with that. After all, it didn't hurt Doyle, and, in the daydream, I had nothing to do with his demise. So how could God fault me for wishing he was gone? I would never have to talk to Doyle again or deal with trying to protect the girls from him. My attention turned back to the sermon.

"Like it says in Ephesians 4:31-32: 'Get rid of all bitterness, rage and anger, brawling and slander, along with every form of malice. Be kind and compassionate to one another, forgiving each other, just as Christ has forgiven you.' It's not an easy thing to do, but love and forgiveness are choices. Once we make the choice, God gives us the grace we need to walk it out.

"GOD LOVES EVERYONE AND FORGIVES ALL – let us always remember that is why He sent His son to shed His blood for the forgiveness of ALL of our sins. And that we are victorious over it all because He defeated death and rose from the grave.

GOD LOVES US ALL. Let us pray."

God Loves Everyone and forgives all, God loves everyone and forgives all, God loves everyone and forgives all... kept echoing through my mind.

I didn't make eye contact with anyone when I slipped out during the chorus of the last song, "Let There Be Peace on Earth." What a fake song, I thought, as its melody followed me down the hall. There is no peace in this lifetime. I was living proof of it!

My thoughts were rushing like a turbulent waterfall drowning me while I fixed lunch for the girls in silence.

Jaime smiled sweetly as she wiggled back and forth. "Do we get to see Daddy today?" she asked.

Stinging words formed in my mind, tempting me to release them, I bit my tongue. Smiling back, I softly said, "I'm sorry Jaime not today." I was confounded by her desire to spend time with him, even if he was her father. I read a story to the girls, then put them down for a nap.

I was about to turn on the TV when the words *God Loves Everyone* started harassing me, consuming me.

I got angry at the words that would not leave, and shouted at the air, "No, you don't! You can't love a child molester! You can't love Doyle! Doesn't your word say in Matthew 18:6; If anyone abuses one of these little ones who believe in me, it would be better for him to have a heavy boulder tied around his neck and be hurled into the deepest sea than to face the punishment he deserves!"

I railed against these words I felt God was harassing me with. The fuming continued for several minutes, then exhaustion overtook me, and I couldn't speak. I sat there in silence waiting to be struck dead for speaking my mind so boldly.

That's when I heard a still small voice, "Yes, I love everyone - even Doyle."

I couldn't believe what I was hearing. I knew they weren't my thoughts.

My heart screamed, "But you can't! You just can't love someone who would do such a thing."

"I do love everyone," whispered Truth into my spirit.

"But what about Your judgment? Your word says we will be judged for every word, every act and every deed."

"Everyone will be judged because I love everyone," Truth whispered back.

Then Truth asked, "Do your children have consequences for their actions so they will learn from them?"

"Yes."

Then Truth asked, "And that is because?"

"I love them," I admitted.

I started to weep. I understood what God was showing me -- His truth. He wanted me to accept it. "OK, so you love Doyle - well I don't. I'm sure you can understand that." Silence.

"Oh, really? Now you have nothing to say?" The words slipped out before I could stop them. I looked around the room sure the walls would collapse on top of me!

Then I heard, "Forgiveness."

"What? Forgive Doyle? If I do that, then I can't protect my Jaime!" I was confused.

"Forgiveness is for you; it brings My peace."

I picked up my Bible and searched His word for more truth. Isaiah 43:25-26 said: "I blot out your transgressions, for my sake and remember your sins no more. Review the past for me, let us argue the matter together; state the case for your innocence."

I had chills and felt a heavy peaceful presence. The scripture alluded to what I was experiencing, and I knew the Holy Spirit was in the room with me. It was His voice I heard. I was in awe of His presence and a reverent fear came over me. God was speaking His truth to me, the truth I needed to hear. I realized I sinned by not forgiving Doyle. The unforgiveness resulted in anger and hatred. I had been tormented by them long enough. My behavior, even if just in my thoughts, were not a reflection of who God created me to be.

My eyes were pools of tears as I whispered, "God, I want to forgive Doyle for abusing me and molesting Jaime. Give me the strength to forgive him because I don't have the power to do this on my own. Please forgive me for my anger and hatred of him."

Immediately, I envisioned what Doyle would face when he stood before a Holy God, giving an account of the abuse he put us through. I felt sorry for him and instantly understood the wrath he could endure unless he gave his heart to God in true repentance.

"God, please move on Doyle's heart, draw him close with Your love so he will repent of his sin and be with You in eternity," I earnestly prayed.

The weight I'd dragged around for all those months lifted. I felt free. An indescribable elation and jubilance welled up in me, lifting me higher into His presence. A kind of euphoria enveloped my whole body, creating a desire in me to stay right there in God's presence forever.

*"Sometimes the love of your life
comes after the mistake of your life."*

~ Unknown

CHAPTER 14

The bright sunshine pierced through the ominous black clouds on the drive home from the store. It had been six months since I had forgiven Doyle. I had passed through fierce times, like a tumultuous spring that turned into a glorious summer, and now I was excited about the future. I struggled to carry the heavy bags of groceries into the apartment, barely lifting them onto the kitchen countertop when the phone rang.

"Hi Denise. Man, work was crazy today, wasn't it?" Diane complained.

Juggling fruit, I opened the refrigerator door, then balanced the receiver with my shoulder to my ear. "Sure was. I am worn out and seeing cross-eyed from typing so many numbers! Can I call you back? I've got food to put away."

"Real quick. I forgot to ask you something. Are you coming to the company golf outing on Friday?"

"Barry said he had enough help setting up and since I don't play golf, he told me to take the day off."

"Geez, I didn't realize that. I can't go to the outing. The deadline on the Williams job got moved up. Soooo... I was hoping you could take my place offering drinks to the golfers by driving one of the beer carts around? I promise, it will be more fun...than having a day off!" she cajoled.

"Well, I guess I could. OK, you twisted my arm right off. But I'm not sure who I can get to watch the girls."

"Oh, I'm way ahead of you. I asked our dear brother Andy. You remember him?" she joked. "He owed me a favor and I figured he needed to spend more time with his nieces anyway. One more question: Do you know anyone else who would like to drive a beer cart on the other nine?"

I spurted out, "Betty would love to do it with me!"

🙒 🙒 🙒 🙒 🙒 🙒 🙒 🙒 🙒 🙒

Over the next few days as the list of men who were playing in the golf outing grew, I started to regret my decision to drive a beer cart. I knew I would feel uncomfortable around a lot of men I didn't know, but I reminded myself that Betty would make it fun. Besides, I didn't have to make conversation, just hand out drinks.

I saw Betty pull into the parking lot at the Pleasant Run Golf Course just ahead of me. I was dressed in a striped tank top and pink shorts to soak up some sun. True to form, you could see Betty coming in her short dress. It had a scattered mod design of brilliant pink, blue and purple daisies. Except for her ebony hair, Betty's outfit made her the spitting image of a dancing Goldie Hawn from *Laugh-in*.

As I leaned down to hug her, I chided, "Don't you think you might distract the golfers in that outfit?"

"Honey, that is the plan! There might be some men worth meeting out here today!" she teased as she seductively put her hands on her hips, shaking them. I shook my head at her brazenness and looked around, hoping no one had overheard.

We walked to the clubhouse. I greeted Barry and introduced him to Betty. He helped us pack our carts with pop and beer. I noticed Barry eyeing Betty's figure in the colorful dress, which showed every curve. She was oblivious to his attraction.

"It's sunny and there's not a cloud in the sky! At least I am dressed to work on my tan and not distract the golfers," I needled. Barry muffled a smirk.

Using a southern drawl, Betty said, "What? I'm sure the golfers will be concentrating so much they will hardly notice me." Then she pointed to herself and fluttered her eyes. I was doubled over from laughter. This was just the mindless break I needed.

I came upon a group of older guys at the first hole. They seemed pleasant. The golfers continued to focus on their game while I quietly offered them drinks. I started to relax and enjoy riding around with the sunshine warming my back when I came to the fourth hole.

I noticed the men in this foursome were all my age. They were a loud bunch who seemed to be more interested in playing around than winning the game. Flirtatiously, a tall guy with an olive complexion teased, "Hey, Sunshine, you can be my caddy anytime!"

They all stared at me and I could feel the crimson heat creep up my neck. Without saying a word, I quickly handed them each the beer they had requested and walked back to my golf cart.

"Look at that back nine!"

I turned to see who made the remark just in time to see the tall, dark one look away acting like he was in search of his ball.

Then they loudly crooned in unison, "Don't be a stranger. We will need another round soon!" They high-fived one another and broke out in laughter.

I forced a smile and, waving, drove away. I checked my watch. It was 11:30 in the morning. I wondered how crazy this group could get as the day progressed.

The rest of the foursomes that I delivered drinks to were more interested in their golf games than in me, so my nerves calmed down. When I rounded the bend coming up to the next hole, I could hear the wisecracks and jokes before I even saw the guys.

"You're better looking than your twin sister! Let me introduce myself. I'm Jake Lane," he said, extending his hand. I had heard his name before from Diane. I shook his hand.

Oh, Jake was the guy from our parent company who had tried to set Diane up on a couple of dates with a guy named Chris. Jake introduced me to the rest of the foursome. The tall, dark, mischievous cute one was the last to be introduced.

"Denise, this crazy guy who wants you to caddy for him is Chris Fromm." *Oh, this is Chris!* I contained my laughter. I couldn't envision Diane going out with him. She would have decked any stranger brash enough to use a catcall to get her attention.

"Hi," Chris coyly said. I shook his hand, then turned to get drinks out of the cart. When I turned back to give them their cans of beer, I noticed Chris blatantly staring at me. Maybe I had a stain on my shirt or my hair was a mess. I waved goodbye and left. I decided to stop by the clubhouse bathroom before I continued to another hole.

The mirror showed I had no stain on my shirt and every hair was in place. I looked at my reflection again. I had put a little weight back on and was happy with what I saw, but uncomfortable with the attention from the foursome that, by this time, was feeling no pain. I knew as the day progressed and the more they drank, the flirtation directed toward me would only get worse.

I drove around to the back nine to find Betty. "Hey, having fun yet?" I asked.

"Yes, I sure am," Betty cackled. "Your boss is coming on to me! I told you there would be some meat, ah, I mean men worth pursuing today!" She winked.

I chuckled. "I could tell he was checking you out when we first got here, so I'm not surprised. I don't mean to change the subject, but I need you to stay on the back nine, so I can stay on the front."

"Sure. But why don't you want to switch nines?"

"Because one of the guys is making me really uncomfortable and I don't want to continue to run into him." Betty understood where I was coming from and consented to switch places with me for the remainder of the day.

I had just returned my golf cart when I saw Chris barreling towards me from the last green. He wasn't slowing down! Just when I thought he was going to knock me over, he grabbed me up in his strong arms and twirled me around. I ignored the surge of electricity that coursed through my body leaving me limp.

Chris' intense look made my heart flutter when he peered down at me. "Who is he?" he asked. "Betty told us someone was bothering you!" From behind I felt everyone staring at us.

If Betty blabbed to everyone, I'm gonna kill her.

"I...I ...just told Betty that to give her something to talk about. You don't have to rescue me from anyone," I stammered, twisting to get out of his arms.

He gently put me down and continued to stare at me. I knew it was the beer that made him so bold. I could tell I had misjudged this sweet, shy guy. It would crush him if he knew he was the one I was trying to avoid!

"Hey, a bunch of us are going back to my apartment tonight. Would you like to join us?" he invited.

I hesitated for a moment. I didn't know him and, even though he appeared harmless in that moment, I didn't want to take any chances. "Can Betty and my boss, Barry, come along?"

"Sure! I think I saw your boss eyeing her all day."

"I'm sure he was! We can follow you after we pack up the tables and signs."

He looked down and smiled. "I'm sure the tables are heavy. Let me help you." He walked with me to the registration area and I introduced him to Betty and Barry. By the end of the outing everyone knew that one of the golfers had made me feel uncomfortable. They just didn't know who the culprit was—and neither did Chris.

I reprimanded Betty when she got in my car. "How could you tell everyone that one of the guys was upsetting me?"

In a sultry voice and with a devilish grin, she replied, "I just told the truth. But you know what? Those luscious lubed cuties can bother me any day. And your boss! I could just kiss him all over!"

I snickered. "You might need your eyesight checked because Chris is the hot one!"

Chris' apartment was the ultimate bachelor pad with sparse furnishings. One black leather loveseat, conveniently hiding any dirt, sat in the corner of the room, with a couple of lounge chairs and bean bags in the middle of the room. A dining table buried in mail was right outside the kitchen. Dirty dishes were piled high in the sink with open, empty green bean cans lining the countertop. As the night progressed, it was easy to overlook the unkempt room. Chris and his friends had a great sense of humor and kept everyone laughing late into the evening.

Several times I caught Chris looking my way during everyone's larger-than-life golf stories. My blushing became uncontrollable as Jake unmercifully teased me about the crimson color spreading across my face. Betty didn't come to my rescue; she was too busy entertaining Barry on the loveseat and ignoring everyone else.

I was shocked when I glanced down at my watch. I had a forty-five-minute drive home after I dropped Betty off. "I better get going," I announced, looking directly at Betty in the corner with Barry. I wondered what ploy I could use to pry her away from him.

Chris handed me a paper plate and a pen. I turned it over, curious why he'd given it to me. "Can I have your number?" he mumbled.

I laughed.

"Well, it's the only thing I have to write on," he admitted.

"I'm not sure that's a good idea. Didn't I hear Jake mention you are seeing someone?"

He looked disconcerted. "It's not serious. I would really like to see you again. How can I do that without your number?"

"Based on what you've had to drink today, I wouldn't be surprised if you didn't remember me tomorrow," I smirked.

He placed his hands on my shoulders and looked down at me with his translucent amber eyes. His soft voice became serious. "I could never forget you."

My heart melted. "I guess it won't hurt to talk to you over the phone." I wrote my number on the paper plate and handed it back to him.

I went over to Betty and nudged her, hoping she would get the hint. "It's already 10 and I still have to drop you off at the golf course. I promised my brother I wouldn't be too late."

"OK, Mom." She turned to Barry and whined, "Mom says we have to get going."

He smiled at her. "I think Mom is right!"

She walked her fingers up his arm and tapped him on the nose. "Ya'll give me a call soon, Sugar Pie!" she drawled. Barry lost it, and we heard his laughter follow us out the door.

*"Forget your mistakes but remember
what they taught you."*

~ Benjamin Franklin

CHAPTER 15

"*H*i, Sunshine. Been driving any golf carts lately?" Chris joked when I picked up the phone.

"No, but I was beginning to think you lost your 'little black' book," I teased.

"I wouldn't do that. I have it in a very safe place," he assured.

"Let me guess. For safe keeping you wedged the paper plate in the crack between the wall and your phone?"

He chuckled. "How did you know?"

"Just a lucky guess."

"I really called to ask you an important question. Would you like to go get some Mexican food at Chi-Chi's and then see *St. Elmo's Fire* afterwards?"

"Umm, a date? I haven't been on one of those in a while. Well, I guess you're a safe enough guy to go out with..." I chortled.

I had made a decision not to date until I was on my own for at least a year. It had been that long. I had also decided that the girls would not spend time with anyone I dated until it became a serious relationship, and I could trust my instincts that he would not harm them.

"Come on. Don't leave me hanging," he pleaded. "How about Saturday at 6?"

"As long as my sister can watch the girls, I would love to!" *It wouldn't hurt for the girls to just meet him.*

I was elated and couldn't remove the grin from my face when I called Diane.

"Guess who asked me out?" I shrieked in her ear when she answered the phone.

"It's got to be the guy from the golf outing. Chris, right?" she surmised.

"Yes! Ugh, I don't have a thing to wear! And I really need you to babysit so Jaime won't get too upset when I leave. Can you?" I cajoled.

"Sure. I had plans, but I will rearrange my schedule just for you, Sis!"

"Thanks so much. You're the best!"

🙠🙠🙠🙠🙠🙠🙠🙠🙠🙠🙠

The week crawled along and even the pile of work on my desk didn't distract me long enough to make the time fly by, but finally Saturday arrived. Diane came early to play with the girls, so I could get ready. I rummaged through my closet. I had imagined so many outfits, but still couldn't decide which one would be just right. The ruffled blouse was too dressy. The casual t-shirt announced, "You're not important. Therefore, I don't care what I look like." Aha! My high-waist, acid-washed jeans with a white blouse under my new lace and pearl vest, would be perfect! I got dressed and went into the bathroom.

I lifted each teased curl to spritz it with hair spray -- for staying power -- when the thought came to me: Chris is a stranger. What do we have in common? Does he like kids? What does he do for fun? I leaned into the hallway.

"Hey, Diane. What if we don't have anything to talk about? I should have thought this through before I said I'd go. What if he turns out to be like those other creeps I've gone out with? What if Chris is only interested in one thing – like they were?" I lamented and a bit of panic set in.

Diane came down the hall. "OK, take a deep breath. You're getting ahead of yourself. This is a first date, not a lifelong commitment! Relax. Go have fun!" she encouraged.

Just then there was a knock, we saw Jaime race to the door. Diane hugged me and repeated, "Relax. Just go, enjoy dinner and the movie!" She sprinted down the hall after her.

Jaime flung the door opened and a smiling Chris bent down. "Well, hi there!" he said. "I bet you're Jaime and let me see. You must be Samantha! Am I right?"

Jaime became shy all of a sudden, hid behind Diane and nodded her head. Samantha toddled up and hugged Chris' leg.

My sister stuck out her hand. "Hi, I'm Diane, the better-looking twin."

Chris snickered and looked down at Samantha still clinging to his leg.

"Samantha must like you. She usually runs the other way at the sight of strangers!" Diane chuckled.

"Samantha, for goodness sake unhook your arms from around Chris' leg!" I said.

"It's ok. Really. I like the attention! I love kids. They aren't afraid to be themselves," he observed.

I leaned in and gave him a hug. "I'm glad to hear that. It's good to see you again!"

Chris looked at me and smiled. "You've got two cutie pies here!" Then he turned and looked at the girls. "I could stay and play with you two all night, but guess we better get going so we have time to eat before the movie."

"Diane, you can call me at the restaurant or the movie theater if you need anything or if they give you a hard time," I fretted

"The girls and I will be fine. Stop worrying. Just go and have fun!" Diane said.

Chris walked in front of me and opened the car door. *OK, he's a gentleman and loves kids. What is there to worry about?*

We talked about the hot weather, our favorite Mexican dish *and* our jobs on the way to dinner. Chi-Chi's was decorated with fun parrots that sat on swings hanging from the ceiling. Mexican sombreros and woven, striped blankets hung on the walls. The festive surroundings and the margarita I ordered helped me unwind.

We laughed through dinner reminiscing about Betty's antics at the party two weeks earlier. In the movie Chris put his arm around me, his hand lightly brushed against my arm sending a tingle down my spine. The attraction was palpable, a spark was starting to ignite, and I wondered where this would all lead. We walked arm-in-arm, discussing the scenes we liked on the way out to the car.

Chris' mood changed on the drive home; he became distant and quiet. I wondered if his "casual dating" of someone had turned more serious since the golf outing? It was awkward when he escorted me to the door.

"Would you like to come in for a minute? I wanted to ask you about something."

"That's ok. Ask me out here, unless you don't want anyone else to hear," he teased in a whisper.

I chuckled nervously. "No, it's not that. I just thought we could sit down for a minute. Look, Barry just gave me two tickets to the Pointer Sisters concert next weekend, so I thought...well, I was hoping you could go with me."

Chris shifted his weight from foot to foot and looked towards the stairs. *Ugh! Why did I risk him saying no? Here it comes.*

"I really don't like that kind of music. You should take someone who would enjoy it more than me. I had a good time tonight, but I better get going. I have a long drive home."

He gave me a peck on the cheek, then I watched him disappear down the steps and out the door. *Did I say something or do something wrong? He seemed attracted to me and said he had a good time.* I let myself in and saw Diane sleeping in the recliner.

"Diane, wake up. I'm home," I announced.

"Oh, hi. I didn't mean to fall asleep. I must have been wiped out from being outside all day surveying. Well, how did it go?"

"He's nice and I enjoyed the evening, but on the way home he became distant and when I asked him to go to the concert with me next weekend, he turned me down flat! Said he didn't like the music! You know, if I were interested in a guy, I wouldn't care what we were doing together. I would just want to spend time with him! And until Chris drinks a few beers, he doesn't have much to say. And he smokes! So maybe I'm better off," I tried to convince myself.

"That's a shame! He seemed really nice. Maybe how he acted had something to do with the other girl you told me he was dating when he met you. No figuring men out!"

"It doesn't matter. I'm done with dating. I want you to take the tickets and go with Ray. I can't believe you met him at your friend's high school reunion! You two make a cute couple. Someday I'll find the right person. Just not now. Maybe it's for the best with everything else going on in my world."

"Thanks. And I will be happy to make, I mean take, Ray with me to the Pointer Sisters concert! You do know Chris had a valid excuse? Most guys really don't like dance music. And you also know men don't think like women. Yeah, we'd say yes just to be with them – even a demolition derby," she explained as if she had such great insight on the male psyche. Then she abruptly switched the subject. "When do Doyle's monitored visits start up again?"

"He's coming in the morning to pick the girls up. It's been three months since we had to stop his visitation for violating the court order. Can you believe Doyle gets visitation back and on the first visit he's alone with the girls?"

Diane shook her head, "I don't know who he thinks he is!"

"It just couldn't have been a coincidence that I saw Brice at the grocery store after dropping off the girls for their visit with Doyle, three months ago! God wanted me to know Doyle was alone with the girls. I'll never forget the panic I felt, people must have thought I was crazy leaving a cart full of groceries in the middle of the aisle! I've never driven so fast to get home. I was grateful I got a hold of Joe and he was able to file contempt charges the next day. Thank Ray's parents again for me; if they weren't willing to drop everything and go over to Doyle's house to get the girls, I don't know what I would have done. I knew Doyle wouldn't give them a hard time! I figured Doyle wouldn't tell Brice she had to monitor the visits; I heard she blew a gasket when she found out!"

We both chuckled. "Serves him right!" Diane said. "Who is going to monitor the visits now?" Diane asked.

"At last week's visitation hearing Doyle's attorney asked the judge to allow his mom to monitor the visits. Judge Waters agreed; he'd suggested that at the first hearing. But he warned Doyle that he better follow the order this time. We objected since she lives two hours away, but Doyle convinced the judge she would be happy to come down every other weekend. I don't trust him one bit, but I'm trying my best to put it all in God's hands and let Him take care of it."

Diane scowled. She wasn't an advocate of God handling it, unless He was still in the smiting business. "Maybe He could just cause the ground to open up and swallow Doyle," she'd mused. She wasn't in a place where forgiveness was even an option to consider. Though we'd both had a horrific upbringing, I was slowly learning that the healing I needed could only be found in God. Diane still carried anger and bitterness like a badge of honor and she wasn't about to let God take that from her.

I gave Diane a hug and she let herself out as I went down the hall and peeked into the girls' bedroom. The slumbering angels looked so tranquil. I tiptoed across the room, pulled Jaime's blanket up, tucked her in and kissed her on the forehead. I leaned over Samantha's crib and touched her cheek, adoring her precious sweet face. *God, please keep them both safe. Take Jaime's anxiety and nightmares away. And, Lord, please make Yourself known to Doyle.*

When I climbed into bed, the thought of their visit to Doyle's the next day made me anxious. I just couldn't imagine Doyle's mom, Connie, driving over two hours to monitor his visits with the girls every other weekend. I had to find out if Connie was actually there during the visit, but I knew Doyle would not let me just waltz into the house and have a conversation with her.

I ran through scenario after scenario, trying to determine what would work, when it dawned on me that I could call Connie during the visit. If she picked up the phone, I'd know for sure she wasn't at Doyle's house monitoring the visit. I relaxed and drifted into a sound sleep.

Hours later, giggles drifted from across the hall. I turned over in bed and squinted at the ray of light that pierced through the crack in the window blind. I crawled out of bed and stretched. It would be a busy morning, but at least I would have a couple hours with the girls before Doyle arrived.

Jaime saw her backpack by the front door and raced around the living room, excited. "When do we get to see Daddy? When do we get to go? I wanna go now."

"I know, honey. He will be here soon, but you've got to eat some breakfast first," my voice quavered.

Her excitement only increased my apprehension. The *what ifs* popped up again and again in my mind like the "whack-a-mole" game. I tried to hammer them away, but they kept coming back. *What if Connie isn't there and he's alone with them and he touches Jaime again? What if he does something to Samantha this time?*

A waffle popped up from the toaster. I cut it in half and placed one piece on each daughter's plate, then poured syrup on them and put another one in to toast. "Come sit down and eat your waffles while they are hot."

A picture of Doyle flashed through my mind. I hadn't seen him in months and my nerves were on edge. I paced back and forth down the hall several times. Then, on the verge of tears, I ducked into the bathroom. I looked in the mirror. *You have got to get ahold of yourself for the sake of the girls! And you don't want to cry in front of Doyle! Breathe. Breathe!*

My heart rate slowed. *Think of all the positive things: the girls are happy they get to see their dad. He won't try anything because he won't want it coming out in court. I choose to be happy that Jaime gets to see her father.* I sighed. There was a knock at the door; I smiled into the mirror... *You've got this!*

Jaime jumped up from the table and flung the door open. "It's Daddy! It's Daddy!" And then she jumped into Doyle's arms.

"I missed you sooooo much!" Doyle exclaimed.

I scooped up Samantha out of her high chair and picked up their bag, almost feeling sorry for Doyle. My pity dissolved quickly. This was not a man who could be trusted, and I had to make sure my girls remained safe. I'd call Connie's house in an hour or so to confirm she was at Doyle's house.

"Here you go. Everything they need is in the bag and I will pick them up at 5:00. Tell Connie I said, 'Hi.'"

Doyle's smile disappeared, and suspicion flashed crossed his face. I handed him Samantha and the bag. I gave the girls a kiss and shut the door, more determined than ever to make that call to his mother.

"A lie can travel half way around the world
while the truth is putting on its shoes."

~ Charles Spurgeon

CHAPTER 16

"*L*oui, I've got a plan!" I announced.

"Denise? You do know it's proper, when a person answers the phone, to say hello first, right?" MariLu teased.

"I'm sorry. Loui. I'm just wound up like a rubber band about to break! Doyle has his monitored visit today and...."

"I know. I was about to walk out the door to come over there for our "Girls Day Out." Remember?"

"Actually, I forgot. But that's great. I will tell you the plan when you get to my apartment!"

I stepped out of the shower, dried off and quickly threw on a pair of jeans and a t-shirt. I was towel-drying my hair when Loui knocked on the door. "Come on in." I yelled. "Sorry I sounded so crazy on the phone."

"Hey, I get it and that's why I'm here to keep you distracted all day!" Loui leaned in and gave me a tight squeeze.

"You're a great friend and I'm lucky to have you! I have to make a call first before we go anywhere."

"OK. Fill me in on this plan you were talking about."

I told Loui about the idea I'd thought of the night before and about the expression on Doyle's face that morning. I knew he was up to something. "Since the kids have been gone for two hours, I think now would be a good time to call his mom and see if she answers her home phone!"

"OK. Sounds like a good plan."

I dug around my kitchen drawer, located my address book and looked up Connie's number. I took a deep breath, dialed slowly, and heard it ring. Then I lost my nerve and hung up.

"Why'd you do that?" Loui asked.

"What should I say? I know I will recognize her voice, but I don't want her to know I'm calling, do I?"

"All you have to do is let her say hello, then when she does, say "Connie?" When she says "Yes?" hang up! Then you'll know for sure it's her, and she won't recognize your voice," Loui coached. Then she added, "Thank goodness, you can block the number you're calling from!"

I carefully dialed each number and waited for someone to answer. My pulse quickened when someone picked up on the third ring.

"Hello? ...Hello?" I heard Connie say.

"Connie?" I asked.

"Yes, this is Connie." I slammed down the receiver.

"Doyle is alone with the girls!" My body ignited with heat, a deep growl spewed to the surface. "Argggggh... Who does he think he is? He doesn't care what the court order says!" I gritted my teeth. Frustration grew.

"Ughhhhh, I can't leave them over there and I can't go get them. I won't be able to control my anger when I see Doyle!" I ranted.

Loui put her hand on my shoulder. "OK," she said. "Think about what just happened. Doyle didn't expect you to call Connie, right? And when you hung up, I'm sure Connie got suspicious and called Doyle. Maybe Doyle did the same thing to his mom that he did to Brice. Connie might not even know she was supposed to monitor the visits!"

"So, you're saying Doyle got caught red-handed and he's the one that should be shaking in his boots!"

"Yes, that's exactly what I am saying. I don't think Doyle is going to give anyone a hard time today. But just to be safe. Can you get Diane and Ray to go over and get the kids?" she suggested.

"That's a good idea. I'll call her now."

Diane and Ray agreed to go over to Doyle's and get the girls three hours into the visit. Diane told me how surprised Doyle looked when he came to the door. "He didn't hassle Ray at all! He just packed up the girls' things, kissed them on the forehead and told them he'd see them soon."

Knowing Doyle, the way I do, I expected a call from a ranting, raving madman. But the call never came.

First thing Monday morning, I called Joe to tell him that Doyle's visit had not been supervised by his mother and how I'd found out. He filed a contempt motion that morning, citing Doyle's violation of the court order and asked the judge to stop his visits.

I was exhausted by the end of the work week and couldn't wait to get home and have a quiet evening with the girls. Now that Doyle was out of the picture again, the roller coaster I had been riding came to a delightful stop. I didn't have to be on high alert, trying to catch Doyle in his lies, and I didn't have to live in fear that the girls would be harmed. God had led me to discover the truth and I was grateful for the blissful break from the drama. Once we were home from daycare, I had an idea for a fun stay-at-home evening.

"Jaime, how about we order a four-cheese pizza from Cicero's? Then we can watch the *Care Bears* movie."

"Yay! Pizza! I love Care Bears!" she exclaimed, then ran into her bedroom and came out carrying her Tenderheart Care Bear and Baby Hugs, which she handed to Samantha. The girls were hungry when the pizza arrived 30 minutes later and stuffed themselves. They snuggled with their Care Bears, mesmerized through the entire movie. I read them a bedtime story and kissed them good night. It was one of the most peacefully refreshing evenings I'd had with them in a long time.

Time alone was just what I needed so I could write in my journal. I cleared my mind and contemplated the scripture I had just read when a loud ring pierced the silence. I jumped out of the chair. My pulse raced. "Hello?" I said.

"Hey, girl. Wha'sup? I know you have been wondering why I haven't called you lately. I know I left a void in your life."

I recognized the prideful, obnoxious voice. It was the short, creepy guy I'd gone out with once. Billy was my co-worker's cousin. She'd insisted on setting me up with him and convinced me he would be a fun date. The girls were with Doyle that night, so I figured one date couldn't hurt and then she'd quit pestering me.

"Not really. I've been too busy with my girls and you caught me at a bad time."

He had taken me to a disgusting dark hole-in-the-wall bar, then proceeded to brag all night about the logo t-shirts his company designed. They were worn by people all over the country. Then to prove it, for two hours he recited, from memory, the names of every customer who had ever bought his merchandise!

"I'd like to take you out again if you aren't on a diet. You ate like a bird the last time, girl. You know I love it when a girl can eat!" Billy crowed.

Why is he calling? I thought I made it crystal clear I wasn't interested in what he was selling.

"You looked fine on our date and if you've been working out, girl, you'll really look fine! I know you miss my adorable face! I'm right, aren't I?" he bragged.

This guy doesn't take a hint! Oh, brother why did I even pick up the phone!

"No, to be quite honest," I growled.

"What? Girl, you need to have some fun! Don't be mad that I haven't called, I've been hiking in the mountains...." Blah, blah, blah was all I heard as he droned on and on.

My heart lifted up an earnest prayer, *"God help me find some-one who will love me for who I am and not what he can get from me. I need someone who can be my best friend first and love the girls like they are his own. And is it too much to ask for tall and cute? I'm not asking you to send me Robert Redford...just a nice, honest guy."*

Billy continued the conversation with himself, not noticing that I had zoned out.

When he paused to take a breath, I interrupted him.

"Oh no, what was that?" I pretended. "Well, it was nice to hear about your adventure, but it sounds like one of the kids just threw up in the bathroom! Oh my, there are chunks of undigested food sliding down the wall! Poor baby! She must have a virus, ugh, the stench is about to make me... hurl! I gotta go!"

That should make him lose interest and it wasn't a total lie; the bathroom could use a deep cleaning!

"What? OK, girl. Bye," he muttered.

"True love is the best blessing
God ever gave man."

~ Unknown

CHAPTER 17

*I*t had been weeks and I was done waiting for Doyle to call me. I needed an answer. The car payment was due next week and the unpaid bills from my attorney were piled on my desk. I was out of options. I paced around the room, then picked up the phone.

"Hi Doyle. Everyone I know who filed their taxes after us has already received their check. So where is ours?" I demanded.

"Oh, I can't talk right now." Click.

This is the second time he has hung up on me when I asked him about the tax refund!

Since our divorce wasn't finalized, Doyle had convinced me that filing jointly was a good idea. He knew I needed the five hundred dollars, but instinct and history told me I had made a mistake. Once again, I had to find out if Doyle was lying. I thought about calling the IRS, but I knew if I didn't speak to the right person, I wouldn't get the right answer.

The words surfaced again and became stronger: *Call Chris Fromm. He works at the IRS; he'll know the answer.* I pushed away the thought. It had been nine months since we had gone out and I wasn't sure he'd even remember me. And if he did, I sure didn't want him to think I was using a tax fiasco to get a date! Dating was the last thing on my mind. But the thought wouldn't leave me alone. So I called Jake and got Chris' number.

Every time I picked up the phone, I put it back down again. A calm, still voice encouraged me, *"So what if he doesn't remember you? That's even better. Just ask him the question and get off the phone."*

I dialed his number again and he picked up.

I tried not to hyperventilate. "Hi. This is Denise Boese. I don't know if you remember me, but I was hoping you could help me with something."

"I remember you...you wouldn't be my caddie at the golf outing, and I was devastated! But I won't hold that against you. How have you been?"

"Trust me, I don't know anything about golf. So I would have only distracted you from your game. I'm calling because I have a problem with my tax return. I was wondering if you could look up my refund check and tell me if it has been mailed."

"No, I can't look it up, but I can call you on Monday with the name and number of the person who can give you that information."

"That would be great. I really appreciate this! Thank you so much. I'll be expecting your call on Monday then."

"Wait. I have a question..."

Uh, this is awkward. Don't ask me out! Don't ask me out!

"What have your cutie pies, Jaime and Samantha, been up to?"

"Oh, uh...Right now they are at the zoo with Aunt Diane, seeing the baby tigers that were just born, so I could get some things done around here."

Ahh, he called the girls cute and remembered their names!

"That sounds like fun! I must confess I thought about calling you the other day. I realized I messed up big time by not taking you to the Pointer Sisters concert. I'd like to make it up to you. Hey, if your sister could keep the girls, I would love to take you out tonight."

"Well, I think I can talk Diane into that. Sure, I'd love to!" My quick response surprised me. After all, I had made up my mind that I was done with dating.

"I will pick you up at 6:00 and Denise. . . I am glad you called. I can't wait to see you."

"Me too." I felt a familiar tingle and my heart fluttered.

A few minutes later, Diane called to make arrangements to meet for dinner, so I could get the girls back.

"Actually, I was hoping you would keep the girls a little longer. You won't believe this! I just got asked out! I called Chris about the refund check and he asked me to go to dinner!"

"Are you sure you didn't have an ulterior motive when you made that call?" she teased.

"No. Really. I only said yes because . . . I don't know. He remembered the girls' names and asked about them! Any guy who does that is worth giving a second chance."

"Hmm... If you say so. Well, I will feed the girls, bring them home and put them to bed so you can go on your 'so-called' date. But don't blame me if the date is a disaster. The way he just left you hanging and then let so much time pass. To the curb, I say. Kick him to the curb!"

I gave up trying to convince Diane that I didn't used my tax refund check problem to get a date.

I scoured my closet for the right outfit. I decided on a cap sleeve, curve fitting, blue and white flowered dress. I patted my makeup with powder, put on eye shadow and lipstick, then ran a curling iron through my hair and coated it with hair spray. I glanced in the full-length mirror on the back of the bathroom door, twirled around and beamed at my reflection.

Floating into the family room I saw the tape "Up Where We Belong" sitting on my cassette player. I popped it in and turned up the volume. The lyrics filled the room, and my version of the last scene from *An Officer and a Gentleman* came to life. I swayed across the floor imagining myself at my work desk. Lips caress my neck. Startled, I look back to see my handsome Navy officer in his dress uniform. His kisses electrify my body. He swings my chair around, picks me up in his arms and passionately kisses me. My hero carries me out of the office, away from the drudgery of life to live happily ever after.

Are happily-ever-afters only the invention of movies and fairy tales? Or do girls like me get the good guy in the end and sail off into the horizon? Up to this point, that version of the story had eluded me, and I was almost afraid to dream.

There has to be a happily-ever-after! There has to be!

There was a loud knock, withdrawing my mind from the fairy tale I had created. I raced over, pushed the off button and stopped to check my appearance in the mirror on the way to open the door.

It was Chris, wearing a blue oxford cloth button-down shirt and jeans, sporting a grin from ear to ear.

Gasping for air, I blurted out, "Hi. Nice outfit!"

"Thanks! It's my trademark dating apparel since I must be ready at a moment's notice. Girls are constantly calling me with their tax problems and I'm trying to keep them all happy. It's a hard life being an IRS agent!" Chris' head tilted back as he laughed, then he ran his fingers through his thick chestnut colored hair.

His gaze caught mine. "You look gorgeous!"

My face flushed. He leaned over and kissed my hot cheek, his translucent amber eyes made me melt inside. I had forgotten how attractive he was.

He led me to his car. "I made reservations at My Good Friend Donny's downtown. It is a small, quaint place with really good food."

"That sounds great. I love trying new places."

They sat us at a round booth with tufted red velvet cushions on the back and seat. The ornate tin ceiling and the wooden mirrored bar with carved designs at the top and pillars at each end was stunning. The scene transported me to a bygone era out of a movie.

The waitress took our drink order, then told us about the special. "Our master chef has taken 24 hours to prepare a delectable delight for your taste buds this evening. You can only get this mouthwatering dish here!" She thumped her fingers on the table. "Drum roll please...may I suggest...Peking duck with plum sauce!"

We both chuckled at her presentation.

We were savoring every bite of the duck when Chris broke the silence. "I want to explain why I haven't called. Right after I met you, my relationship with Jeanette became serious and we got engaged. She broke up with me a month ago. My friends were relieved because they hated the way she treated me. The break-up saved me from making the biggest mistake of my life."

He continued, "Since I didn't call after our first date, I was pretty sure you wouldn't want to hear from me." A sheepish grin crossed his face. "Just yesterday, I threw out my little black book, aka paper plate, that had your number on it. So, if you didn't have that tax problem and call me, we wouldn't be eating this awesome duck!"

I smiled, any words I had stuck in my throat. A peaceful, warm feeling spread through me. This couldn't be a coincidence. Was this the answer to my 'tall-dark-and-doesn't-have-to-look-like-Robert-Redford' prayer? Only time would tell. I was starting to understand who had prodded me to call Chris.

The waitress came by and picked up our empty plates. "Now that you have had the delectable, mouthwatering duck, you must try Pastry Chef Ivan's world-famous triple layer white cake with a rich fudge center that will melt in your mouth and mocha chocolate frosting, drizzled with caramel on top," she advertised.

I moaned and turned towards Chris. "As wonderful as that sounds, I couldn't possibly eat another bite!"

"I agree! Sorry, we will have to come back to try Chef Ivan's grand creation," he said, flinging his hand in the air to play along with the dramatic waitress. Chris cocked his head to the side and looked at me, then dabbed his napkin in his water. He delicately turned my head slightly and gently wiped a particle of food from the corner of my mouth. My cheeks blushed from the tender touch.

The night air was chilly, and I shivered on the walk to the car. Chris wrapped his arm around me and pulled me close. He opened my door and stared at me, "Your beautiful smile made dinner even more delicious." When he helped me in the car, his hand brushed my shoulder, goosebumps erupted down my arm. *Get a grip on your emotions! You are done with dating... remember? Why did you say yes so quickly?* I smiled back at Chris and wondered how I was going to keep my feelings from betraying me.

Diane met us at the door and reported that the girls had been asleep for an hour. She then turned to Chris and smirked, "I just wanted to thank you. I got to take my boyfriend to the Pointer Sisters concert because you turned my awesome sister down! You missed out on one fun night!" Diane was never one to let things go or to show restraint.

Chris turned and peered into my eyes. "I realized tonight what I fool I was. I should have said yes the moment she asked," he said, his voice deep and smoldering. Diane was rendered speechless. Mouth agape, eyes widened, she walked out the door. We roared with laughter.

"I've never seen Diane speechless!" I chuckled. "Would you like to sit on the couch and talk?"

We sat down, and he put his arm around my shoulder and lightly rubbed my arm with his hand. "Did I tell you I have twin sisters?"

"No, you didn't. Are they identical?"

"Yes. Linda and Sharon are five years older than me..." His words faded. I pictured him gathering me up in his strong arms and tenderly planting his lips on mine. *Stop! Focus! What did he just say?* I smiled to hide the fact that I hadn't heard the last three sentences he'd uttered. I fought to refocus my attention on his words.

"I heard music playing when I came to pick you up," Chris said, pointing to the cassette player. He stood up and walked across the room. "Let me guess . . . Pointer Sisters?"

"No, but "He's So Shy" by the Pointer Sisters would be fitting to play right now," I teased.

"Oh really? "He's so Shy"? What if I just hit this button and see what you were listening to?"

I tried not to panic and nonchalantly got up. "I don't think you need to do that," I said, emphasizing each word.

"Oh really? Now I'm dying of curiosity. I have to push the button."

Before I could stop him, "Up Where We Belong" drifted through the air.

Chris recognized the music and grinned. "Oh, a real romantic, huh? Guess you like the last scene in *An Officer and a Gentleman!*"

As I tried to turn the music off, he grabbed my shoulder and pulled me into his arms. His face was full of desire and I was helpless to resist the surging tide of warmth that left me limp. He bent his head down and caressed my cheek in his hand, pulling my lips toward his. His insistent mouth evoked sensations I didn't think I could feel. The soft, sweet embrace of his lips on mine turned into a deep penetrating kiss I didn't want to end. Lost in the moment, I kissed him back.

I pulled away. "I was wrong "He's So Shy" isn't you. But then again, it's those shy ones..."

Chris' expression intensified. He pulled me back into his arms and covered my mouth with his soft lips, sending wild tremors along my spine. Then he pulled back slightly and said, "Oh, I interrupted you. Let me guess....the shy ones are . . . the ones you have to watch out for?"

I leaned back so I could respond, but he slowly kissed me again, making a searing heat rise up my neck and sparks ignited. The kiss ended, and with intensity, he stared into my eyes.

"Has anyone ever told you your blue eyes have gold flecks in the middle? They're gorgeous! As much as I don't want to leave, I better get going. I have a long drive home."

When Chris released me from his embrace I could feel the crimson heat flush my cheeks. My emotions had betrayed me. It was useless to deny the attraction.

"You're right. It is late, and the girls will be up early." I walked him to the door and smiled up at him.

He wrapped me in his arms, lifting me off the ground and kissed me once more. Then he gently put me down and whispered, "Denise, I am so glad you called me. I will call you tomorrow!" Then he disappeared down the stairs.

On Monday, the cloud I was floating on disintegrated and reality smacked me in the face. The IRS agent that Chris recommended I call told me the check had been sent out, endorsed with both of our names and cashed. When he faxed me a copy of the check, sure enough, Doyle had signed my name. Since we were still married, the only thing I could do was take Doyle to court for my half of the tax refund.

I had neither energy or money left to file another charge against Doyle. The bigamy trial was in two weeks, and at the last visitation hearing, the judge had ordered everyone to have a psychological assessment. My appointments with the doctor were creatively rescheduled on several occasions to buy time to find the extra money to pay his fee and protect Jaime. Doyle had recently pushed for a final court date to determine visitation, so I couldn't stall any longer. The extra money from the tax refund was going to help me catch up. Now I could only hope my attorney would give me grace and the bank would allow me to add a car payment onto the end of my loan.

In the past my emotions would have left me tangled and stuck in the web of lies Doyle had spun, but now I chose to focus on Chris and our amorous phone conversations every night. By the end of the week I came to believe he was the answer to my 'tall-dark-and-doesn't-have-to-look-like-Robert-Redford' prayer! Maybe I was headed for my own happily-ever-after.

*"Suffering has been stronger than
all other teaching,
I have been bent and broken,
but – I hope – into a better shape."*

~ Charles Dickens

CHAPTER 18

Three Months Later

*S*nuggling in Jaime's bed with the girls was my favorite part of the day. I held them close, breathing in the berry scent of their hair from the Strawberry Shortcake shampoo while I read to them.

"But Mommy...why did God...tell Noah to build an ark?" she attempted to ask between yawns.

I looked down at Jaime and admired her flawless, delicate features and brilliant mind that questioned every part of *Noah's Ark*.

"Because God knew a big flood was coming and He wanted to save all the animals! Good idea, huh?" I added and kissed them both on the cheek.

Minutes later, when I turned the book around to show the animals walking up the ramp two by two, Samantha and Jaime were asleep.

"Let's finish this tomorrow night," I whispered, then gently pulled the covers up and kissed Jaime on the forehead and put Samantha in her crib. Tiptoeing out of the bedroom, I gently shut the door. Just then the phone rang, startling me. I raced down the hall to grab it before the girls woke up.

"How are my three sweethearts today?" The sound of Chris' chipper voice made me smile. I then remembered what I had promised myself and struggled to respond.

"Fine. They fell asleep during their bedtime story, so mission accomplished," I mumbled. *Tell him and get it over with.* "So how was your day?" *Go ahead, avoid the subject, chicken.*

"You don't sound all right. Is something wrong?"

That question was all it took. I blurted out, "Yes. A lot is wrong that I haven't told you about and you deserve to know the truth. My life is a disaster and I would completely understand if you don't want to see me anymore."

"Hey, wait a minute. Before you make up my mind for me, tell me what kind of disaster you're talking about."

"OK, brace yourself. It's an ugly story, but you have a right to know what storm you've walked into."

I took a deep breath, scarcely knowing where to begin. "Jaime wakes up almost every night terrified and screaming, 'There are monsters in my bed.' Then she runs into my room and sleeps with me the rest of the night. Around the time this started, Doyle told his attorney that the babysitter's husband had molested Jaime. Now she has separation anxiety, which means she cries and throws tantrums most of the time when I leave her. That's the short version of the story. Through counseling, we discovered Doyle was the one sexually abusing her. Visitation has been stopped and I am currently going to court to try to protect Jaime from her own father. I'm sorry I didn't tell you sooner." I closed my eyes, cringed and bit my lip waiting for a response.

I was sure the hellish truth I was living through would end this fairytale love story. I certainly could relate to Cinderella, although an evil stepmother wasn't nearly as much a deterrent as an evil ex-husband.

Silence. More silence. My heart skipped a beat. It seemed like an eternity before Chris spoke. "I thought Doyle was a scum bag for stealing half of your tax return, but I had no idea that even he could sink lower than scum. I'm so sorry for everything you and Jaime are going through. You know how deeply I care about you and the girls. Denise, I don't plan on going anywhere."

I choked back tears, then mumbled, "You might want to go find another 'good Catholic' girl before it's too late."

"It's already too late, Denise! I'm in love with you."

"I love you, too. You don't even know how your love and support has kept me going the last several months. But wait, this absurd, outrageous story gets better! I had to go court today because I pressed bigamy charges against Doyle."

"What? But you're in the process of getting divorced!"

"I know, but Doyle thought he could get away with getting married in the middle of our divorce! He went to Gulfport, Mississippi several months ago and got married on a beach to a woman he works with named Brice. So, I pressed bigamy charges, hoping it would help me protect Jaime and show Doyle he couldn't control me anymore. But the judge said we didn't prove they consummated the marriage! Can you believe that? After the hearing Joe, my attorney, overheard Doyle's attorney telling him how lucky he was that the judge was just caught cheating on his wife! Joe said he was surprised at the decision with the evidence we had, but now it all makes sense. The judge ruled that way to justify his own behavior!"

"That's messed up!"

"At least now Doyle knows I'm not afraid to stand up to him and I won't back down from a fight. I hope he's so worried I will take him back to court, he will never touch Jaime again!"

"I hate Doyle for what he's done to Jaime. It's going to be hard for me to forgive and not punch him when I see him! I can't even imagine how hard this is on you and Jaime, but I want you to know that you can tell me anything. You're not alone anymore."

I hesitated. "I come with a lot of baggage. You should be headin' for the hills about now."

"Nothing you have shared changes my feelings for you or the girls. We will face this together!" Chris reassured.

"You might want to wait to make that decision. Soon I will be able to tell you if I am officially crazy! At the last visitation hearing the juvenile judge ordered everyone to be evaluated by a psychologist, Dr. Frank Robbe. All the evaluations on Doyle, the kids and I were just completed. The judge thinks the doctor will be able to determine if the abuse happened. I'm so frustrated! It's been over a year since Jaime told the counselor 'Daddy said it's a secret', then showed the counselor where he'd touched her. She drew two pictures of penises after she was in therapy for a while. I can't stand to think about what Jaime has been through!"

"Pictures of a penis, huh? That sounds like overwhelming evidence to me, proving it happened."

"You would think, but the pictures were ignored by the judge and Doyle's attorney when my therapist showed them in court. I have little hope that Jaime opened up to a complete stranger and told him something that happened when she was three and a half! Although I know she remembers everything and that's why she has nightmares and separation anxiety. Her mind is trying to process what has happened when she sleeps. Jaime's mind buried the memories deep in her subconscious to survive. Doyle is so manipulative. I'm sure he smiled his way through the whole interview and came out smelling like a rose instead of the pond scum that he is. Every time I think about going to the hearing next week my stomach lurches and I run for the bathroom. The psychologist will share his opinion at the hearing and then the judge will make his final decision."

"Certainly, the judge will weigh everything and not make a decision based solely on the report of a psychologist!"

"Especially since we've had to stop visitation for a third time! Several weeks ago, we filed another contempt motion because Doyle was found alone with the girls again. His mom was supposed to be there monitoring their visit. Samantha said Doyle took a bath with them. It was the middle of the day and there was no reason for them to be bathing at his house. I can't repeat the rest of what she said...it's too upsetting. Doyle doesn't respect anything the court orders! There will be no way for me to protect them from their own father if he gets back visitation next week."

"Do you think with Doyle's new wife in the picture he will continue to abuse the girls?"

"That is my only hope! I pray he will be too busy controlling her to even think of abusing them. I recently read that domestic violence and abuse go hand in hand. It's about exerting control over another person to feel powerful. I'm pretty sure he will be focused on controlling Brice, and by now he knows I will take him back to court if anything else happens!"

"Hey, you know you can call me anytime, day or night, to talk and I will listen."

Chris' compassionate, loving response encouraged me and boosted my strength to keep going. Now I had someone in my corner. I wasn't fighting alone.

కావకావకావకావకావకావ

Intimidation loomed before me as I stood and looked up at the massive courthouse steps and pillars. They seemed to taunt me: "You will not find justice here." The power the cold, hard landscape exuded was a reminder of the unwelcoming courtroom that awaited me inside. Joe Schwartz came around the corner in a three-piece suit. "How are you doing?" he asked.

"I'm nervous. How do you think it will go today?"

"I have no idea. Doyle is on his third attorney, Shannon Beck. I have tried several times in the last three weeks to reach her and she never returned my calls. At the last hearing, when I made a motion for the 'penis-in-action' picture Jaime drew to be seen as evidence and it was not allowed, I was baffled. I hate to say this, but Doyle may likely get visitation back. And if he does, I plan on requesting that his visits remain supervised."

My heart sank, my stomach tightened, and any hope I had, dissipated. Joe escorted me up the steps into the courthouse in silence.

My thoughts screamed as we walked down the hall. *Why can't the justice system protect my girls? After all, an experienced counselor believed what Jaime had shared, and it wasn't a stretch to understand from Jaime's words exactly what Doyle had done to her. So how could a judge not believe or understand what had happened?*

In 1986 the "good old boys club" was alive and well in the court system. They couldn't fathom the possibility of a father sexually abusing his daughter and any wrong verdict would keep an "innocent" father from his children. One agonizing question never left my mind: **Why aren't our children more important than protecting the "good old boys club"?** I fumed to myself. Forcing down the blind rage that brewed inside, I became numb, so I could get through the hearing.

The bailiff opened the courtroom door for us, and Doyle's laughter bellowed into the hallway. The evil haughtiness of his demeanor made me cringe. The spiritual curtain from an unseen realm was pulled back and I witnessed a ghastly scene. Hundreds of snakes were hanging from light fixtures all over the room. One slithered across the judge's bench and onto the floor. Then it slinked over, curled around Doyle's leg and up his torso. The snake opened his mouth and hissed lies into Doyle's ear for him to repeat. Then its sharp fangs plunged into his neck. I expected to see him writhe in pain on the floor.

"Are you, all right?" Joe asked.

I shook my head and glanced around. "I'm... I'm not sure...I just saw..."

Judge Waters slammed down his gavel and called the court to order.

I mumbled, "Never mind. I couldn't explain it even if I tried."

The judge called both attorneys to the bench, handed them a copy of the psychologist's report and asked them to give Doyle and me a copy to read through. He then called Dr. Robbe to the stand. This was the moment of truth. The paper shook in my quivering hand when I took the report from Joe. I took control of my emotions and focused on the words in the report. It started out with the basic facts and then went into what Doyle had told the psychologist.

"Jaime told me when I gave her a bath, the babysitter's husband 'touched me in the genital area.' I became concerned and told Denise" the report read.

What? Wait. Told me? He never told me anything; he told his attorney that story! And Jaime doesn't use the word "genital". Doyle went on to tell the doctor, "I'm surprised that I'm being blamed when I'm the one that brought up the possibility that someone molested my daughters." *Daughters? He never told his attorney they both were molested!*

Then came lie after lie. Doyle said Samantha was an unplanned pregnancy. The truth was that Doyle and I decided together to go off the pill and get pregnant! Then the report said Doyle and Brice planned for the child she was pregnant with.

What? She's pregnant? At the bigamy hearing a week ago, they'd said we didn't prove they had consummated the marriage! I wanted to scream, 'Liar, Liar, pants on fire!'

I skimmed the rest of the report that was about me and saw that Dr. Robbe had reported all the details of the abuse Jaime shared at the therapist office and the pictures she drew. But he had twisted some of the things I'd said in such a way that I looked like a neurotic, emotional, crazy person who couldn't handle stress. He even pinned me with a mental disorder! Everything I told him was accurate. I was upset when I met with him and shared about Jaime's abuse. Any mother would be. How could he not see the truth? The mountain of lies Doyle had told piled up by the end of the report. The rope around my chest and the throbbing in my ears told me my blood pressure was through the roof. The temptation to point to each lie and blurt out the truth was unbearable!

The judge called the doctor up to testify. "Dr. Robbe," he began, "I know you have met with all the parties involved here. Please summarize your findings for the court as it pertains to the defendant, Mr. Boese."

Frank Robbe was a thin, quiet and inconspicuous man that you wouldn't notice if you passed him on the street. But on the stand, he seemed to come alive. He spoke with confidence and authority. "Mr. Boese denies ever touching his daughter inappropriately and denies taking a bath with her. Psychological testing and the interview with Mr. Boese indicate that he is defensive and evasive when talking about issues. He has a general pattern of handling anxieties and conflict by not recognizing their presence, but his psychological makeup does not appear to be one of a chronic child-molester."

Your tests and interview just proved that he is defensive and evasive, but you believed him when he said he didn't touch Jaime! Of course, he doesn't appear to be a "chronic child molester" because he has manipulated you with his charisma and by masking his true identity with a three-piece suit!

The doctor smiled and continued, "Assessing child abuse in young children is particularly difficult and, in this case, it was over a year after the alleged abuse. As a result of the evaluations, no clinical evidence was found to support the allegations of sexual abuse. But I must add, since I examined her long after the alleged abuse, I cannot be certain that the abuse did not occur. It is known that even normal-appearing individuals can regress under stressful circumstances, such as divorce and engage in sexual abuse of children. It cannot be stated with 100% certainty that it did not occur but, in my opinion, there are minimal factors in his clinical picture to suggest that he abused his daughter. It is my recommendation that Mr. Boese be permitted to have normal visitation with his daughters."

How could this so-called professional not catch on to Doyle's lies?

My attorney stood to his feet and addressed the bench. "Your Honor, over a year ago we provided this court with overwhelming evidence that Mr. Boese did sexually abuse his daughter! That evidence should not be denied! I am requesting that you re-examine the testimonies and pictures and that Mr. Boese's visitation remain supervised."

Finally, someone is standing up for the truth!

The judge asked for both attorneys to approach the bench. After a brief discussion he announced, "The psychologist's report, along with my order that Mr. Boese's visitation be unsupervised, will be put in the court record."

My pulse quickened. I threw my head back and closed my eyes. I just wanted to run far, far away and escape with the girls to that deserted island I so often dreamed of! But the vicious wolf showed up too often, invading the scene to chase me down and devour my flesh. There was no way to hide from the monsters that lived in our house now. We would have to find a way to survive in spite of them. The tears came in torrents. I didn't even try to stop them.

Before the attorneys could sit down, the yearning to bolt took over, I vanished from the courtroom, disappearing down the hall.

A few minutes later, Joe found me leaning against a wall. He led me over to a bench and when we sat down, gut-wrenching sobs shook my whole body. There was no way to fight the mire of quicksand that sucked me down into despair. It was over. I would never be able to protect my girls from Doyle's abuse now.

"I know how upsetting this is, but his visits are limited to twice a month. Doyle's attorney wants to know what time he can pick them up on Thanksgiving."

"You don't understand! How could you understand?" I wailed and blotted the tears from my face with a tissue. I got up and felt the stares penetrating my back as the eyes of strangers followed me out the door. I pulled my jacket collar up to block the cool, fall wind that quickly became a soothing compress to my inflamed red cheeks and puffy eyes.

I sprinted to my car, jumped in, started the engine and reclined my seat. It was a sanctuary, hiding me away from the ugly reality of the cruel world. I closed my eyes and fought to block out the *what ifs* that tried to bombard my mind.

Ten minutes later I was startled by a loud rap on my window and I sprang upright in the seat. There stood Doyle with a sanctimonious smile looking down at me. I revved the engine with delight, put the car in drive and sped away. Doyle stood, dumfounded, in the middle of a dusty cloud kicked up from the gravel parking lot. He could wait two weeks to find out when I would be dropping the girls off for Thanksgiving.

The hearing finished just in time. It was almost noon and Chris would be having his lunch outside at City Garden. He often went there to get a break from his work and the overheated, stuffy government building. I needed to feel his big arms wrapped around me; I needed to feel safe. It was only ten blocks from the courthouse to the beautiful garden with its water features and sculptures in the middle of downtown, yet it felt like every slow driver pulled out in front of me and pumped their brakes. Finally, a parking spot came into view. I pulled in and spotted Chris sitting on a granite bench under a tree. Across from him were a stack of painted pumpkins in brilliant colors left over from a city-wide art competition, their backdrop a huge rock waterfall. This oasis in the middle of an urban jungle was just the cathartic place I needed to be.

The sun peaked out and warmed my back. I was glad the buildings blocked most of the fall breeze. I ambled up behind Chris, trying not startle him and asked, "Would you like company for lunch?"

He put down his drink, got up and came around the bench, smiling. He grabbed me up in his arms and whispered in my ear, "I just tossed a coin in the waterfall, made a wish and you appeared." Then he gently kissed me. Looking into my eyes, he said, "You've been crying. Guess the outcome wasn't good."

"No, it was awful! He got visitation back like I feared he would. Now I must empower Jaime to protect herself! I've already taught her the difference between a 'good' and 'bad' touch, so hopefully she will tell me if he ever harms her again! But I'm exhausted and I don't want to spend our time talking about it. I just want to enjoy your company and sit here with you where I feel safe."

Chris grinned at me. "I want to make you feel safe for the rest of our lives. How about we go out Saturday and make it official?"

I grinned back and turned on my southern charm. "If I was a betting woman, I would say it sounds like you plan to ask for my hand in marriage," I said with one hand on my chin while pointing a finger at him. I felt heat flush my cheeks.

He chuckled at my antics and said, "Yes, that is exactly what I plan on doing! We've been dating long enough. We know we're in love, and you know I'm crazy about the girls! I would adopt them if I could. You know that I would never hurt you or the girls. I think we're ready. Don't you?"

"Yes! There's no one I trust more. I love you, Chris Fromm!"

We sat on the bench. Chris draped his arm around my shoulder and I leaned against his chest, elated about the future. He offered me half of his sandwich and I took it, happy to fill my growling stomach. The sound of the waterfall helped soothe my nerves and the bright pumpkins lifted my spirit.

Sandy, my counselor, listened patiently to the struggles I shared about trusting men, especially men I might date. I was skeptical that there were any good men left when I started to date Chris, but I took Sandy's advice. Intentionally, I observed how Chris' dad, Steve, treated his mom, Ellen, and how Chris' brother, Paul, treated his wife, Carol. What I witnessed warmed my heart. Steve was a sweetheart, gentle and caring to Ellen, his wife of thirty-five years. Ellen had developed Multiple Sclerosis ten years earlier and now needed care 24 hours a day. Steve didn't mind caring for Ellen and was attentive to her every need. He fed her. He bathed her. I never knew love like that existed.

Paul had learned well from their father's example. He was so tender and very loving towards Carol, and Paul always showed her respect. I knew that God had answered my prayer by putting Chris in my path. Whenever I spent time with Chris' family, his parents, his twin sisters, Linda and Sharon, and Paul and Carol, I felt like I'd stepped into a Norman Rockwell painting. They enjoyed one another, and their love was palpable. There was no doubt that I could trust my heart to this man. Chris' kindness and tenderness were not an act. His love was a safe place, a haven.

That night, as I drifted off to sleep, the vision I had in the courtroom vividly replayed in my mind. The scene of the vicious snake coiled around Doyle's chest spewing venomous lies into Doyle's ear made me shutter. Then I heard the quiet voice of Truth whisper, "I allowed you to see Doyle being controlled be a malicious, deceitful spirit. Forgive his haughtiness and deceit, so you can be free. I have revealed the truth to stop the abuse. Rejoice."

I marveled at God's goodness to me. I once again made the choice to forgive Doyle and peaceful sleep was my reward.

*"Once in a while, right in the middle of
an ordinary life, love gives us a fairy tale."*

~ Unknown

CHAPTER 19

September 1987

"You've got to eat something!" begged Diane.

"I know but there is too much going on to be hungry. The hairdresser is going to be here any minute and the photographer had to get a picture before I put on my makeup. You know, so he can do that fancy before-and-after merged image thing he keeps trying to explain to us. I just can't concentrate on what he is saying right now... I've got to get the girls in their dresses before I can get in my gown and leave for the church."

"I will take care of the girls getting dressed, but you can't do any of that other stuff if you don't eat. We certainly don't need a repeat performance of you fainting at your own wedding like you did at mine six weeks ago. Thank goodness, it was during the pictures and not the ceremony!" Diane reminded.

"And who kept telling them to fill my wine glass every time my back was turned? Huh?" I accused.

"Go ahead. Blame me. My nerves were on edge! I thought you had eaten like the rest of us. I didn't know it would hit you that hard!" Diane snickered. "But I promised Chris I would make sure you ate something today!"

I picked up a sandwich from the tray on the kitchen counter. Crossing my eyes while taking a huge bite and chewing, I mumbled, "There! Are you happy?"

"Yes, but you have to eat it all...or no wedding cake for dessert!" Diane burst out laughing.

"OK, Mom! Speaking of Mom, where is she? I gave her good directions to get to Chris' parents' house."

"Oh, I meant to tell you. She didn't think she needed to be here because you had enough help. She's going to come with Dad and meet us at the church for family pictures before the ceremony."

"Why am I not surprised? She has been against a big church wedding from the moment we got engaged. Remember the day we were going to shop for my wedding dress? We were literally on our way out the door and she called to say she wasn't coming. She was embarrassed that I was going to wear a white dress! She is more concerned about what others think than what Chris and I want."

"I'm not concerned about what others think! You deserve a nice wedding after all you have been through and the first ceremony with that monster could hardly be called a wedding!" Diane vented.

I reminded her, "Now you know the rule: no talking about Doyle today!"

"Sorry. It slipped out," Diane coyly admitted.

"I never told you this, but Mom's negative comments invaded my thoughts to the point that I had convinced myself she was right. The closer it got to the wedding, the more I felt like everything I was doing was wrong. I called Chris and told him we should just go to the courthouse and get married. But my knight in shining armor wouldn't listen and bravely stood up to her. Chris told her he was the one who insisted on having a big traditional wedding. Since he was paying for everything, she had no ammunition to fight back with!"

"He's brave all right! Finish that sandwich so you can get your wedding dress on . . .and eat it all!"

Stuffing another bite in my mouth, I did an eye roll at Diane and shooed her out of the room. A conversation with my mom echoed in my ear. "Do you really expect my friends to pay for their own mixed drinks at the wedding reception? It will be downright embarrassing!" she'd said.

"We are paying for beer and wine, Mom. Mixed drinks are just too expensive! Surely, your friends won't mind and can afford to buy their own drinks."

She never said another word to me about the wedding.

Two hours later, everyone was dressed, pictures taken, and we were loading into the stretch limo. All the conversations blurred into one and my mind wandered off to the first time I'd met Chris and the scene he made on the golf course. He barreled towards me from the last green and knocked me off my feet as he grabbed me up in his arms, demanding to know which guy was bothering me. I never had the heart to tell Chris he was the culprit that day. The huge chip on my shoulder formed by abuse dissolved from the unconditional love Chris gave me the last year and a half we had been together. His easy-going, positive spirit and humor about mundane things brightened my day. He never belittled me or anything I did, and the kindness and respect he showed me were a comforting balm that helped to mend the gaping wounds in my soul.

Excited giggles from the flower girls --Jaime, Samantha and their soon-to-be cousin, Caroline, who was Chris' niece, and the same age as Jaime, snapped me out of my thoughts. They were beautiful in their teal satin flower girl dresses. A seamstress had made them with white lace accents that formed a 'V' design on the front that went over the puffy sleeves and down the back with the same white lace around the bottom of the hem. I smiled down at the girls, then noticed Chris' twin sisters, Linda and Sharon, staring at me.

They said in unison, "Now remember what we told you when you got engaged: No returns. Chris is yours for good now!"

"I remember. It made me nervous wondering why you were anxious to get rid of him!"

"No reason in particular. Baby brothers can just be a pain!" Linda joked.

The old Gothic, stone church came into view with its bell tower and copper steeple. In less than an hour I would be Mrs. Chris Fromm! I was nervous about walking down the aisle in front of so many people, but excited to start our future together.

MariLu helped the girls get out of the limo and Diane held up the train of my dress so I could climb out. Once inside I looked up to admire the interior of the church. Massive white flying buttresses supported high vaulted ceilings and light streamed in through colorful stained-glass windows. It looked like an enchanted scene out of a romantic movie. Marrying Chris in this spectacular building made the day feel surreal. The wedding party gathered in the back of the church and lined up in front of me. A lump formed in my throat and grew bigger at the sight of Jaime and Samantha throwing flower petals in front of each step they took. My bridesmaids followed them.

My dad danced up beside me with a mischievous grin. "Are you ready to do this again? Let's see if it sticks this time!" he bellowed.

I scowled at him. "Yes, I'm more than ready. Dad, just for today behave yourself, please." My eyes continued to plead with him. He smiled, took my arm and we walked down the aisle in silence.

I saw my tall, tan fiancé in his handsome white, long tail tuxedo jacket with black tie and pants, standing at the altar. All my nervous thoughts disappeared, along with the anxiety from the last few moments. His bright smiling face was all I could see walking down the aisle to Wagner's Bridal Chorus, better known as "Here Comes the Bride." The chaotic drama-filled life I once knew would finally be over. I hoped the new life that awaited me would be far from chaotic or plagued with drama.

I faced Chris, held his hands and gazed into his eyes. Before I knew it, we had recited our vows and we were kissing as husband and wife. God was raining down His blessings, and I felt His love enveloped me when everyone started to sing "Amazing Grace" at the end of the nuptials. Steve, Chris' father and I both loved that hymn. Steve had told Chris to get on the first bus out of town when he found out I was a divorcee and Jaime had been abused. I had agreed, telling Chris he would be better off with the "good Catholic" girl he dated before me. But Chris would hear none of it and had said, "You'll have to break up with me! I'm not going anywhere."

Joy swelled up in me during the last verse of "Amazing Grace" as I remembered what Steve had later admitted to Chris. "Denise and the girls are best thing that ever happened to you," he'd said, "I'm so glad you found each other."

God uses everything to answer prayer, even deceit over a tax refund check. God knew I would look for answers when I didn't receive the refund, so He nudged me to call Chris, knowing he would never call me, and now here we were headed up the aisle, a married couple! The girls and I had moved out of our apartment and had been staying in Linda's duplex. Jaime had started the first grade two weeks before the wedding, and Linda's duplex was five minutes away from her school. After the honeymoon on the sandy beaches of Anna Maria Island in Florida, we would be moving into our newly purchased home, a two story with three bedrooms. Paul and Carol lived down the street from our new home and would be watching the girls while we were on our honeymoon.

๛๛๛๛๛๛๛๛๛๛

When I heard Chris walk in the front door; a giddiness surged through me. It would take all my control to keep from blurting out the news and ruining the surprise. A card with the announcement waited for him on his dresser.

"Hi honey! Wow, dinner smells good! Did you get my message about golf being canceled tonight?" Chris asked when he walked into the kitchen.

"Yes, thanks for letting me know. That's why I made your favorite casserole -- chicken wrapped in bacon, smothered in white creamy garlic sauce -- to ease the pain of not getting to hit a little white ball around for hours!" Chris smirked, leaned down and kissed me, squeezing me tight. He then walked down the hallway to our bedroom.

Smiling and listening, I put the casserole into the oven. *Here it comes...any minute now...I should hear his response to the news...*

"What? Oh honey, are you sure? Whoooa! I'm gonna be a father!"

And there it was --Chris' jubilant response, the response I had waited all day to hear. Chris bounded into the kitchen and swept me off my feet, twirling me around almost knocking things off the counter. "I can't believe it! I thought it would take longer...We are expecting a child?" I smiled and nodded. "I'm going to be a father!" he shouted.

Jaime, now seven years old, and Samantha, five, heard the commotion and came running upstairs from the family room, clueless.

"What's going on?" Jaime hollered as she hit the top step.

I knelt and pulled the girls close, hugging them tight. "I've been waiting all day to tell you something. In the spring, eight months from now, we are going to have a new addition to our family. We're going to have a baby! You both are going to be big sisters to a baby brother or sister!"

Samantha started jumping up and down, "Yay! A baby! A baby! Yay!"

"Isn't this exciting? You've been asking for one for a long time, haven't you?" She nodded, and tears filled her eyes.

"Will I get to hold the baby and change the baby's diaper?" she asked.

I hugged Samantha again. "Of course! It's going to be so much fun to have a little one to love and take care of, won't it?"

Jaime hesitated. "But will you still love us?"

I looked into her eyes and repeated the poem I often read to them from their favorite book, "'I'll love you forever, I'll like you for always, as long as I'm living, my baby you'll be!' And that will never change! And the baby will love you, too!"

"I'm too old to be your baby, Mom!" Jaime grinned.

I smothered her with kisses till she giggled and pushed away. Then I grabbed Samantha and did the same. Chris scooped them up, one in each arm, and kissed them.

Eight months later a joyful bundle named Daniel came in to our lives, completing our family.

*"Darkness cannot drive out darkness;
only light can do that."*

~Martin Luther King Jr.

CHAPTER 20

*C*hris and I sat in a cushy blue velvet 's' shaped kissing bench, facing opposite directions holding hands in the Grand Hall. Brilliant orange and yellow stained-glass windows cast a glow throughout the iconic historical jewel that sat in the middle of the St. Louis Union Station Hotel. Mesmerized, we stared up at the gold leaf Romanesque vaulted arches that formed the high ceiling above the hall. Without saying a word, Chris leaned over and nibbled on my neck. The silence turned into giddiness when he whispered, "This place is almost as beautiful as you are." My heart fluttered.

Curious stares landed in our direction. We felt like two smitten teenagers during a secret rendezvous. This was a rare opportunity for a weekend away at the Abundant Life Family Conference. It was an easy escape from the kids, now ten, seven and two years old, who were excited to stay with their cousins down the street.

After a leisurely breakfast, we walked arm-in-arm and followed the conference signs that led us to the Regency Ballroom. The décor was a mix of old world charm and twentieth century modern. The walls had wainscot paneling and the carpet was a vibrant, geometric pattern of golds and blues. The smell of fresh coffee lured us to the front of the room where we each fixed a cup. The family conference had been a recommended follow-up to the marriage conference we had attended a few months earlier. Understanding what wasn't working in our marriage and how to heal those sore spots did wonders for our relationship. We found seats near the front and sat at the end of a row. The morning's keynote speaker came to the podium.

"Welcome to the Abundant Life Family Conference. I'm glad to see you made it! You never know what you're going to get in late February, fighting rush hour traffic in the snow and ice, then add crying kids who didn't want you to leave this morning and you've got Armageddon! Am I right? So, give yourselves a round of applause. You made it! I promise it will all be worth it!"

Chris smirked and nudged me. He hated fighting rush hour traffic, so he'd booked an extra night, weeks ago at Union Station. He gloated during breakfast that morning in the Grand Hall. "Now don't you think my idea to get here the night before was well worth the extra money? Think of all the drivers we avoided, slipping and sliding on the treacherous Glendale roads!"

The speaker began, "By the end of this morning's session you will be able to recognize the foundation your family of origin built when you were growing up and how that foundation affects your family unit today. The teaching I am going to share is based on Luke 6:47-49 from the New International Version." And then he read the verses aloud.

"As for everyone who comes to me and hears my words and puts them into practice, I will show you what they are like. They are like a man building a house, who dug down deep and laid the foundation on rock. When a flood came, the torrent struck that house but could not shake it, because it was well built. But the one who hears my words and does not put them into practice is like a man who built a house on the ground without a foundation. The moment the torrent struck that house, it collapsed, and its destruction was complete."

He explained, "The concept of building a house is the same as building a life. I am going to ask you to reflect today on the foundation your family of origin built as I elaborate on this passage from Luke. The truth is everyone wants to have a vibrant, dynamic, strong family. But everybody will be affected by the storms of this life, the negative realities of life may not be the same for everyone, but one thing is true for all of us—it will rain cats and dogs and the sunshine may not come out for days!" I under uncrossed my legs and leaned into Chris who smiled at the comment, then he wrapped his arm around me.

"So, let me ask you to consider these questions: Was your family of origin built on a solid foundation or no foundation? What kind of foundation do you want for your family?

"The wise man built his house well on a rock foundation and the foolish man had no foundation for his house. These two men, or let's say families, are fundamentally different. One was intentional in how the house was built and the other wasn't. But in one way they were both exactly alike -- they both had storms.

"The biggest contrast is the results, because it says one house stood and another house totally collapsed. If you were to observe these two families from a distance or even talk to them, you might not see a fundamental distinction. The only time you would discover there was a difference between these two families was during the storm. Only a storm reveals the nature of your foundation. But there is one thing you need to understand about foundations: you can't pour them when it's raining. You need to do it while the sun is shining."

My heart swelled, and I grinned. We were intentionally build-ing a strong foundation! We prayed with the kids and taught them God's word. But what was the family I'd grown up in built on?

"Right now, I would like everyone to find a quiet place in the hotel, so you can take some time to reflect and write down the char-acteristics of the family you grew up in. Did you grow up hearing God's word? Knowing His unconditional love for you? If not, what was your family's home built on and how does it affect you today? Then I would like you to go over your answers together as a cou-ple and discuss your past foundations. Then write down what your current foundation is and how it might need to change so when the storm comes, your family is strong and doesn't collapse in a crisis. And don't worry if I went over all that too fast. The binder we handed you when you came in has all the questions I just mentioned."

Chris and I found a table in the lobby café and sat down across from each other. The uneasy feeling that tightened in my chest grew. This wasn't what I expected. Parenting tips, yes, but not a discussion with Chris about my murky past and his delightful childhood. I did well to leave my childhood in the rearview mirror and focus on raising godly kids.

My jaw clenched. It would only take one sentence to answer those questions. My parents were too self-absorbed to teach us about God's unconditional love, let alone give us unconditional love. Love was conditional in our home. It was "Do as I say, not as I do." And in our household, God was a four-letter word. There you have it. Mine was a shifting foundation of sand built by the foolish! It struck me that the foundation laid by my parents had caused me to struggle to believe what God's word said about me. If they didn't love me unconditionally, why would God?

A deluge of memories started to unlock themselves from a dark vault, my right heel tapped incessantly on the hard-concrete floor while my mind went back in time.

I was on my dad's lap. He was saying words I didn't understand. "You get knocked up, I'll disown you." 'Knocked up' meant nothing to me at six years old, but now my face grew hot with shame at the implication of those words. Then another distant memory took the place of the ugly words.

It was a warm summer morning and our mom, still in her bathrobe, pushed Diane and me out the front door of our ranch home. "Go play and don't come back until dinner time," she said as she thrust a sleeve of saltine crackers in my hand. "These are for when you get hungry." Then she pointed to the garden hose laying in the front yard. "And you can get a drink from there to wash them down with." When she turned to go inside, I saw her reach down and pat the spotted head of our black and white Dalmatian saying, "They won't be running down the hall making you nervous any more today!" A knife of rejection stabbed hard and deep with the realization that the dog was more important than we were.

Then another memory surfaced. We were playing tag and laughing as we ran barefoot through a field of buzzing bees that landed on a thick carpet of purple clover at our friend's house. Suddenly the laughter turned to tears and we gingerly limped home in excruciating pain. We sat down next to a puddle by our driveway and winced in agony as we pulled out each stinger one by one. Then we scooped up some mud in our hands and mixed it with water to make a paste. We smeared the damp earth onto every bee sting to draw out the venom. *Where in the world had we learned that?* Unsympathetic, angry voices from the past echoed, "Don't come home crying about getting stung by bees! Haven't we told you over and over again to wear shoes?" our parents screamed.

Was it really our fault? We were forgetful, adventurous young girls. Wasn't it their job to make sure we wore shoes? My sketchy memories seemed to rise out of a vast, deep black hole somewhere and surface after invasive questions. I imagined gathering them all up and dumping them right back down into the abyss, but it was too late. They had escaped. The radiant joy I had that morning dissipated into a gray cloud of sadness.

I glanced up at a smiling Chris, speed-writing his memories that were popping to the surface. I looked down and stared at the paper in front of me wishing I had something positive to write, anything that included God or encouragement or love. Nothing.

The realization hit me hard. Diane and I were terribly neglected! No wonder I felt unworthy of love and tended to push Chris, and even God, away. Now I understood how the foundation my family built provoked negative emotions in my everyday life. My mother didn't have time for us, but where was our dad?

I remembered him being home a lot with us along with his business partner, Pete Reginelle. My dad and Pete had started a business building homes. Just then, ironically, I remembered Dad explaining how they built a foundation for a house. They would put a layer of pea gravel down before pouring the concrete to make it strong. He was intentional about the way he built a foundation for a home, but he wasn't at all intentional about what he let happen in our family. That triggered a familiar memory, the one from years earlier, when I left the counselor's office with Jaime.

Diane and I were walking out of our bedroom, down the hall and into the family room, where we saw Pete sitting on a barstool at the end of the kitchen counter. A ray of sun streamed in through an open window and a breeze made the curtain billow. Pete grabbed my wrist with force as I walked by, "Sit here, sweetie," he said. I grimaced in pain as he pulled me up into his lap. "There. Are you comfortable? You are such a towhead!" I rubbed my wrist and frowned; something didn't feel right. He slipped his hand under my shirt and started to rub my back while he carried on a conversation with our dad across the room. His gentle touch relaxed me. Then several minutes later he started to rub my chest, and then he slipped his hand down my pants. I squeezed my legs together, but he forced his hand between my legs! I froze and my whole body became rigid and my stomach started to hurt.

Why didn't I jump down and run from the room! Why hadn't I protected myself? It's my fault. The questions made my heart pound out of rhythm and a huge lump formed in my throat. I breathed deep to hold back the tears of shame.

Where was Diane? The question made more vivid details flooded in; Diane was on our dad's lap, sitting on the couch across the room from me. He was rubbing her back under her shirt. Instinctively I knew he was touching her like Pete was touching me!

This can't be true! My stomach churned violently, and the back of my mouth started to water. I swallowed hard, so I wouldn't throw up. My dad was in the room watching Pete molest me while he was molesting Diane! I was in disbelief. How could he be doing the same thing to Diane? Why wouldn't our dad protect us?

My heart raced harder and I dropped my head into my hands. The torrent of tears that I had tried to hold back fell hard onto the paper while I sobbed. Within seconds I felt Chris' warm embrace around my shaking shoulders.

"Let's go outside and get some fresh air," he whispered into my ear as he handed me a Kleenex.

Chris held up my coat and I slipped my arms in. We walked out of the Grand Hall down the stairs and onto the front lawn. Chris led me over to a concrete bench by a tree that blocked the view of the busy hotel entrance. He used the edge of the conference binder to brush off powdery snow from a bench and we sat down. The morning snow storm was only a memory now, replaced by bright sun that had peeked out from behind a cloud and now warmed my face.

"Unpleasant memories, huh?" Chris asked.

"No, worse than unpleasant...much worse."

How can I tell Chris? Why would he or anyone believe me? Maybe it didn't happen. Maybe my mind is playing a sick game on me and I made it all up.

"I don't think I can talk about it...I ... I can't think straight right now. I really need to leave! Would you mind if we just go home?"

"Not at all. Whatever you need to do is OK with me." He squeezed my shoulder and kissed my cheek. "Let me know when you're ready to go back to the room and get our things."

I leaned against him, shut my puffy eyes and started to day-dream. My toes were covered by soft white sand as I sat on the beach watching the ocean, glistening diamonds from the sun danced on the rolling waves. I longed to stay in this euphoric place far away from the memories and the pain they evoked. The vision calmed my nerves.

"Thanks for understanding. I'm ready to go."

On the way home, I stared out the car window. The buildings blurred into one while the horrific act played like a movie reel, repeating the scene until it suffocated me. Accusatory words bombarded my mind. *This is your fault! You're worthless! That's why Dad didn't protect you!* I could barely breathe. *I'm losing it...I've got to talk to Diane. She can tell me if it really happened.*

Chris got the bags out of the car. "I'll get the kids later this afternoon, so you can rest," he said.

"Thanks. I'm going upstairs."

I tried to push the nagging memories and biting words from my mind. The urge to call Diane consumed me. I looked at the clock; it was a little after one. My three-year-old niece, Breanna, should be taking her nap. A nervousness rose up. With a shaking hand, I dialed Diane's number.

"Hey, Denise! I was just going to call you, so we could catch up, but then I remembered you were at that family conference. Did it end early?" Diane asked.

"Hi. No, not exactly. We left before it was over." I paused.

"Are you OK? You sound. . . strange."

I took a deep breath. "We were asked to think about our memories from childhood, so we could consider what kind of foundation our parents built for our lives and I remembered..." I choked on the words trying to escape my lips and started to cry. "I remembered Mom shoving us out the door and being on our own all day, eating crackers, drinking from the garden hose, going from one friend's house to the other because we weren't allowed to go home. Getting stung by bees. But then I remembered something even worse, and you are the only one that can tell me if it really happened!"

"I haven't thought about any of that in a long time. We had a lousy childhood, but why are you getting so emotional now? It's not a big deal. And it's over," Diane stated, almost nonchalantly.

"I already told you, we were asked to reflect on our past. I've got to know if Dad's business partner, Pete, you know... touched us?" I tremored.

"Hell yeah, that man had his hands down our pants every time he came over, but that was over thirty years ago."

"How can you be so flippant?" I sniffled into the phone.

"Why are you letting it get to you? You can't do anything about it!"

"Aren't you mad – angry that we weren't protected? Dad didn't protect us!" I shrieked.

"Yeah, well at least Pete didn't leave you with a permanent scar. I was laying on the couch once and Pete took a lit cigarette, jabbed it into my thigh, then twisted it deep into my skin to put it out. Man, did it hurt! Dad stood over me laughing. They were both sons of bitches, but it's not going to ruin my life. You need to stop thinking about it and move on," she coldly said.

Move on? You have got to be kidding me!

I thought she would be the one person on earth who would help me understand why it happened. The one person I could cry with. Disappointment flooded in.

"Thanks for letting me know I'm not crazy. I need to go get the kids," I snapped, and I hung up not waiting for a response.

I collapsed on the bed and pulled a pillow over my head. The memories wouldn't stop playing in my mind like an automatic loop on a video tape. The anger inside me was like scorching hot steam that shook the lid of a pressure cooker as it tried to find a way of escape. I had to find the valve to release the pressure before it destroyed me, but I didn't know how. Then the sting from Diane's angry, uncaring response brought back the torrential downpour of tears. Worn out, from the crashing waves of guilt and shame, I fell asleep within minutes.

Late in the day I felt someone lean over me and kiss my cheek. Samantha laid her head on my shoulder, hugged me and said, "Chris wanted me to tell you dinner is ready."

"Thanks, honey," I said, rolling over I grabbed her and kissed her cheek. "I love you so much!"

"I love you, too!" Her smile faded into dolefulness. "Mom, if people love one another, why do they hurt each other?"

Fear rose up. Did she somehow know what I was dealing with? I composed myself and asked softly, "I'm not sure I can answer that question. Can you tell me what you're talking about?"

"When I'm over at Dad's house, he yells at my little brother Timmy for nothing. And last weekend...he ... he slapped him across the face and Timmy fell down the stairs. He's only five and was just playing, being a kid, but Dad expects him to...to be... I don't know. . . perfect," she mumbled and looked away.

"Oh, Sam, I had no idea. I'm so sorry. That is very sad. Are you afraid of your dad? Do you feel safe when you're there on weekends?"

"He never treats us like he treats Timmy, but I hate the yelling. It hurts my ears!"

"I will talk to your dad and let him know it bothers you and hurts Timmy."

"Dad will be mad I told you. Please don't talk to him."

I kissed her on the forehead. "You know what? I just heard your tummy growl! Let's go eat some dinner and talk about this later."

It took every ounce of energy I had to push my body out of bed and force a smile on my face. *Sleeping for days would make all of this go away.* The thought tempted me to fall right back into bed, but my desire to see the kids beckoned me downstairs. I stretched as I got out of bed and hugged Sam. We went down the hall, then maneuvered past shoes and books on the stairs.

Daniel dropped the train he was playing with in the family room and ran into my arms. "Hi, Mommy! Missed is you!" he exclaimed. The raging emotional waterfall that I dreaded would let loose, vanished in his warm hug and I carried him over to the table. I forced away the devastating childhood recollections and the upsetting words Sam had just shared.

"Glad to see you're up. Sam set the table and I just picked up a wood roasted chicken pizza and fresh salad from Katie's Pizza and Pasta!" Chris said, proud as a peacock that he had figured out dinner on his own.

"That sounds wonderful. Thanks honey," I said and strapped Daniel in his highchair. "Thanks for setting the table, Sam."

She sat down across from Daniel and smiled at me. We had just moved into a new two-story house we had built six months before. The kitchen was the center of activity with a breakfast room next to it that had a bay window overlooking a two-tier Koi fish pond. The family room, on the other side of it, had a vaulted ceiling and sliding glass doors leading out to a big deck surrounded by trees. The new house gave us two more bedrooms and a bigger yard with privacy.

I walked into the family room and blocked the TV where Jaime sat in a bean bag chair, glued to her favorite show, *Clarissa Explains it All*. "Earth to Jaime. We're ready to eat," I announced. I pulled her up into my arms, hugged her, and smothered her with kisses. She giggled and hugged me back. We walked, arm-in-arm, to the table.

After dinner and Daniel's bath, Jaime picked out the book, *If You Give a Moose a Muffin*, to read to Daniel for a bedtime story. Sam and I chuckled as she embellished the details. The girls then said prayers with Daniel and helped me tuck him into bed. They went to the finished basement to play cards until their bedtime. The warm glow of a fire in the hearth greeted me when I walked into the family room. Chris handed me a glass of red wine and then pulled me next to him on the couch.

"So how is my favorite person doing tonight?"

"Fine when I am taking care of the kids and not in my head thinking about my past! But right now, we need to talk about what Sam told me before dinner. I'm really afraid."

Chris' countenance dropped. He moved away from my side and looked at me.

"Sam said Doyle is yelling a lot at Timmy and even hit him last weekend. She doesn't want me to talk to Doyle. I'm afraid it will escalate, and he will become violent with the girls!" Tears welled up in my eyes.

"Is Sam afraid Doyle will hit her?" Chris asked.

"No. Sam said he treats Jaime and her totally different. He seems to be taking all his anger out on Timmy. Doyle needs help, or he will never stop. He really needs to be reported to Children's Services. I can't stand to think of the damage this is doing to Timmy and the girls. After the conference today, I understand how the foundation a parent builds affects children -- especially when parents are abusive!"

"Honey, I understand. But I'm not sure we can or should do anything. If Doyle was doing this to Sam or Jaime, it would be a different story. But Brice is perfectly capable of calling the authorities. I don't think it's our place and it will just create more drama for us with weekend visits."

"So once again I have no power to protect my children or anyone else's! What kind of demented world do we live in! Well, I can tell you one thing I'm going to do...I'm going to set up an appointment with that psychic. She'll be able to see into the future and tell me if he's going to hurt the girls. I can't stand to think about my sweet, innocent girls being exposed to the abuse he is putting Timmy through. It's harming them!"

"If that gives you comfort, then go for it. But do you really want to know the future? It may cause more stress."

"That's where you're wrong. The unknown future causes me stress. Maybe knowing what will happen can help me know what to do. When I went to the psychic the first time I didn't tell her anything about you or our relationship. It was like she knew you, knew us and peered right into our future like she was watching a movie in her mind, right before my very eyes! She kept saying how much you loved and respected me and that our future together would be wonderful. I couldn't trust my feelings at the time. I had to know I wasn't making another mistake! That visit to the psychic and counseling helped me overcome my fear of marrying you, didn't it?" I leaned over and kissed his cheek. "I've got to know what will happen to the girls in the future and if he's going to start taking his anger out on them."

Chris pulled me into his arms and looked down at me. "Everything will be OK. I understand your motivation. Just don't ask her to reveal any of my hidden secrets!" His lips brushed my cheek, lingered on my neck, sending a tingle down my spine. His hand rested on my side. He tickled me. Giggling erupted. I tried to push his hand away. And then in a dramatic Romanian accent, he declared, "I can see into the future and there is no escape from me!"

I became hysterical with laughter. It felt so good. But then suddenly, I rolled onto the floor, pushed myself up and ran to the bathroom, making it just in time.

"Thank God we don't look like
what we've been through."

~ Unknown

CHAPTER 21

"Honey, wake up," Chris said as he gently rubbed my back.

I opened one eye and his solemn face, worry etched in every line, came into focus. "Ugh...you interrupted my dream," I grumbled. I rolled towards him and wiped the crusty sleep from my eyes.

"Do you know what time it is? It's eleven. You've been asleep fourteen hours! I made your favorite breakfast, French toast, to coax you out of bed."

"I just feel like I could sleep for days. I guess it's because I keep waking up all night and can't get back to sleep. My mind just won't turn off... Hmmm, French toast. That was so nice of you. I'm just not sure I can eat it right now. Guess the kids loved it."

"They sure did! Honey, I know you haven't wanted to talk but we can't keep living like this. You've barely eaten anything in three days. I think you're depressed," Chris said.

"You're right...I feel like I'm sinking in emotional quicksand. I couldn't stop crying yesterday after I spilled milk all over the floor. Then I spent half the day wandering from room to room, unable to remember what I was doing."

"Do you think you can tell me what upset you at the conference? It might make you feel better to share it with me. If not, maybe you could talk to a professional?" he softly asked.

"I don't think anything will help the way I feel. Sit down." I scooted over and patted the bed.

"One childhood memory after the other surfaced at the conference, but when I remembered my dad's business partner..." Tears filled my eyes. ". . . pulling me onto his lap and touching me inappropriately, that's when I fell apart. If that's not bad enough, my dad was doing the same thing to Diane. The shame of it all will never leave. If my dad loved me, he wouldn't have allowed this to happen. It has to be my fault. I feel so worthless," I murmured, defeated, and I turned away from Chris as tears streamed down my cheek.

Chris pulled me back towards him. "That is a lie! You are not worthless. I love you so much and so do the kids! You are an awesome person. He is the one who is worthless!" Anger flashed in his eyes and he tightened his hand into a fist. "I don't know how I will control my anger the next time we see your dad."

He pulled a Kleenex out of the box on the night stand, hugged me and gently caressed my head in his hand. "Now I understand why this has been so hard for you. But I think you need to talk to someone."

"Now it makes even more sense why I get so upset about not being able to protect the girls from Doyle's abuse. I somehow knew no one protected me. All I ever wanted to do was keep them safe." Tears welled up again. "I haven't talked to Sandy for a long time, but I'm sure she's still practicing. I'll call her today." I blew my nose hard.

Chris got up, pulled me out of bed and grabbed my robe off the bench at the end of the bed. He wrapped it around me. "You have to eat something!" he urged.

My belly growled at the mention of food. "I can't believe you made me French toast!"

ぬぬぬぬぬぬぬぬぬぬ

I repeatedly slapped the rolled-up homework assignment in the palm of my hand as I walked through the damp parking garage to my car. It would be easy to tell that sorry excuse for a father exactly what I thought of him, especially now that someone had given me permission! I never spoke my mind around my father; he was to be revered. But I didn't revere him. I was just plain scared to death of him. I got in my car, threw the assignment onto the passenger seat and started the engine. Sandy's words echoed in my mind, "By writing a letter to your dad you can lay the blame and shame right back where it belongs--on the abuser." A rage ignited deep from within me and I stomped on the brake as hard as I could. An irate scream let loose from my lips, the hatred exploded, and it felt so good. Alone in the car, it was safe to lift the lid off the pressure cooker and let the scalding stream escape. I took a cleansing breath and pulled out of the parking garage. The conversation Sandy and I had replayed during the drive home.

"Writing about the abuse and the emotion it created will externalize the memories and make them less overwhelming, so the feelings don't control you. Writing is a wonderful tool. It will help you move beyond the trauma," Sandy explained.

"I don't know how I will ever be able to talk to my dad again, especially after he reads the letter!" I vehemently said during the session.

"Let's not get ahead of the process. I just want you to write about what he did and how you feel. Write about anything that comes to your mind that you want to say to your dad. It would be good to include what he did to you in specific detail, so you don't sugar coat the abuse and how it has affected your life. This will keep you from getting stuck in self-blame. You will want to rewrite the letter numerous times until you feel the anger dissipate."

Sandy continued, "Since your abuser is your dad, you may want to give yourself permission to cut contact with him during this time. This way you can do the hard work it will take to totally focus on caring for your inner child, so you can heal from your abuse. But let me warn you, it's going to be a battle. You will have to fight the persistent guilt that will likely pursue you as you move into this new territory."

That advice sparked something inside of me. My parents always expected me to be the obedient child, but I needed to feel like an adult who was in control of her own life. It was time to grow up. I would never gain their approval, as much as I still wanted it. But now I wanted my freedom more.

Exhaustion had set in and made my legs feel like rubber; they almost buckled underneath me when I got out of the car in the garage. I shuffled into the mud room and opened the door into the family room. Daniel, still dressed in his PJs, saw me and squealed as he ran towards me, and wrapped his arms around my legs. I bent down and picked him up. I licked my thumb and wiped the strawberry jam from the corner of his mouth. "I love you so much!" I kissed his cheek and hugged him.

Chris walked up, hugged us both, then asked, "How did it go?"

"It's a lot to digest, but the session has already helped me understand some things. She gave me a homework assignment that I'm anxious to do. Would you mind if I went upstairs and got started on it?"

"Not at all. Daniel and I were just going to go outside on this fine May day, so he can ride his bike... after we get dressed, of course. Right buddy?" Daniel nodded, squirmed out of my embrace and raced up the stairs. "I knew that would work to get him out of those

PJ's! Oh, and the girls are still at their sleepover, so you'll have peace and quiet."

The desk sat in front of the dormer window in our multi-purpose room above the garage. The blank tablet of lined yellow paper on the desk taunted me: *Go ahead! Let him have it. He can't hurt you anymore!* Guilt hounded me: *You can't write down how you really feel. What if someone sees it?* Besides it felt foolish to believe that writing anything down on paper would keep my emotions from eating me alive. But I had to try. My lungs filled with air and I let out a deep groan. I put the pen on the paper and wrote whatever came to mind. Questions came flooding out.

What was wrong with me that you didn't love me enough to protect me? I was trapped on his lap, desperate to make him stop touching me so I could get away, but you did nothing! Furious, I stood up and paced back and forth, so repulsed by the thought that my stomach started to churn.

Bewildered, I wrote: *Why didn't it bother you that I was being hurt? How could you be in the same room when it was happening and not stop it?!?* I seethed. *How could you do the same thing to Diane...* A darkness crushed my soul.

The anguish created from not being able to protect the girls rose up. If I had been in the room when Doyle abused Jaime, no one could have stopped me from protecting her! I continued writing: *You allowed us to be used for another man's sick pleasure! Do you even care that it created unseen, ghastly scars that may never heal? The abuse has changed who I am. Now I am deformed and ugly!*

I screamed out loud, "You should have been a father who adored me and cherished me like a princess!" I glanced at the closed door behind me, hoping no one heard. I looked out the window in front of the desk to the driveway below. Chris and Daniel were out in the front yard, playing tag and chasing each other.

I violently started to scribble the words that I could not say out loud: *You are a twisted, vile, self-centered good for nothing, who only cared about watching TV and drinking beer!* Turbulent bitterness overtook me. *I hate you for not protecting me and I hate Pete! I was a worthless nobody who counted for nothing in your world. I was just there to be used and treated like trash! I want you to say you are sorry! I want you to feel the pain I feel. I want you to be ashamed of what you did to me! But you don't feel remorse for anything and I will never be able to say this to your face. You are dangerous, and I can't give you another opportunity to hurt me.*

An idling car engine startled me. I looked out the window and saw Samantha and Jaime climbing out of the backseat of a car. The dark tunnel I had been traveling down had depleted my energy, so I decided to stop writing. I slid the desk drawer open and shoved the legal tablet inside.

"Hey, Mom, we're home!" the girls yelled as they sprinted up the stairway.

I got up and greeted them in the hall with a hug. "So how was the sleepover?"

"Great! We stayed up late and played games. Then we got yelled at for being too loud at 3 in the morning!"

My hand rubbed the knot that had formed in my shoulder and I winced in pain. "Typical sleepover then, huh? I wanted to talk to you both about going to your dad's. Samantha, you said that your dad yelled at Timmy and hit him the last time you were over there. It's very important that you tell me if it happens again. I want you both to be safe."

"Dad did say he was sorry to Timmy," Samantha said.

"Sam was just being a big baby because her ears hurt when people yell. Timmy deserved it. He kept throwing stuff down the stairs! Really, Mom, it's no big deal!" Jaime said.

"OK. I hope it wasn't like it sounded because I love you both too much," my voice cracked, and tears formed. "I just don't want anything to happen to you. Please promise me you will tell me if he hurts Timmy again."

Jaime looked confused. "OK, but we have fun at Dad's! Can we go play video games in the basement?"

"Sure. But don't forget you're going to help me make tacos for dinner before you get picked up." Before I could finish, they raced each other down the stairs to the basement.

I went down the hall to our bathroom and turned on the water to fill the tub. I squirted some moisturizing Calgon honeysuckle-scented bath bubbles into the hot running water. Then I went over to the TV that sat on a shelf above my makeup table and turned on a rerun of *WKRP in Cincinnati*. I dropped my clothes on the floor and climbed into the relaxing, warm sudsy water. It was the "Turkeys Away" episode, and the radio promotion dropping live turkeys from a helicopter had gone horribly wrong. Les Nessman reported, "The turkeys are hitting the ground like sacks of wet cement!" I laughed until my ribs hurt. Then station manager, Arthur Carlson, said, "As God is my witness, I thought turkeys could fly!" My whole stomach ached from the uncontrollable giggling.

I closed my eyes. I wanted to stay in that tub until the laughter erased all the sorrow. That moment of joy in the midst of extreme pain made me believe that the shattered pieces of my childhood heart could heal.

"All the darkness in the world cannot extinguish the light of a single candle."

~ Francis of Assisi

CHAPTER 22

y trembling hands kneaded the dry onion mix into the hamburger and I struggled to form it into a loaf. A tingling sensation ran down my arm as I washed my hands. I patted them dry, then rubbed my arm. Likely another panic attack. This was the third one in ten days. When the first one struck I was convinced it was a heart attack, but the EMT assured me it wasn't. My vital signs were normal. So now I fought my way through them, but this one seemed more intense.

Determined to finish the recipe, I poured crème of mushroom soup over it, slid it into the oven and set the timer. I held on to the countertop and fought for breath as my throat constricted. I stumbled across the kitchen to a chair, sat down at the table and put my head between my knees to ward off the fainting spell. The room started to spin. The haunting dream from the night before reappeared in my mind. I stood in a doorway of a small room, the broken pieces from a table that had been blown up, were scattered all over the floor behind me. My dad approached the doorway. I held up my hand and blocked his view and said, "Don't look. Don't look. Don't look."

It seemed like I was trying to protect him from the truth of what had caused the table to shatter. I tried to analyze the dream further when palpitations started in my chest. The dream seemed to be triggered after the call from my dad two weeks earlier.

"Do you know what day it is?" he bellowed without saying hello.

"Well, yes. It's Tuesday," I answered.

"You should look at a calendar once in a while! You forgot your mother's birthday! Do you know how hurt she is?"

"I didn't know. I'm sorry."

"I expected better from you, and your mother deserves better! Don't let it happen again!" Click!

My chest had tightened, and I couldn't breathe. I had called 911, never guessing it was a panic attack. I never told Chris. It was tax filing season, and he didn't need to worry about me.

I sat with my head on the table. I had 30 minutes to pull it together before the kids got home from school. I knew fear was at the root of it all: the fear of not knowing if the girls would be hurt during Doyle visits. Dealing with my own abuse made the fear of what could happen more real and intense. *If I just knew what the future holds I wouldn't be stressed out.* I dug in the kitchen drawer, pulled out my address book and I found the psychic's number. Wendy answered the phone on the first ring. I almost joked, "You knew I was going to call," then thought better of it. She had an opening the following day at 1:00.

The front door opened, Jaime and Samantha walked in and threw their backpacks on the stairs.

"Mom, I'm hungry! Is that meat loaf I smell? Yuk!" Jaime whined.

"I'm sorry. I'll fix spaghetti tomorrow." Jaime smiled. She and her sister rifled through the pantry, got fruit roll ups, then went downstairs to watch TV before doing homework.

I didn't tell Chris that night about my meeting with Wendy. My plan was to get rid of the panic attacks by seeing the psychic. He would not have to know about either one, and life would be good again.

During the drive over to Wendy's house, I decided not to give her any of the intimate details about my new life since marrying Chris. I knocked on her door and Wendy greeted me with a warm, genuine smile. She looked to be in her early fifties and had blonde hair that fell to her shoulders. She was dressed casually in jeans and a sweatshirt that had a whimsical cat face airbrushed on it.

"Hi. Good to see you again. I believe I have already received insight into your situation."

"Really?" My curiosity was in overdrive.

"Yes, I am very in tune with the spiritual world. They are guiding me. I have little control over what I receive and when I was meditating this morning I got an impression. We'll see how it comes up in the session. But I can tell you, you will receive what you need -- not necessarily what you want. My intuition helps me specialize in information about life and relationships – you know information about the future. But no psychic can see one hundred percent into the future. They see opportunities and obstacles in your life. So basically, I provide insight into the choices presented to you. You just need to listen, and the credible details that mean something to you will stand out. And please don't share anything about yourself. It's better to just start and see where the session goes. Shall we start?"

"OK, sounds good to me!"

Wendy took my hand. "I see different auras of light or colors around you. White is the predominate one; it means truth. Truth is very important to you, and I get the impression you have tried to make a truth known, to protect someone from danger, so they wouldn't get hurt. The other color I see is gold. You are connected to God in service of mankind. You aren't serving yet but will be. You have a daughter . . . no two daughters. They visit someone. Their father, yes?"

"Yes, they visit their father. We are divorced."

"Awe, yes. It is the younger one I am seeing, and she is the one I saw earlier when I was meditating. Very soon she will not want to visit her father anymore. It is a strong impression. You should not make her go on these visits."

"Wow! OK. I don't know how that will go over with her dad or the court, but I will be happy not to send her on visits! But what about my older daughter?"

"The older one will want to continue to go. Their father will not object to your younger daughter staying behind."

I thanked Wendy, gave her the fee we had agreed upon and left. I was amazed at what she shared and decided not to tell Chris, or anyone, unless it came true. What Wendy said made logical sense. Sam was already sensitive and upset about Timmy being hurt. I would have to wait-and-see now.

The fear and panic didn't go away. It only got worse. The *what-ifs* rose up and haunted me all night. What if Sam does stop going on visits? Then that gives Doyle more time alone with Jaime! The anxiety made me regret my visit to Wendy. I realized I was no better off than before. Exhausted, deep slumber finally overtook me hours later.

With each slow step I took down the hall, my aching body fought me. "Girls, it's late! Get up and get dressed fast!" I announced.

I heard Jaime grumble from her room, "Can't you take us to school?"

"Not today. If you move it, you'll be ready by the time the bus is here! Get dressed and brush your teeth. You can eat cereal or a granola bar while you watch for the bus."

I went into Sam's room. She was out of bed already, tugging on the jeans we'd laid out the night before. I grabbed the brush off the dresser, smoothed out her long, thick hair and she pulled on her pink cotton sweater. I heard Daniel stir in his crib across the hall.

"Mommy, want out!" he squawked. I smiled at the sound of his squeaky adorable, almost three-year-old voice.

"Hold on, buddy. I'll get to you in a minute."

I went back into Jaime's room and brushed her hair back into a pony tail while she pulled on her faded jeans. She threw a denim vest over her tie-dyed long sleeve t-shirt, and I went into Daniel's room. I lifted the side of his crib and slid it down. He climbed over it, hanging there by one arm while pretending to squirt a sticky web from the sleeve of his Spiderman pajama top at the unseen villain in the corner of his room. "You got the bad guy! Good job!" We didn't dare deviate from this part of the morning routine or we were sure to witness a toddler tantrum of epic proportions.

The girls were in the hall bathroom, brushing their teeth when I walked by holding Daniel in my arms and started down the stairs. I could hear them scramble to finish, and when we were on the third step the girls breezed by us, beating us to the bottom step. "We did it and you have 15 minutes to spare!"

I put Daniel down in the kitchen, opened the freezer, dug out two cherry toaster strudels and popped them into the toaster. "Get your jackets and backpacks on while you wait." I got two napkins, and after hearing the ding of the toaster, put a strudel in each one and took them to the girls standing by the front door.

"Ah, Mom, what about the frosting?" Sam complained.

"No time. Besides it's too messy. You'll live without it! And there's the bus! OK, say it with me on your way out the door...We love our mom and she is always right!" They shot me a scowling frown and turned to leave.

Sam took two steps back, reached out and hugged me, "Thanks, Mom!"

After lunchtime, Daniel held my hand and counted each step on the stairs while climbing to the top for his nap. We entered his room, painted corn yellow with a wide wallpaper boarder depicting teddy bears sitting on a shelf. *Very soon he would be too old for this décor*, I thought. One day, when Daniel was three months old, I'd held him for hours, fed him and rocked him while he slept. I never put him down that day until the girls came home from school. I knew I would never have another baby to hold; Daniel was my last. I squeezed him tight and kissed him when I lifted him into his crib. He rolled over and grabbed his octopus with the eight different colored legs, then pointed to each leg and said the color. I pulled his blanket over him. "You sure know your colors! Sleep good, sweetie," I said.

A palpable cloud of dark fear greeted me when I walked into the hallway. I could feel the panic start to rise, and I leaned against the wall. I had to fight against it and take back control of my life! I heard the words *Go write*. I was hoping to catch up on my soap opera, but it had been weeks since I first started to unleash my feelings in a letter to my dad. Maybe finishing the letter would help me get to a better place. I steadied myself, pushed away from the wall, and walked down the hall into the multi-purpose room. I sat at my desk, pulled out the yellow lined tablet out of the drawer and read the words I had scribbled there. Their intensity surprised me. I picked up where I had stopped and wrote for an hour, filling page after page with every emotion that flowed out.

I ended the letter with a declaration: *I will not be your victim anymore! I despise the word victim! If I am a victim, I am powerless and can't change how I view the past. And I am more than a survivor because I will thrive despite what you have done to me! I will overcome and heal from the damage you have inflicted upon me.*

I felt a sudden release of rage and, one by one, the chains of hatred and bitterness broke off, freeing me from their bondage.

When I left to go to counseling that night, the girls were doing homework with Chris at the table, and Daniel was drawing circles on a piece of paper in his highchair. Completing the letter that day made me feel like I was up for an award. The pain had subsided, and I was relieved to be done dealing with it. I was anxious to tell Sandy all about my hard work, convinced the panic attacks would stop. I walked down the hall of the church building and into her waiting room. Ten minutes later she greeted me and led me back to her office.

"Well, Denise, it's been several weeks since we have met. Tell me, how have things been going?"

"Things have been weird, but I got the letter done."

"Weird in what way?"

"Well, my dad called me a few weeks back and he let me have it because I forgot my mom's birthday. Then I had this crazy dream about being in a rundown shack with a smashed-up table behind me and when my dad came to the doorway, I held up my hand and said, 'Don't look, don't look.' Then after the call and the dream, I started having panic attacks! They've been just awful, but I finished the letter today that you asked me to write to my dad."

"Wow, that is a lot going on! OK, I want to talk about each thing separately. Do you usually remember your mom's birthday? Does your family make a big deal out of birthdays?"

"Yeah, I guess I usually remember her birthday. I wasn't paying attention to what date it was. Besides, I didn't do it on purpose! It's not like *he* was going to make a big deal out of her birthday. Our family doesn't make a big deal out of anything."

"How did his call make you feel?" Sandy asked.

"Worthless and belittled."

"How did the dream make you feel?"

"It felt like I was protecting him from the truth of why the table was in pieces. Like it would be my fault if he saw the table and got angry about it. But I didn't feel bad about the table being shattered. I felt bad about him or anyone finding out," I answered.

"I think the call from your dad is the reason you had the dream. It sounds like he expects you to do everything right, but that makes you feel like you will never measure up – leaving you to feel insignificant and demeaned. The dream is very significant. If the table in the dream represents a person, who do you think it would be?"

"I didn't think about the table representing a person. Me? Wow, the shattered table represents how the abuse broke my life into pieces? Yes, it makes sense because if my dad knew I was talking about how he abused me and writing a letter about it, he would be so angry."

"I think you're right. That shattered table does represents you. How did writing the letter make you feel?" Sandy asked.

"It actually felt good to get my feelings out and to be able to say whatever came to mind. And the anger seemed to disappear the more I wrote. But now I wish the panic attacks would stop. They are controlling my life."

"Letter writing is the first exercise I use with clients to help them release feelings around traumatic events. You have done a great job and seem to be in a much better place! But I would like to try something new today: prayer therapy. I will ask the Holy Spirit to show you the truth that has led you to believe a lie about yourself. The root cause of the lie is buried in your subconscious. It influences your actions and thoughts about yourself. A couple words from Jesus through the Holy Spirit changes the lie that led to the belief. I think the panic attacks will be gone after a couple of prayer therapy sessions."

∾∾∾∾∾∾∾∾∾∾

The day had warmed up quickly and the cool breeze against my cheek gave me relief from the bright sun overhead. Walking on the paved trail at Legacy Park brought clarity to the prayer session Sandy had just completed with me. Each lie uncovered from my childhood was a brick, building up a wall around me, suffocating me. Once each lie was destroyed by the truth of Jesus, the wall built by shame came tumbling down. Peace filled the empty cavern inside my soul where the imposed guilt and shame had resided. I chose to forgive an unforgiveable act, and the Holy Spirit gave me the power to forgive Pete and my dad.

At our last session, Sandy did an exercise with me and told me to visualize my seven-year-old self. "Tell seven-year-old Denise that it was not her fault, that she was only a child."

I visualized holding her and rocking back and forth. "I am so sorry you had to endure the horror of abuse and a father full of hatred, but you are worthy of love, especially my love!"

It had been weeks since my last counseling session and the panic attacks had not returned. The storm had passed, and I was grateful to God for leading me through it. I felt like a new person.

It was Friday night. Chris and I had a sitter for Daniel, and the girls were being picked up by Doyle. We were looking forward to going out to dinner for pizza and a movie. Sam bounded down the stairs and said, "I really don't want to go to Dad's this weekend. Is it OK if I stay home?"

Chris looked at me bewildered while I responded, "That is fine with me, but don't you think your dad will object?"

"I don't care. He was really mean to Timmy last time and I don't want to go over to his house again!"

"I understand and would never make you go, but what about your sister? Won't you miss her?"

"It doesn't bother her. All she does is play with the dogs. She loves that Dad takes us out to eat and to fun places, but I don't care about that stuff."

"OK, I will tell your dad when he gets here."

"No, Mom. I will go out and tell him," Sam said.

Jaime hugged me, said good-bye, then ran out the door with her overnight bag. Sam trailed behind.

"Chris, would it be OK with you if we took Sam on our date tonight? I think she needs some time alone with us."

"I agree. I think that is exactly what she needs. There goes our steamy, romantic date!"

I reached up and hugged him. "You really are the best!!"

The following Sunday, after adult Sunday school, I went into fellowship hall to find Daniel and make sure he wasn't eating too many donuts. Chris tended to look the other way and Daniel would gorge himself.

"Hi, Denise. You are just the person I was looking for." I turned around and saw Rose, a senior member of our church, who was one of the wisest women I had ever met, and who neither looked nor acted her age. Her vermilion colored hair made it easy to spot her from across the sanctuary and it perfectly accented her feisty personality "Do you have a minute to talk?" she asked.

"Sure. I was just trying to find Daniel before he goes into a sugar coma, but he must be with Chris upstairs in the nursery."

"During my prayer time yesterday, I got an impression from the Holy Spirit. Your face flashed before me and He said, 'She's opened the door to the occult.'"

"The occult? You mean like black magic, séances and Ouija boards? Of course not!"

"Just think about it. Something might come to mind. It's dangerous territory! Even if you unknowingly dabbled in the occult, you'll want to shut that door!"

I thanked Rose for sharing, went upstairs and found Chris in the sanctuary. I had trouble concentrating on the message. I racked my brain trying to think of what it might be, and my mind was blank.

The next Sunday the scene was repeated with Rose finding me in fellowship hall and relaying the same message from the Holy Spirit.

"OK, now you're scaring me! Rose, can you explain to me what 'occult' means? Because I haven't been involved in witchcraft or anything crazy like that!"

"The occult isn't just participating in séances while using Ouija boards...it's the action or influence of the supernatural. Let me ask you this. Have you ever been to a psychic before?"

My heart sank. "Actually, I have. But I was desperate to know the future."

"That's it! Going to a psychic opens the door to the enemy!"

"But everything she told me came true! The psychic said Sam would no longer want to go on visits with Doyle, and Sam just came to us and asked to stop going to her dad's! Although it did cause fear to rise up in me, thinking Jaime would be abused by Doyle again because Sam wouldn't be there with her."

"If the word given to you breeds fear, then we know it is not from God because God didn't give us a spirit of fear. Real psychics were born with a true gift but choose their own path and not God's path. They don't seek the spirit of God, but rather they seek a familiar spirit. I think it's in 1 John where the apostle says, 'Test every spirit to see if they are from God, because many false prophets have gone out into the world.' And what it says in Leviticus is really scary: 'I will turn against those who commit spiritual prostitution by putting their trust in mediums, so set yourselves apart to be holy.' Think about it. Spiritual prostitution! Let me ask you this. Did she pray and listen for God's voice? Or did she take the credit for the power she had?"

"No, she didn't pray and, yes, she took credit for her gift. But I went months ago before Pastor Whit gave the sermon about the gift of prophecy being alive today and that God still speaks through His people. I didn't know then that God would speak through others to give me comfort and hope. And I certainly don't want to commit the sin of 'spiritual prostitution' so I would never go back to a psychic now," I insisted.

"I'm glad to hear that, but you have opened a spiritual door to the dark realm and we need to shut it. God has brought this to your attention to protect you, and all you need to do is repent from putting your trust in a psychic instead of God. We can pray about this right now if you like?"

"Of course! Let's find a quiet room."

"All things work together;
For God's glory and my good."

CHAPTER 23

Four Years Later

"I can't believe we're late again," I muttered as I stared at the parking lot full of cars but void of people. The contemporary, upbeat music from inside Kirkwood United Methodist church confirmed that Pastor Whit had already made announcements and the service had started without us.

Daniel was already walking in with Chris; Samantha and I waited for Jaime to get out of the car. She was slouched in the back seat, staring out the window into deep space. I had hoped to slip into church quickly without causing a scene, but now I wondered how much cajoling I would have to do to get her to move. Her defiant behavior had become worse in recent months and now daily it reared its ugly head. "Jaime, Jaimeee! May I have your attention, please. We have arrived at our destination." She snapped out of her thoughts and shot me an annoying look. "Sorry to interrupt your daydream, but we're late," I announced.

"If you had just left me at home, you wouldn't be late, Mom," she snarled.

"But what fun would that be? Come on let's get going."

She hesitantly climbed out of the car and lethargically walked up to the church doors; Samantha and I followed.

Chris slowly opened one of the double doors that led into the sanctuary. A few heads turned in our direction, but most of the congregation kept their attention on the screen as the pastor ran through the list of announcements and upcoming events. We took seats in the next-to-last row of pews.

Across the aisle, I saw my friend Tina and her husband, George. We'd met in Bible study three years earlier. I had learned a lot from observing Tina's relationship with the Lord and listening to her passionate stories of His activity in her life. She might have been soft spoken, but she was His flaming torch that lit the path for others to follow. Her wavy, flowing dark hair was striking against the lacy princess cut, ecru dress she was wearing. They sat with a tall, lanky man I didn't recognize, and they whispered back and forth. When Tina saw me, she gestured hello with a wave towards me.

I stifled a laugh at the memory of the previous Friday night when we all went to a spirit-filled service across the river at Living Spirit Fellowship.

"You wouldn't believe how many times this week I've read or heard the story of Jonah. My Bible falls open to the book of Jonah, or when I turn on the TV, a pastor is preaching about Jonah and the focus of our Bible study this week was on Jonah!" an exasperated Tina had shared on the way to the Friday night service.

"I guess you better figure out what you're running from and why God wants you to turn around and go back. You wouldn't want to get thrown overboard and end up in a whale!" I joked. We had a good laugh walking into the building.

The Friday service was already crowded because it attracted people from many denominations all over the tri-state area who anticipated emotional and physical healings. People raised their hands while swaying and clapping to the lively praise music. At the front of the church, some of the worshipers waved colorful silk banners with dazzling gold and orange flames of fire, representing the Holy Spirit. The freedom during worship was exhilarating and His presence flowed over me like warm honey.

After the worship time ended, Pastor Kenny began preaching. He stopped right in the middle of a sentence and walked right up to Tina. He pointed at her saying, "The Lord is telling me that you are a Jonah running from God and His will for your life! He is telling me to encourage you to, *Stop Running*. He has given you a great work to complete – Do not fear! Take His hand and let Him lead you!" Then he turned around, went back to the front and continued preaching. We both looked at each other, astonished.

Tina went up for prayer at the end of the service and God replaced her anxiety with peace. Tina and I were still shaking our heads in reverent awe during the trip home.

"Can you believe what just happened? It was a spirit of fear that made me run from God and I've been running long enough! Now I'm free to start a dance ministry and use my passion to glorify God!" Tina said on the drive home.

It was exhilarating to experience God's presence! At Living Spirit, His word became alive when I witnessed first-hand the things I read about in the Bible. Jesus sent the Holy Spirit to pour out His gifts; like an encouraging word, healing or a warning for His people. That is exactly what God did on those Friday nights. God became a living presence I could access. No longer was He floating up in the clouds somewhere, ignoring me. God's love and compassion to heal broken hearts and bodies gave me a passion to know Him more. The intimate discussions, after those services with my mature Christian friends, deepened my understanding of what we were experiencing.

I refocused my attention on our new Kirkwood worship band while they sang one of my favorites, "Shout to the Lord" by Hillsong. It always made me emotional. It reminded me that God's mighty love had been my comfort, my shelter, my refuge and strength through so many tough times, even before I had accepted Jesus.

Tina caught me after the service in the foyer and introduced me to the gentleman she'd been sitting with, Don Watchmen. Don's piercing eyes seemed to look right into my heart.

"I met Don at a Friday night Living Spirit service a few weeks ago. I think that was the Friday you were out of town. George and I have been amazed at his prophetic gift. He just walks up to strangers and tells them what God directs him to say. And he is so on point that the people he ministers to are always stunned by what he says. So much so that they become overwhelmed with emotions."

I nodded at Don, smiled and shook his hand. I was excited to meet someone who God was working through in such a powerful way.

Don's attention suddenly turned towards Daniel. "He already has the Spirit of the Lord on him. He will become a preacher who shares with boldness and in front of many someday." A grin appeared on Daniel's face. This didn't seem to be a revelation to him. I was flabbergasted. Daniel was only seven! I'd witnessed a lot of awesome things at Living Spirit, but how could someone make a statement about such a young boy and without even knowing him?

Even before Daniel was born, I had prayed like Hannah in the Bible, dedicating him to the Lord. On many occasions, I'd sensed the Holy Spirit's warm presence wrap Daniel in a cozy blanket when he would sit with Tina and me during our prayer time. Daniel was only five when he adamantly announced that Easter 'shouldn't be called Easter; it should be called Resurrection Day!' But this Don guy didn't know any of that. God was definitely working through this man... unless Tina had talked to him about my family. That could be why the word is so specific and on target. Yes, that must be it.

Don gazed at my husband, compassion pouring from his eyes. He said, "Your family has been going through a lot lately."

I shot Tina a questioning look. But Tina's wide-eyed expression indicated that she was just as surprised by Don's words as I was.

"A dark spirit of depression has a stranglehold over you." He glanced at me, then back at Chris. "And this has had a profound effect on your wife."

My jaw dropped. A few years before, Chris had been hit hard by a spirit of anxiety and depression. Lately, I saw this persistent entity revisiting him with a vengeance! The fun, easy-going man I had married constantly worried about everything and rarely got off the couch unless he had to. I had considered divorce because I could no longer handle the gloomy oppression in the house. Chris had tried numerous medications, professional counseling, and even electric shock therapy. And, of course, countless prayers. Some of it seemed to work—temporarily. But the oppression always returned.

Don looked at Jaime. "And you are being seduced by the occult."

Now, hold on just a minute. My daughter was a typical four-teen-year-old girl—moody, manipulative, sneaky, constantly try-ing new ways to get her parents to let her do what she wanted. But the occult? No way. I didn't even let her watch scary movies at home, mostly because I didn't like them myself.

But the look in Jaime's eyes told me he'd struck a chord.

Tina saw that this attention Jaime was getting right there in the middle of foyer was making her uncomfortable. She interjected, "Would you guys mind if we came with Don to your house and prayed with all of you next week?"

My heart stirred with hope. I had been in prayer for weeks, asking God to do a mighty work in my family's life. Could this man be the one God wanted to work through to answer those prayers?

I glanced at Chris, whose eyes darted around the foyer while he anxiously shifted his weight from one foot to the other. I could tell he wished he could disappear. "Thank you for your offer," he quietly said, "but we're fine. We have to get home now." He didn't like sharing personal details of his life, even with friends.

"We could just pray over the kids, then," Tina added, sensing his discomfort.

George and Don nodded, silently offering their support.

To my surprise, Chris appeased them. "I guess that'd be OK."

This must be God moving! Chris is such an introvert; he never would have said yes to something like this.

The following Wednesday, Don, Tina, and George arrived on our doorstep. I greeted them with excited anticipation and invited them to make themselves comfortable in the family room. Chris and the kids took seats across from Don.

After some small talk and snacks, Don said, "I'd like to share with you how God has moved in my life." He described an alarming night when he'd contemplated suicide. "I could no longer take the evil whispers that had plagued me for hours, telling me, *You're worthless. No one will miss you. Just end it.*"

I shuddered. A memory of Chris in the worst of his depression came to my mind. He sat on the floor in the corner of our bedroom with his knees pulled up, rocking back and forth sobbing, "I can't take the pain anymore. I'm gonna kill myself."

Chris had been a happy-go-lucky guy when we met, but things started to change when his mom died three months after we were married, and Daniel was born a year later. He became anxious doing everyday things like walking the dog, then it spiraled into depression and fear gripped him constantly.

Don continued, "Just as I was about to pull the trigger of the gun I had aimed at my head, a bright light shone all around me. I heard the voice of God whisper, '*I have great plans for you. If you do this, you will never complete them.*' I had never encountered God before, and I knew in that moment He was real and that my life was precious to Him. That very night, I threw away the gun and started reading the Bible."

My heart leapt for joy. I felt convinced that God had led Don to us, so He could work though him to heal Chris. We were all amazed at what the Lord had done in Don's life. He said he wanted to prayed with each of us individually, then he prayed and asked God to move in a mighty way to accomplish His will in each one of our lives. When he prayed with me, the Holy Spirit poured over my head like warm honey and a blanket of tranquility wrapped around me.

When Don got to Jaime, he asked us to go into the living room, so he could pray with her privately. I felt a little uncomfortable leaving her in a room with a man I had just met. I wanted to hear what God would say through Don but decided I could pry it out of him later. Jaime was in trouble at school. She had skipped classes and was close to failing them as a result. She didn't share things with me like she once had, but I'd just attributed that to hormones. And she wasn't sharing her thoughts with Doyle either. His sweet talk had lost its power a couple of years ago, soon after she turned 12. She preferred her friends over visiting him, unless there was a birthday present or Christmas gift to be picked up. Maybe she'd be more willing to open up if we weren't present. We all got comfortable in the living room and continued to pray while Don talked to Jaime.

A few minutes later Jaime and Don joined us. Her face looked so serene.

Don looked concerned. "Denise, may I speak to you and your husband in the family room?"

Tina, George and the kids grabbed a bowl of popcorn and went into the dining room to play one of their favorite card games, Kings in the Corner. Chris and I sat on the couch with Don. My mind swirled with questions. *What on earth did he need to tell us? Was Jaime in more trouble than we thought?*

"God gave me a vision while I was praying with Jaime."

I'd heard of people having visions, but I had never experienced such a thing myself. Nor had I met anyone who had them—at least not to my knowledge.

"What kind of vision?" I inquired.

"In my mind, I saw Jaime being drawn into the woods where a group of people were worshipping demonic spirits. I got the impression that God wants to stop this now before something horrific happens," Don gently explained.

Wow! That lines up with what Don told us at church when he looked at Jaime, but that's crazy! Jaime wouldn't be involved in something like that, or does that explain her attitude lately? Chris looked confused and remained silent.

Concern showed on my face and Don placed his hand on my shoulder. "It's going to be okay. God allowed the Holy Spirit to show me this, so He can give Jaime an understanding of the demonic realm and demonstrate His power at work."

"Did …" I stammered, trying to clear the lump out of my throat. "Did you tell Jaime about this vision?"

He nodded.

"What did she say?" Chris asked.

"She admitted that it has already happened."

What? No! It couldn't be true. How? I was so intentional about what my children watched on television and listened to on the radio. I read the Bible to them and prayed with them every night. When Jaime became a teenager, she loved to watch scary movies when she was out with her friends and go to haunted houses at Halloween. But this was so out of character for sweet, sensitive Jaime who hated cruelty of any kind. She constantly rescued abandoned cats and dogs from the side of the road, parks, anywhere she found them. I could never picture her getting involved in such a thing. How could she even want anything to do with demons? It didn't make sense. And worse, I'd missed it.

Don continued, "I prayed for her and asked God to show her the real side of evil so that she will not be intrigued by it anymore. I assure you that God will protect her and your family." I fought to process what this man of God had just shared. I gazed up at Chris, and he looked as confused as I felt.

Don took Chris's hands and started to pray in tongues. I'd heard a few people at Living Spirit and in our congregation whisper strange sounds during meditation or between praise songs. But Don prayed out loud—and fervently. It sounded so strange, yet I felt indescribable serenity.

He ended his prayer with, "Amen!" and sat quietly for a few moments. Then he opened his eyes and looked intently at Chris. "The Lord showed me that the depression you have suffered has come and gone for quite some time. Are you ready for it to be gone for good?"

Chris was quiet for a moment and I could tell was he debating. He looked skeptical but desperate, and finally announced, "Yes, I don't want to be anxious and sad all the time. The doctors thought the electric shock therapy treatments would get rid of the depression, but it has come back and I'm tired of living this way. I want it gone for good."

Chris had submitted himself to what amounted to torture when he went through the shock therapy. They would strap him to a gurney, stick a tongue protector in his mouth and attach electrodes to his head. Then they would send volts of electricity to shock his brain, making his body violently contort. Every time they brought him out after these treatments Chris looked fragile and disheveled. The worst part was the treatments could make him lose his long-term memory. I cried every time I saw him.

Don laid his hand on my husband's head and cried out in a loud, commanding voice, "You deceiving, lying spirit of depression, come out! Release this man. Release him now, in Jesus' name. Return to the pit of hell where you belong. I plead the shed blood of Jesus over this child of God. You have held this man hostage long enough. And you will not return!"

Chris' head was back, and his eyes were closed, immediately his demeanor changed. The fearful, anxious lines crisscrossing his face disappeared and a serene, quiet peace took their place.

Don removed his hand from Chris's head. "How do you feel?" he asked.

My husband's eyes shone brightly. "I don't know how to explain it. It feels like a hot flame of fire has just erupted, releasing pressure from my head!! I feel ... I feel . . .free."

"Thank you, God!" Don shouted. "You have been delivered!"

My husband and I were in awe as we hugged each other, soaking in the contentment that surrounded us. I knew Chris would take a wait-and-see approach to what had just happened but, at that moment, I firmly believed that his depression would never again haunt us. Tina, George and the kids joined us when they heard all the commotion.

"Now," Don cautioned Chris, "you have a responsibility to make sure the depression does not return. For the Bible tells us in Matthew 12:45, once a person has been delivered from an evil spirit oppressing them, if the house or soul is not filled with God's presence, the malicious spirit finds seven other spirits more wicked than itself, and they all enter the person and live there. And so that person is worse off than before."

Don went on methodically explaining, "You have to be diligent about reading the Bible

and believe what you read. If you do this, you will assure there is not a void where the evil entity

can come back and oppress you. Remember, Ephesians 6:12 says, for we are not fighting against flesh-and-blood enemies, but against evil rulers and authorities of the unseen world, against mighty powers in this dark world, and against evil spirits in the heavenly places."

I'd heard those Bible passages quoted in church several times, but never fully understood them. But now they were personal and meant so much.

Chris smiled. "Thanks, Don. This thing came so close to destroying everything I love. I will do whatever I need to do to keep it from coming back."

Don patted Chris on the back and Tina hugged him.

"Thank You, God," Don shouted. "You are faithful to fulfill Your word!"

Daniel and Samantha were perplexed, and I admit a little unfazed by what was going on, until I explained to them that their father's depression was gone and would not come back!! Daniel beamed, and high-fived his dad; Samantha gave Chris a peck on the cheek.

But Jaime held back. With arms crossed and a darkness in her eyes, she leaned against the wall as if she couldn't decide whether to run out of the room or launch an attack against us.

"Every knee will bow and every tongue will confess that Jesus is Lord."

~ Philippians 2:10-11

CHAPTER 24

*J*t had been a week since Chris' miraculous healing. A bright morning sun peeked out from behind a cloud, a light breeze tousled my hair as I stood on the porch looking up at Chris.

"It's gonna be a beautiful day. I will pick up something for dinner on my way home from work. You just take it easy. OK?" he said.

I was surprised and delighted by his offer. For so long he had isolated himself in the house when he got home from work. He never wanted to do anything with the family. But now I realized he really was different. He was smiling. *Was the easy-going, fun-loving husband I'd married back?*

"Are you sure you want to do that? I mean you haven't liked being in crowds or shopping. I don't want you to go back to. . ."

He smiled down at me, "Denise, I'm healed! Remember? I feel great and I'm ready to get back to living!"

I was speechless and knew if I said one more thing, I would dissolve in tears. Yes, he was healed. Since Don had prayed with him; it was like Chris walked out of a cave into the light. He was noticeably changed and our whole household was changed as well. There was laughter and joy. I hugged him, and he leaned down to kiss me goodbye. I listened to a dove coo its morning call, the sun warming my face. Chris disappeared down the driveway.

I was tempted to get a cup of coffee and stay right there, thanking God for what He had done for our family, but I still had to get the kids up for school. When I reached Jaime's room, I noticed that something was just not right. She wasn't in her bed. I peeked into Samantha's room, and there was Jaime, sound asleep with Samantha's arm around her. *This is strange. They never slept together when they were younger. So why now?*

"Jaime, wake up," I coaxed, and I shook her. She turned over and finally opened her eyes.

"What are you doing in Samantha's bed?" I probed.

"Oh, Mom. Let me wake up, would you?" She seemed to remember something and suddenly came alive. "You won't believe what happened! I woke up in the middle of the night and saw the face of Chucky—you know, from the movie? It was in my mirror where my Precious Moments doll's face should have been!" she exclaimed, fascinated.

Now this was a first. She had never talked about anything like this before.

"OK. But don't you think it was a dream?" I suggested.

"No, Mom, because I got up and touched my mirror and it didn't go away! You know in the TV commercials for the movie where the puppet's face was all gnarly! He had jagged teeth, red glowing eyes with freckles on his cheeks and an evil smile," she explained, using animated gestures to prove her point.

OK, now I know it was not a vivid dream; she has way too many details!

All I could think to say was, "Well, thank God, it's not here now! You've got to get ready for school and it's already late. So let's get going."

When I passed her room a few minutes later, fear tried to grip me, but I brushed it aside, deciding to take a look at the angelic image of the Precious Moments doll in the mirror for myself. I laid down on her bed to determine if I could see the Precious Moments doll from that angle. And sure enough, I could see the cute doll's face reflected in her mirror! A shiver ran down my spine as I got up. It was clear to me that she had seen something last night! I couldn't get through the morning routine quick enough.

On the way to school, I questioned Jaime more about what had happened. Again, she told me the same story, adding even more grisly details about the "Chucky Face." She was animated and almost excited, more enthralled by it than frightened.

I, on the other hand, was not intrigued at all by anything that remotely hinted at the demonic. I never understood how anyone could be entertained by a horror movie or actually want to walk through a haunted house! And to be willing to pay for the ghastly activity was beyond my comprehension. I couldn't even go to a movie, full of intrigue and suspense with a dangerous guy prowling around or I would squirm in my seat and hide my face! A light-hearted romantic comedy, like *Overboard* with Goldie Hawn and Kurt Russell, was more my style.

By the time I got home, I was so disturbed that I decided something had to be done to deal with whatever had happened in Jaime's room. I called Tina. She had a lot of experience with spiritual things. Surely, she would know how to keep it from happening again.

My voice quivered as I relayed the story to Tina. She hesitated, then gasped, "Don't you remember what Don prayed?"

I thought for a minute. "Oh, no... now I do. God is showing Jaime the *real side of evil*!" Panic set in and I lost it. "I just can't handle this happening in my house. I would freak out if I saw a demon! And Jaime just jumps out of bed in the middle of the night and goes up to the mirror and touches it? What am I supposed to do? Do you believe Jaime is telling the truth?" I rattled on and on. Tina just listened.

"Of course, I believe it happened. God is allowing Jaime to experience this because she has no fear of it. She needs to see that she's playing with fire and will get burnt if she continues to be fascinated by these entities. But the good news is Jesus has power over all demonic spirits!" Tina exclaimed.

I bet you would not be this joyful if it were happening in your house!

I had hoped I could convince Tina to come over, but she was already late for a meeting.

"Write down the scriptures I give you and recite them out loud in her room. Pray in Jesus' name and plead the power of His shed blood against the demonic activity. The demons will have to flee," she instructed with confidence.

Tina prayed in a way I don't recall ever hearing her pray before. She came against the evil forces and asked for God's protection over me. I thanked her for her encouragement and I hung up.

I have authority in Christ! I can do this!

Then I prayed, "Please, Jesus, don't let me see that chilling Chucky Face or anything else that might be lurking around!" I spoke scripture over Jaime's room and prayed with passion. When I was done, my mind wandered back to the times when I was a single mom.

The memory of Jaime being scared to death in the middle of the night because of monsters in her bed came to mind. I had wanted so much to protect her then but couldn't. I had so much regret that I didn't do more, but surely now I can pray so this thing won't come back, and she will be protected.

Suddenly, I felt a calm presence and heard the still small voice of Truth inside me whisper, "I protected her all those years ago by showing you the truth. I protected her from the real enemy who worked through Doyle. Pray for My power in her life because I AM her Protector!" This reality gave me the assurance that He was in control. No matter what we faced, He would use it for His glory and our good.

The realization that He loved me enough to go willingly to the cross, shed His blood, die and then overcome death for my sins, consumed me at that moment. I now could invoke the precious gift of His authority to put a stop to the enemy! That morning, the whole time I prayed in Jaime's room, I felt euphoric in His presence. I could not wait until Jaime got home from school, so I could tell her about my prayer time and what Jesus had done. My excitement was squelched when I thought of Jaime's recent attitude shift. The mere mention of Jesus usually ended up with a disgusted look from Jaime thrown my way. She frankly made it known she wasn't interested and didn't want to hear about Him.

Shortly after 3:30 Jaime charged into the house, shed her backpack in the foyer and took two steps at a time up the stairs, racing into her room with me in hot pursuit. She was pulling off her navy sweater as I entered her room and sat on her bed. She then unzipped and drop- kicked her jeans across the floor. She frantically pulled on shorts and a t-shirt for drill team practice.

Interrupting the process, I pleaded, "Jaime, please sit down next to me for a minute. I need to tell you something."

"Ahh, Mom, I don't have time. My ride is going to be here any minute. We are trying to get extra practice time in. The new routine is impossible; even the seniors are messing it up. Oh, and you don't have to come to the competition early this weekend to help with my hair and makeup. I can do it by myself."

"*I do...I do.*" A two-year-old version of Jaime, attempting to pull on her snow boots, flashed through my mind while I watched her struggle to get on her gym shoes. The arrow, she unknowingly threw, pierced hard and deep into my heart. She was not a baby anymore and needed me less and less.

This activity for the past two years before competitions gave us common ground; she needed me for something. I would comb her hair, putting it up in braids or a ponytail, and then spray it with copious amounts of hairspray. Then I'd help her get her makeup just right. The excited banter about boys and their weekend exploits between her and her teammates made the prep time fly by. Anticipation would rise, and things would grow quiet as the girls got into their outfits before they went into the gymnasium to perform intricate dance moves in front of hundreds of people. But lately, Jaime kept me at arm's length, and more recently the division between us had grown as enormous as the Grand Canyon. I longed to find a way to cross the divide.

"All right, all right! I just want to let you know that I called Tina and she told me how to pray over your room. You will not see any more Chucky faces tonight."

Jaime swiftly turned around to face me, indignant at my report. She bellowed, "But Mom, I want to see it again!"

I was dumbfounded! "Really? Do you understand what can happen? Aren't you afraid to see it again? You can't be serious!"

She flippantly retorted, "Yes, Mom, I am serious. And no... I'm not afraid. I want to see it again to know if it's real."

The words of Don's prayer echoed in my spirit. I turned and walked out of the room. I had no logic left to reason with her irrational desire. I didn't want my child to experience any of this if I could help it. I had to trust God. I had prayed and was hopeful she would not experience it again. But God wouldn't override Jaime's free will, just as Don had prayed.

I went into her room one morning when she did not come down for breakfast. Stepping over shoes and a backpack as I snaked my way to her bed, I sat down and gently started to rub her back.

"Good morning, sleepy head."

Jaime rolled over and peered at me through puffy eyes, underlined by smeared mascara. It was evident she had been crying.

"Sweetie, what's the matter?"

"Mom, it came back last night! It looked just like it did before, but this time I couldn't move I just laid in bed and hoped it would go away," she quavered.

"Jaime, God has allowed this to happen because you wanted to know if evil is real. So, if you want it to stop, we can pray together to get rid of it."

She snapped back, "I don't believe in all that prayer junk, Mom. It was probably just my imagination. Leave it alone."

"Well, if you change your mind, I will be happy to pray with you." Then I forcefully added, "Your fascination with the demonic realm has opened the door, so it will come back, unless you shut that door."

That afternoon, I felt a strong urge to go into Jaime's room and pray for a while. I sat on her bed, hushed my thoughts and prayed.

A visual picture of a wall materialized in my mind. One by one, red droplets appeared at the top of the wall and started to trickle down the surface, forming streaks of blood that gave me goose bumps. I felt an ominous presence. Then a pool of blood started to form on the ceiling above my head. I feared this blob of plasma would split open and saturate me!

One drop of blood hit my hand and instantly it turned to water. Immediately, I was immersed in a deep intimate love; I had never experienced anything this powerful before. The Holy Spirit spoke to my heart: "This blood is so powerful, it only takes one drop to purify the whole world!"

The next day when I had lunch with our Bible study group from church, I mentioned the vision. Most of them just listened engrossed in the story, but Rose spoke up. Everyone respected Rose, and since she had prayed with me to close the door I had opened by consulting a psychic, I knew I could trust her to interpret the vision.

"Denise, you know Jesus overcame death on the cross. The instant His work was done over 2000 years ago, it healed us all for eternity! It is a gift. Jesus has already done the work and all we must do is receive it. The Holy Spirit is impressing upon me that the blood streaming down the wall epitomizes evil, but the drop of blood from the ceiling symbolized His shed blood. When that drop of blood hit your hand, it turned to water; His blood cleanses all from sin and gives us the authority to triumph over evil!" Rose rejoiced.

Now I had deep revelation of the redemptive power of Jesus through this mesmerizing vision. Like one droplet that sends a ripple through a body of water—only this wave continues through the whole universe! I felt exhilaration. Everyone has the privilege to choose Him and walk with Him in freedom!

Rose paused for a moment, then continued, "The impression I am getting from the Holy Spirit is that the vision He gave you demonstrates that Jesus has already won the war. Jaime is in a battle right now, but the minute she surrenders her life to Him, God wins, and the demonic visitations will stop!" Everyone was silent as they digested what Rose was saying.

Then that small still voice I was growing accustomed to hearing whispered, *"If only people believed and accepted what I have done."* My mountaintop elation turned into heartbreaking despair. This gift of unending life I accepted from Him had become my priceless treasure. I longed for others to experience it. This extraordinary vision had astounded me and now a desire resonated in my heart. *Jesus, I will tell of Your Love for them.*

I decided to take a walk in the park and warm up in the sunshine so I could ponder everything God had revealed to me. The tulips were in full bloom, showing off their vibrant hues of canary, fuchsia and peach, and I was grateful for the time to bask in the beauty of His creation. Butterflies fluttered from flower to flower while my thoughts wandered back to the vision. I felt encouraged, no matter what the future held. I looked at my watch; I had just enough time to pick up the kids and then throw something together for the church potluck that night.

Chris sat with George, so they could talk sports; the kids found their friends and made a swift exit to eat outside. I sat with Tina and filled her in on the vision God had given me. I told her what the Holy Spirit said through Rose, but without warning tears of frustration filled my eyes.

"Jaime doesn't believe the 'Chucky face' is real and she won't pray with me about it. I don't know how much more I can take. I want my house free from this demonic stuff!"

Tina hugged me. "You know you can call me anytime, day or night, if things get worse. Jesus is protecting Jaime and your family, even if it doesn't seem like it."

"I know you're right. I know God is giving Jaime time to understand the devil is real, so she won't want anything to do with it. But she is so stubborn! I'm afraid we'll have to live with the 'things that go bump in the night' for the rest of our lives!" An empathetic Tina patted me on the back as we made our way out the door to find the kids.

The next night everyone was accounted for; Jaime was home from drill team practice, Samantha and Daniel didn't have cheerleading or softball. This gave us the rare opportunity to enjoy dinner together.

Jaime was sullen and withdrawn. She looked down at her plate while she pushed her food around it. I prodded, "Jaime, we would love to hear about your latest dance routine. Tell us what you like most about it."

"It's really hard, but I do like the music. The back flips are..."

Daniel interrupted her flow with his rendition from *The Princess Bride*. "Hello! My name is Inigo Montoya. You killed my father. Prepare to die!" he said with a nearly perfect Spanish accent. Sam tried to wedge in a word or two, leaving Chris and me to decipher the blended conversation. The evening routine went fast. I was exhausted from the day's activities. I slowly climbed the stairs and ambled down the hall to go to bed.

I was awakened by a police siren in the middle of the night. Just as I drifted back to sleep, I heard a voice shriek in terror.

"Help me! Something's in here!"

Chris and I bolted out of bed and he trailed behind me down the hall. The screams came from Jaime's room. When I barged through the door, she was shaking uncontrollably. Chris was rubbing his eyes and leaning against the door jam. "Go back to bed honey," I said. "I think I know what's wrong." Chris yawned and turned to leave.

I sat on the bed and held Jaime. "Mom, it was horrible! Something made my whole bed shake! It felt like a bowling ball fell from the ceiling and hit my bed. I thought it was a dream, but it happened again a second later. Make it stop! Make it stop!" she sobbed.

Finally, she has seen enough of the real side of evil and is done playing with it. This deceitful, ghastly spirit, must go!

I helped Jaime down stairs and made her some cocoa while she sat at the kitchen table.

"If it is OK with you, I would like to call Tina and ask her to pray with us."

This time Jaime didn't argue. She just nodded her head in agreement.

Tina picked up on the fourth ring. I was grateful to hear her voice since it was just a few short hours before the sunrise. She sounded groggy but came to life once I told her what had happened.

"I am so glad you called. It sounds like the thing is getting more aggressive. Can you put me on speaker, so I can talk directly to Jaime?"

"No problem," I said and switch the phone from the handset to speaker.

"Jaime? Can you hear me?" Tina asked.

"Yes," Jaime mumbled, still visibly shaken.

"Hi, honey. I'm sorry you've had a rough night. Would it be all right if I read some scriptures with you?" Tina sweetly said.

Jaime agreed, and I went upstairs and got Jaime's Bible. Tina started reading scriptures leading Jaime back and forth through the Bible, to show Jaime who Jesus is and His love for her. Tina explained to her that He willingly laid down His life, so she would not have to die.

"Jaime, do you believe what the Bible says about Jesus and who He is?" Tina asked.

Jaime meekly replied, "Yes."

"Do you want to accept what Jesus has done on the cross to cover your sins? Remember what we just read in Romans that all have sinned and have fallen short of the holiness of God."

"Yes, I do."

"Congratulations!" Tina celebrated. "You belong to Jesus now. Nothing can come against you unless you allow it, for you now have authority in Jesus and it has to flee!"

Jaime thanked Tina. A smile spread across Jaime's radiant face and Tina rejoiced with me.

"Tina, can you hold on a minute?"

"Sure."

I took Jaime upstairs, settled her back into bed, then gave her a lengthy hug. "I love you soooo much!" She looked so peaceful. I knew she would have no trouble falling back to sleep.

Downstairs, I picked up the phone, and switched Tina back to the handset. "Tina, what if she has accepted Jesus *just* to make the demonic activity stop?"

"He knows her heart and accepts her motivation, no matter what it is. Remember He uses everything for His glory and our good!" she assured.

I closed my eyes and inaudibly proclaimed, "You sure work through everything to accomplish Your will. Even a teenager's curiosity and stubbornness. God, You always win the war!"

Now Jaime knew the Truth and no longer wanted anything to do with the wicked forces of this dark world. Jaime was never bothered again by anything in her bedroom.

*"A person who truly loves you, is someone
who sees the pain in your eyes, while everyone else
believes the smile on your face."*

~ Unknown

CHAPTER 25

I tripped over one of Chris' stray shoes and sprinted up the stairs from the laundry room, barely able to catch the phone on the fifth ring. I strained to catch my breath, "Hello, Grand Central Station," I joked, expecting to hear Chris' voice.

An unfamiliar voice laughed, "Oh, your day must be as crazy as mine! Hi. I'm Louise Cantor, Jaime's art teacher."

"Oh gosh, I am so sorry. My husband usually calls about this time and I had to run for the...well... never mind. I hope Jaime isn't in some kind of trouble in class."

"No, not at all. She's a great student, but I am very worried about her. I wanted you to come in and see a picture Jaime created in class last week."

"Sure. Would you like me to come by this afternoon right before school lets out?"

"That would be great. My class is in the right wing of the building, room 304."

It was a ten-minute drive to the school, but my curiosity and every red traffic light made the drive seem like an eternity. By the time I arrived, I was a ball of anxiety. I couldn't imagine what Jaime could possibly have drawn that would cause her teacher enough concern to contact me. The art room was abuzz with activity as students hurried to put away their art supplies before the last bell rang. Colorful works of art, all shapes and sizes, hung on the walls. I could barely take my eyes off them. The art teacher thanked me for coming and then pointed to a picture directly in front of us.

"This is the picture Jaime did last week," she explained. "I assigned them a watercolor picture to do that expresses a deep-seated emotion from a time they have not shared with anyone. You can see by the picture she is deeply saddened by something in her life."

I was astonished and in awe of Jaime's artistic ability. She had a real gift. As soon as I looked at it, I understood why the teacher was concerned. Other pictures showed the typical adolescent angst. But Jaime's was no ordinary rendition of some eighth grader's thoughts. This was a picture that expressed something much deeper than a boy that didn't like her or not being a part of the popular clique.

The portrait depicted a beautiful, serene, angelic girl, with huge tears on her cheeks, lying in a bed. Her face was surrounded by beautiful orbs of blue and purple hues. In those spheres, small images surrounded her head and suggested she was deep in thought, evoking extreme sadness. I got the impression this self-portrait, with melancholy memories not well-defined, put her in an alternate universe she could not escape. Jaime's picture depicted a child in desperate need of comfort.

Did this have something to do with her childhood? Perhaps Jaime's memories, locked in her subconscious, were rising to the surface trying to get her to deal with the pain from her abuse. The emotions she denied were unconstrained in her art.

"This is amazing. I can't believe her talent. I think I understand what the unhappiness she has expressed in this portrait is from. Is it possible to take this home?"

"No, Jaime owns the artwork. I just thought it was important for you to see it," Louise explained apologetically.

That afternoon when Jaime got home, I sat her down in the living room to talk with her, "Honey, Mrs. Cantor called me today about a picture you did. She showed me the beautiful painting of a tearful girl deep in thought. It concerned her."

"Why would she do that? I didn't want anyone to see that picture, especially you!" Jaime retorted.

"Jaime, sweetheart you are a wonderful artist! I am blown away by what you created. Mrs. Cantor just wanted to make sure you were OK. Can you tell me what you were thinking about when you did it?"

"No, Mom, I can't because I wasn't thinking about anything!" She turned and stomped out of the room. The next day Mrs. Cantor called, saying Jaime came to the art room before the first bell, tore up the picture and put it in the trash. I never saw any more of her artwork. To this day, I mourn the artistic ability in Jaime that lays dormant, never to be explored or expressed.

Jaime was determined not to share her emotions with anyone. All the counselors we took her to could not climb the five-foot-high wall she hid behind, isolating herself from anyone that could help. She avoided pain – physical and emotional -- at all costs. She'd been in drill team since sixth grade and it had taken a toll on her knees. Walking had become an effort; the pain registered in every step, especially at drill team practice. She had tried for as long as possible to hide the pain because she so loved being on the drill team, but eventually the pain won out. The orthopedic doctor we took her to recommended arthroscopic surgery. So we set the date for the procedure at the hospital.

Jaime was very nervous the day of the procedure. Nothing I said seemed to calm her. I had never seen her so terrified. In the hospital parking lot, she moved from anxious to downright contentious.

"I don't understand why I have to have this surgery! I can just drop out of drill team, then my knee will be fine. I can manage it just the way it is," she groaned.

Exasperated, I replied, "You limp around all the time! The doctor told us every day you are doing more damage to your knee, so this is not about drill team! Let's just get this over with so you can feel better."

Begrudgingly, she made her way out of the car, hobbling beside me into the lobby. Once they checked her in, they led us to a room and gave her a gown to put on. I tried to keep her from thinking about the surgery and brought up the latest antics at drill team practice. Unfortunately, it was not working. Now Jaime's anxiety, as she limped around the room refusing to put on the gown, was building from a slow burn to an explosion waiting to ignite, consuming anyone in her path. Suddenly her knee buckled, and she winced in pain. I managed to catch her and coax her into the bed.

Forty minutes later, after two nurses prepped her for the operation, I could see the growing panic in Jaime's eyes. She now had on her hospital gown and her clothes were stored in a locker. A big stern looking nurse came into the room to administer Jaime's IV for surgery. This was the tipping point.

Genghis Khan was not here to play games. "You have wasted enough of our time! Give me your right arm now so I can stick the biggest vein," she growled.

Jaime hid her arm under the sheet and when she didn't reveal it quickly enough, Genghis yanked it out. She forced Jaime to straighten her arm and then looked for a vein.

Jaime burst into tears. She rolled out of bed and pushed past the mammoth nurse. In a fierce guttural voice, Jaime demanded, "Give me back my clothes, now!" The emotional volcano had erupted.

I tried to mollify her. "Come on, Jaime. You can't leave; you need this surgery. I'll be here the whole time. Everyone is trying to help you." All to no avail. I silently scolded myself. *She would have listened to Chris. Why didn't I bring him?*

"I will not get back in that bed! Give me my clothes! I have rights too, you know!" she snarled.

The agitated nurse left the room, only to be replaced by a more daunting and determined one. "Show some respect and get back into bed. You have put us behind schedule!" she snapped.

"Shame on you for caring about your schedule more than a frightened teenager! We are leaving. Please get Jaime's clothes, now!" I demanded. The nurse scowled, but silently acquiesced.

Jaime got dressed and I helped her hobble out to the car. *Where was the nurses' empathy for her? Why wouldn't they take the time to talk to her, to at least, try to calm her down. Instead of trying to win Jaime over, they had made it a war!*

A memory of four-year-old Jaime's panicked and blanched face as she fought off the doctor who had manhandled her at Children's Hospital, came flooding back. Then another memory surfaced of her own pediatrician's frustration at Jaime's uncontrollable outburst during a visit. This had nothing to do with her fear of the unknown, but with trust. She felt victimized! How could she trust anyone? Even her own father had victimized her. She did not trust anyone, not even me. And how could I blame her? All these professionals only victimized her further. Why would I expect any other reaction?

There was nothing but silence between us on the drive home. Jaime got out, slammed the car door behind her and shuffled into the house. I walked into the kitchen to see someone who didn't resemble my daughter at all. A wide-eyed Jaime was already on the phone talking in an animated whisper to someone. I heard her mumble goodbye and then she scuttled out the door. I peered out the window to see her speed-gimping down the driveway.

"Where do you think you're going?" I yelled out the window.

She kept going without looking back. I was certain she was on her way over to her boyfriend's house. We had plenty of conversations about dating and the fact that she was too young, but to keep her from sneaking around to see Scott, we allowed him to come to our house, so we could keep an eye on them. He was polite and always fun to talk to, so I had concluded, if anyone was a bad influence, it was her not him. Now Jaime was going to do even more damage speed-limping for miles on her bad knee!

Now every ounce of energy, from the adrenalin pumping through my veins at the hospital, drained from my body, leaving me spent and exhausted. I collapsed in a chair and called Chris at work. His cheerful voice answered the phone. "Hi honey. How did surgery go?"

"Surgery?" I snorted. "It didn't go! And now she has run away—most likely to Scott's house."

"What do you mean... it didn't go?"

"Jaime got very upset at the hospital and refused to let them give her an IV. She insisted we leave. The minute we got home, she called Scott . . . well, at least, I think that's who she called, and limped out the door. I can't go after her. Daniel will be home any minute from school. Can you go find her?" I moaned.

"I'll leave right now," Chris said and then he softly added, "Hey, Denise ... I love you. Hang in there. It will be all right." He was a calming force in my life and as he spoke I felt peace.

Jaime had indeed made it to Scott's house. He lived two miles from us and they had been seeing each other for the last six months. Their relationship seemed innocent enough, more like a friendship than anything serious, so I hoped that Scott would convince Jaime to have the surgery. Chris walked in forty minutes later with Jaime who grimaced in pain from every step as she leaned against Chris' side.

"How could you take off like that? You scared the daylights out of me, Jaime!" I spontaneously hugged her and didn't let her go. Her whole body went limp in my arms; she was exhausted. "Let's get you upstairs into bed so you can rest. I'll bring up some dinner for you later."

We went up to her room. I helped her get into her pajamas, tucked her in and smoothed her hair back out of her eyes. "We're going to help you through this. It's gonna be all right," I promised. Then I kissed her forehead and prayed she would not disappear again.

*"Sometimes the people who hurt us the most
are the people who were hurt more than us."*

~ Unknown

CHAPTER 26

*J*aime's reaction to the surgery and the fact that she'd taken off, hobbling to Scott's house miles away in pain, was the last straw. I immediately set up three weekly counseling sessions to help her cope with the necessary surgery and rescheduled it for the beginning of her summer break, four weeks later. This would give her knee time to heal so she could start her first day of high school without crutches. She reluctantly went to the first appointment, and by the second session Jaime accepted the fact that the surgery was in her best interest. Her doctor prescribed a valium for her to take an hour before we left for the procedure to calm her nerves. This time I talked to the hospital staff to make sure the nurses who were prepping Jaime for surgery understood her fear. It was a huge relief when they wheeled her out of surgery. Jaime's recovery time was pleasant. The daughter who constantly pushed me away needed me again.

Jaime was resting soundly on her make-shift bed, the family room couch, when Chris walked through the door. "Hi, Honey. How was your day?" I whispered and pointed to our Sleeping Beauty.

"Good. It looks like you succeeded in your plan to get her to rest," Chris said. I nodded and pointed toward the living room. He tiptoed out behind me.

"I know we have made the decision to send Daniel to Fellowship Christian for second grade and the thought came to me that an all-girls Catholic school for Jaime's sophomore year might be just what she needs. All Saints High School would give her a new start and she could still be in drill team. What do you think?" I asked. Her junior high school went through the ninth grade, so everyone Jaime knew would be starting at a new school that fall.

"Well, it might raise her self-esteem, and help her graduate. And it should help take her focus off the boys," he surmised.

"OK, let's talk to her tonight about the idea. I pray it doesn't start World War III, but we must do something to give her the opportunity to make better friends who stay out of trouble and care about their grades."

Jaime woke up an hour later in pain, asking for Motrin. Later that evening, when she felt better and had been awake for a while, we shared our idea with her.

"Jaime," I began, "you know we have made the decision to send Daniel to Fellowship next year. Since you will move on to the high school and will meet new people anyway, we had an idea. We think you need a fresh start. We would like to send you to All Saints High School."

She crossed her arms tightly around her middle and clenched her teeth. "Really! I have no say in this? I can't go to school with a bunch of girls whining about every little thing that goes wrong all day! Ugh.... their ugly uniforms! I'd rather die than be seen in one of those!" she protested.

"I hear you and understand, but we really feel like you need a new, positive environment where you can meet new friends. We also think an all-girls school will help you focus on studying. We have to make this decision now because the latest we can enroll you is the first of August," I firmly added. I had dropped a bombshell.

By the end of June, Jaime's knee was healing well. During her recovery, she reminded us constantly that she hated the idea of attending All Saints, but we made the decision and enrolled her despite her protests.

Samantha walked into the family room and sat on one end of the couch; Jaime was propped up by pillows on the other end. She had been sequestered in the middle of the house with no privacy since surgery, and it would be a few more weeks until she was able to walk up the stairs to her bedroom. Jaime gave her sister a weak smile and Samantha reached over and hugged her.

"Hey, everyone just signed my yearbook at the party last night. Wanna see it?" Samantha asked her sister. Jaime nodded her head, and Samantha bolted upstairs to retrieve her new prized possession.

I stared at my girls as they paged through the yearbook together. Samantha had an impish smile, her dad's sky-blue, wide-set eyes, and thick chestnut hair that flowed down the middle of her back. She and Jaime were on opposite ends of the DNA spectrum. Samantha's face was round; Jaime's was oval. Sam would get tan in the sun; Jaime's pail skin would burn. Despite their differences, they were both beautiful.

In a few weeks Samantha would be in junior high. Where had the years gone? She was my sweet, compliant one, who loved to play with dolls for hours and never fought going to bed. This year she had surrounded herself with a fun, close-knit group of girlfriends who did everything together. They weren't interested in boys and loved having sleepovers at each other's house, playing music and games till the wee morning hours. Samantha loved kids so much that she had started a play group for pre-school children in the neighborhood. Several of her friends would come over after school, two days a week, and help her do activities with the kids. I was grateful that I never had to worry about her grades or her friends.

My handsome son was the spitting image of his father. Same hazel eyes, same light brown hair, same olive complexion. They both had a thin, straight nose with freckles across the bridge. Daniel was smart for his age, and we became frustrated with the school system when they did not offer him more challenging work in first grade. He would breeze through the math assignments, and then sit bored in class until they moved on to the next subject. After investigating Fellowship Christian School and praying about enrolling Daniel there, we had peace and knew that was where God wanted him. Daniel and Jaime would both be headed off to new schools soon, and I prayed it would be a good experience for them both. We explored the option of Samantha attending a Christian school that year as well. But she didn't want to leave her friends, and we knew our budget was stretched thin enough paying tuition at two private schools.

Daniel bounced through the door. He had been playing next door with his best friend, Kerry.

"Hey, Mom, can I get some cookies and go with Kerry to our fort in the woods?" he asked. Kerry's father had built a fort up the hill behind our house from wood left over from a shed he'd built. The boys loved to hang out there.

"Sure, honey," I answered, "but don't go anywhere else, so you can hear me when I call you in for dinner. OK?"

He agreed, grabbed the snack and headed out the door. I watched him sprint up the hill towards the grove of trees that surrounded the fort, and then I turned my attention back to my girls as they laughed together. It warmed my heart to see them on the couch, enjoying one another. The demands of drill team, nine months out of the year with its practices and weekend competitions, had left little family time. Chris took Daniel to his softball games when they were at the same time as Jaime's competitions. It had been a nice change of pace to attend his games and be home more. I relished moments like this and prayed there would be more.

᪥᪥᪥᪥᪥᪥᪥᪥᪥᪥

Jaime's first day at All Saints High School in late August was rocky. She threatened to stay in the car when we pulled up to the front steps. But after seven months, she seemed to click with many of her teachers, and I had high hopes her religion class would help her connect with God. My hopes soared when Jaime came home from school one day and shared that God had spoken to her in religion class about the Holocaust! She asked God how He could allow such an atrocity to happen. Then she heard His quiet voice say, "It was not My will. Evil forces influenced one man, but I empowered many to stop it."

That spring morning, Jaime jumped into the car, smiling as she flung her bookbag in the backseat. Her straight blonde hair was full of small, sawtooth waves created by her crimping iron, half of the wild mass on top of her head contained in a shell clip. She looked cute in her new faded jeans and navy t-shirt embossed with the All Saints logo, an ethereal being with a halo. "You look pretty this morning!" I observed.

She gushed, "The All Saints Walk to raise money for school is today, and I get to hang with my friends!"

"That's fun and you get to be out of that dismal uniform you hate! It would be nice if each class got to design their own uniforms, you know, so you would feel good in them and like how you look," I teased.

She just tossed me one of her 'don't-be-ridiculous-Mom' looks, her eyes flashed with a hint of indignation. She turned her head and stared out the window the rest of the drive to the school. I'd done it again. I had ruined the moment. I never seemed to know the right thing to say. Navigating through adolescence had proven to be more like an obstacle course than parenting. We pulled up to the front of the historic school building with its tall, massive white pillars and sprawling staircase. Jaime hopped out of the car without turning back to say goodbye. A familiar pain penetrated my heart. I missed the real Jaime who had been replaced by this obstinate adolescent. To distract myself from dwelling on what I could not change, I mentally repeated my lengthy 'to do' list on the way home.

Later that afternoon, while relaxing, sipping a cup of tea and engrossed in my favorite talk show, the phone rang. It was Jaime's principal, Kathy Steffens. Her voice was tense and urgent. "I am calling to inform you that Jaime, along with several other girls, were caught with LSD during the All Saints Walk."

Wait. What? People don't do LSD these days! And besides, Jaime doesn't do drugs!

"I'm sorry," I interjected. "Did you say my daughter had LSD on her? You must be mistaken."

"I wish I were mistaken. A teacher saw her ingest the drug and Jaime confessed that it was LSD and she took it. You will need to come and get her immediately. She is expelled for the rest of the year and may not return next year unless she completes a drug rehab," Principal Steffens informed.

I was mystified. I'd thought she was doing so well in school! What had I missed? I was numb and disheartened by the time I arrived at All Saints. Mrs. Steffens was very compassionate about the situation and repeated what she had told me over the phone while Jaime sat in the hallway. She then explained, "Jaime admitted to having and using the LSD along with the other girls and we only want the best for Jaime. Therefore, it will be mandatory for Jaime to complete drug rehab. Once she has done that, then and only then, can we consider her as an applicant for next year."

I couldn't imagine my daughter using any drug, especially LSD. How could I have missed something like that? I hadn't noticed anything in her behavior that would indicate drugs. Then my mind wandered back to an evening not long ago. I'd been awakened in the middle of the night by the sound of a car engine idling and had gotten out of bed and looked out our bedroom window. A taxi had pulled up in front of our house. I went down the hall and as I flew down the steps to investigate; I almost tripped over Jaime who was sitting on the stairs. She was startled and rambled off some elaborate story about friends who had pranked her by sending a taxi to our house. Jaime said that she was watching the street, so she could tell the driver to leave. "Go back to bed!" I hissed. Then I went outside and reprimanded the driver for being willing to pick up a teenager in the middle of the night. Now it was clear Jaime lied about the whole thing. She made up the story to cover her tracks! My realization that day, as I listened to the principal, was later confirmed by Jaime. She confessed. She had indeed, on two different occasions, called a taxi in the middle of the night to go do drugs.

So many things were beginning to make sense now. Just a few weeks before the All Saints Walk, Jaime had asked me repeatedly to take her to a teen dance club that all the kids were going to. Every weekend the begging would start.

"Come on, Mom, you were young once. Remember how much you like to dance? Just take Seria, my friend from school, and me... just this one time...please?" she pleaded.

That weekend I relented and told her, "Only on one condition. The police on duty at the club will have to assure me, beyond any doubt, that it is a safe environment. You also need to make sure that Seria's mom can give you a ride home no later than midnight."

I had scarcely gotten the words out my mouth before Jaime grabbed me, gave me a big hug. "Sure, Mom!" she conceded. "No problem! I love you!" And she was off to call Seria with the news.

When we pulled into the parking lot of Caddy's, I saw a police officer and went right over to him before I even let the girls out of the car. "Officer, I am glad to see you here, but how safe are the teenagers at this club?"

"Ma'am, I can guarantee you they will be safe. We have a zero-tolerance policy for drugs. If kids show up high or with drugs, we arrest them and they are banned from returning to the club," he explained with absolute authority.

Jaime and Seria had hopped out of the car and stood there while the officer spoke to me. The minute he finished, they disappeared into a sea of teenagers entering Caddy's and I pulled out of the parking lot. Even with the officer's assurance, my gut instinct told me something was wrong. I considered making a U-turn, going inside the club, scouring every nook and cranny until I found them, insisting they leave. The last thing I wanted to do, however, was embarrass Jaime by dragging her out in front of her friends. Was I really that mom? I didn't want to be, and silenced the inner voice warning me. I should have listened. The tragic events that followed left scars on both our hearts, for which I'd never forgive myself.

Exhaustion overrode the ominous feeling, and I slid into bed while reminding myself: *Jaime is spending the night at Seria's house. She assured me Seria's mom was picking them up. She will be fine.*

Three hours later I was dead asleep when the phone woke me. It was Jaime. I rubbed my eyes, glanced at the clock, then raced down the hall to keep from waking Chris up and whispered, "It's 2 in the morning. Where are you?"

"We're at Seria's house and I want to come home," she choked out.

"Did you just get to her house?" I asked, confused.

Her voiced laced with panic, Jaime replied, "Yes. Her mom had trouble picking us up and we had to get another ride home. Mom, I don't want to stay here. Please just come get me."

"OK, I will be right there."

Chris was snoring loud enough to wake the dead when I tiptoed back into the bedroom and grabbed my jeans and t-shirt off the floor. He had a headache and took a sleeping pill before going to bed. The last thing he needed was to deal with Jaime's shenanigans. So many questions assaulted my mind on the drive. *What is going on? Why hadn't I listened to my gut? I knew something was wrong. What kind of mother ignores her instinct? I should never have let her stay at that club. Who gave them a ride home? Why hadn't Seria's mom picked them up as she had promised? If anything bad happened to Jaime, I'd have no one else to blame but myself.*

It was a dark, eerie, moonless night, the streets were not well-lit, and I struggled to find Seria's house. It seemed strange that both Jaime and Seria were standing on the front porch waiting for me when I pulled up. I just knew they were hiding something. Jaime's raccoon eyes made by her smeared mascara stared at me when she climbed into the car, and her usually neat hair was a matted mess. Something was horribly wrong, but I felt it would be a fight to get her to open up about what really happened. I decided to wait until morning.

Chris sat at the side of the bed and I rubbed his back and I silently debated when to tell him. *I might as well get it over with.*

"You slept soundly, didn't you?"

"Sure did. Guess I was tired! I didn't wake up once." He stretched while yawning, he turned around, kissed me, then grabbed me, hugging me tightly.

I gently pushed him away, so I could look him in the eyes. "I need to fill you in on what you...ah, missed last night."

His eyes widened and he frowned. "Don't tell me Jaime has pulled the 'calling-a-taxi-in-the-middle-of-the-night' routine again?"

"Well, not exactly. I think it is a lot worse than that," I mumbled, "but I can't put my finger on it. I know something horrible happened to her last night. She called in a panic at two in the morning from Seria's house, asking me to come get her."

"Denise, why in the world didn't you get me up? You know I would never have let you go alone in the middle of the night to get her!" he declared.

"I'm sorry, but I felt so guilty that I let her go to that stupid dance club in the first place. And since you weren't feeling well, I wasn't about to wake you up at 2 in the morning!" I confessed.

He wrapped his arms around me. "It will be OK. She's home safe now."

Jaime slept until noon, giving my imagination more time to whip my emotions into a frenzy. I needed to reel in my feelings, so I could approach Jaime calmly. I had to know the truth about what had happened. I couldn't afford contention. "God, give me wisdom and the right words to say." When Jaime came downstairs, I had a bacon and egg casserole waiting for her in hopes I could ease her into a conversation while she ate.

"It smells great, Mom, and I'm starving!" she declared, while pouring herself a glass of milk.

She was sitting at the breakfast bar on a stool, wolfing down the first few bites when I asked, "So what happened last night? Why didn't Seria's mom get you?"

Jaime looked up and hastily replied, "She ended up having something to do, so a friend of Seria's took us to her house."

"But why did you get home at 2 in the morning when the club closed at 12? And why didn't you have them bring you home instead of going to Seria's?" The questions came in rapid-fire succession. She looked at me, her face wrinkled in annoyance, and I watched the door slam shut on her eagerness to engage in conversation.

Anger erupted. "Don't you trust me?" she retorted.

"No, I don't. Quite honestly, the whole thing seems fishy. You assured me Seria's mom would pick you up and you would be home by 12. There is something you're not telling me. Now tell me what really happened, or we will be here all day! I'm not letting this go until I know the truth. I had a dreadful feeling when I left you at Caddy's. You will not be going back! Now spill the beans!" I snapped loudly.

The floodgates opened, and she started weeping. Between heaves, she gasped, "I will only tell you if you do not make a big deal of it."

"OK. Just tell me what happened. Tell me the truth."

"We were stranded at the club because we couldn't reach Seria's mom. A guy Seria had met once before offered to take us home. We thought it would get us home quicker, but when we were coming up Southwest Avenue the guy turned onto a street. We asked where he was going, and he wouldn't answer us. I was so scared when the car pulled up in front of a vacant, creepy house." She started to cry again.

"We just kept telling him to take us home. But he said there were guys he wanted to introduce us to in the house and that he would take us home after we met them. We thought the sooner we went in, the sooner they would take us home. I had an awful feeling and kept insisting that we leave. The guy Seria knew told her to sit on the couch in the front room, then he disappeared into a bedroom. His friend grabbed my arm and dragged me into the same bedroom. I yanked my arm as hard as I could, trying to get away and then went limp, thinking he would let go. But he just dragged me across the floor! Then he threw me onto a mattress in the middle of the room...I started kicking and screaming but I couldn't get him off of me...Mom...I've never been so scared! Seria listened to me scream from the other room." The words came out in gasps as she relived the nightmare. The blood drained from my face as I processed what she was telling me.

I walked around beside her and held her, stoking her hair as she sobbed into my chest. "We'll get through this, I love you so much!" I assured her.

Rape? My beautiful, adorable daughter had been violently raped? Hurt again? Her innocence in childhood was violated and destroyed by her father and now these monsters? What gashes had they created in the middle of her already wounded soul? How would she ever heal?

I was numb inside. I felt my heart shattering into a million pieces, and tears streamed down my cheeks. I felt I had been violated right along with her! This was all my fault and my thoughts screamed: *WHY COULDN'T I PROTECT HER?*

I continued rocking Jaime in my arms, stroking her hair. It seemed too little too late, but it was all I had to offer in the moment. I would not let these barbarians get away with this. After a few minutes Jaime's tears subsided, and she got up and laid on the family room couch. I followed her and calmly said, "I'm so sorry, but this is not your fault." Then I added gently, "We have got to call the police, sweetie."

"No, Mom! I can't talk to anyone about this! You promised you wouldn't make a big deal out if it!" She rolled over and buried her face in the couch, groaning.

My anger smoldered, but I managed to remain calm. I sat beside her, turned her face towards me and cradled it in my hands while looking into her eyes, now swollen from the deluge of tears. "Baby, look at me," I whispered. "You don't want this to happen to anyone else, do you? If they hurt you, they'll hurt some other girls." Then another thought occurred to me. "Why did they leave Seria alone?"

She whimpered, "I guess she wasn't their type."

She wasn't their type? These animals had to be found and held accountable for what they had done to these precious girls! They could not get away with this! I could feel a black cloud of gloom settling over me from the sucker punch to the gut I had just been dealt.

Jaime continued, "Mom, I don't want to talk about this any-more. Call Seria, if you want to. I think she remembers where the house is..." Then she muttered, "Seria knows the name of the guy who hurt me. Call the police if you want."

Exhausted, Jaime fell asleep on the couch while I rubbed her back. She wouldn't have allowed herself to be vulnerable if Saman-tha and Daniel were traipsing through the house, and I was grate-ful Samantha was at a friend's house and Daniel was next door at Kerry's.

Samantha and Jaime no longer huddled together on one of their beds, laughing and sharing. In fact, Samantha had started to avoid Jaime soon after the school year had started. It puzzled me, but I assumed Jaime's biting attitude might have caused the distance in their relationship. Even Chris escaped to different areas of the house every time Jaime came home, hoping to avoid conflict. Every question or request became a reason for her to fight with us. It felt like we were on opposing sides during a battle, and Jaime was the enemy. But I knew she wasn't the enemy. Nothing was adding up, and we were at a stalemate, going nowhere.

My stomach churned with each step I took up the stairs to tell Chris. As I relayed the horrific details, he stared at me shaking his head in disbelief. We hugged, and I was grateful to have him by my side, even if he did retreat during the battles to keep from getting shot.

"Jaime needs your love and reassurance right now that it is not her fault," I said.

Chris' eyes filled with tears and he couldn't say anything. He only shook his head in agreement.

I called Seria and she agreed to go with me to try to find the house, so I could call the police. Chris had agreed that Seria would be more comfortable if I took her by myself. She told me on the phone that she had no intention of telling her mom what had happened the night before. I felt I had no choice but to respect her decision, even if she was underage. Jaime stayed at home; she didn't want to go anywhere near the place.

"Thank you Seria, for showing me where the house is. Are you doing OK?" I asked. She nodded and looked out the window. "I just want you to know none of this is your fault, I hope someday...you can tell your mom what happened."

She continued to look out the window. "My mom was getting high on god-knows-what and that is why she couldn't come get us. I'm sure she could care less about what happened! I'm just so sorry...Jaime got...hurt." Her voice trailed off and I could see a tear run down her cheek.

Her mom does drugs? Parents don't do drugs!

Compassion for Seria filled my heart as she directed me onto Main Street which ran off Southwest Avenue. I decided I might do more damage if I bombarded her with questions that should be left for a detective to ask.

We passed house after house with boarded up windows, peeling paint and overgrown bushes. Beer bottles had been tossed to the curb and stray dogs pawed through knocked over trash cans. A lump formed in my throat as I fought back tears, trying not to think about the haunting images of what had taken place the night before.

"It's that one right there!" Seria rattled off the house number and pointed to a small house with white siding falling off and trash strewn all over the front yard. I turned the car around. My stomach started to churn, and goose bumps crawled up my arms. I could sense a foreboding evil presence, and I couldn't get out of there fast enough!

Chris was waiting for me when I walked in the door. He was surprised we had found the house so quickly. He sat at the table with me while I called the police and choked out the details of the girls' horrendous story. Detective Hamilton called me back. She was very kind as she coached me on how to talk to Jaime, so she wouldn't be victimized further. She talked to Jaime briefly and set up a time for the girls to come in the next day.

Samantha appeared at the bottom of the stairs, and asked, "Why does Jaime have her door locked? When I tried to open it, she told me to go away and leave her alone." She fought back tears.

"Honey, Jaime's had a rough day. Let's go into the family room and ..."

Just then Daniel breezed by us standing in the front hall, he stopped and turned around.

"Girl talk...Yuk...I'm going to watch cartoons," he said and bounded down the steps to the basement. He was the easiest one to love, the easiest to care for. He went with the flow and just loved life! If my experience had taught me anything; girls were just more complicated and could hang on to a grudge for eternity. But boys never thought too long about anything. They were simple.

Samantha's face brightened, a grin replaced her sadness. I rolled my eyes at Daniel's comment, thankful he was still obvious to the harsh realities of life.

I retold Jaime's story, leaving out a lot of the gruesome details. Samantha retorted in anger, "Jaime deserves it for putting herself in that situation!"

"Samantha! Do you really think she is to blame? Jaime had no way of knowing what would happen. I can understand your anger. I know she's had a bad attitude about everything lately. But no one deserves what she's been through!"

The anger in Samantha's eyes softened and she hugged me. "I know. You're right, Mom."

I was exhausted by the time I fell into bed that night, but my mind continued to race. I blamed myself for not keeping Jaime safe. She had been through so much! I took mental inventory, which only tormented me further until a torrent of tears drenched my pillow. When I finally drifted off to sleep, the terrifying images of the girls being pushed out of a car and then dragged into a house of horrors plagued my mind. A scream escaped my lips and I woke up with my heart racing. How I wished it was only a nightmare and not reality!

Chris held me until I fell back to sleep.

The girls were somber during the ride to the police station the next morning. A no-nonsense, bulky female detective introduced herself, then directed us into a drab, windowless office.

"All right, ladies, tell me what you know. Don't leave anything out. It may help us to catch these guys," Detective Hamilton began. The girls gave detail after detail. I cringed at every word and tried desperately to contain my rage.

"Unfortunately, we know that street and that house all too well. It's a drug flop house. The guy who owns it doesn't live there. He just lets druggies come and go. They pay him to use it, which makes catching these guys almost impossible," she stated matter-of-factly. "The guys you left the club with...are they drug dealers? Did you leave the club with them because you were gonna hang out and do drugs?" she interrogated.

"No, we weren't going there to do drugs with them!" came Jaime's defensive reply, her eyes fixed on a spot on the floor.

"We just wanted a ride home," added Seria.

The detective's eyes narrowed, and she scoffed, "Now come on. I have had a lot of women in here relaying the same story with the same details, and it all came down to the same thing. They were there with those guys so they could get drugs."

I was incensed at the implication. "Jaime has never done drugs and I don't care what other stories you have heard. She was raped! Aren't you even going to try and catch these guys?"

The detective looked at me as if she couldn't believe my naïveté. Then the look in her eyes softened. "I understand you're concerned, but over the years we have received numerous reports of rape from the women that live on Main Street. It has been impossible to make any arrests; there is never enough evidence. But you must understand that in most cases, the women were lured to that house with the promise of drugs."

This wasn't about drugs; it was about justice! Just because those women happened to live on the wrong street, they were targets for rapists? Was there no recourse for them? Once again women were at the mercy of a powerless judicial system that could do nothing to make their street safe! The danger I felt that day on Main Street now made sense. Compassion for all those women flooded my heart.

I had dismissed the idea of drugs. Until the moment I found myself sitting in the school principal's office, I wouldn't have put Jaime and drugs in the same sentence. But now. . .

How did she get the drugs and how long had she been experimenting? I knew drugs were readily available at the public school. But a Catholic school?

Jaime should be having fun in high school, but instead she continued to put herself in dangerous situations. Now I understood why. Drugs! Drugs motivated all her actions and resulted in serious consequences, creating a downward spiral which could have been even worse.

With all we'd been through with Jaime over the years, I instinctively knew that a short-term drug rehab was not the answer. She had become extremely depressed after the rape, and now that I knew drugs were involved, I understood why her personality had changed. My sweet, caring, beautiful Jaime had become an ill-tempered, paranoid mess. She no longer even cared what she looked like. A friend who worked with teens suggested I take her to Children's Hospital for the weekend to get a mental health evaluation. They would assess what kind of help she needed. This also gave us time to figure out where she could get long-term care.

It was heart-wrenching to make the decision to take her to the hospital. Jaime was miserable. She didn't want to go anywhere. But she was a runner and when things got tough, I knew she would take off. I had no choice but to try and keep her safe from the destructive decisions she was making.

During the weekend hospital stay, several professionals made it clear; she needed to be admitted into a long-term drug rehab.

*"When they walk through the valley of weeping,
it will become a place of refreshing springs."*

~ Psalm 84:6 NLT

CHAPTER 27

I caught a glimpse of Samantha, who had just turned twelve, going into the family room. I watched with curiosity as she searched through every built-in cabinet on both sides of the fireplace. She pulled out every photo album she found and sat in the middle of the floor. She wildly flipped through the albums, stopping when she came to a picture she wanted and carefully took it out. Satisfied with the collection of photos she had retrieved; she gathered them up, climbed the stairs and disappeared into her bedroom.

An hour later I peeked in Samantha's room. She was sitting on her bed, cross-legged, with a finished collection of pictures of her and Jaime from birth to the present, arranged on a 16 x 20 piece of poster board. She had taken a picture off her wall to use the frame for the collage. She held it up to view it from every angle. Then satisfied with the outcome, she fastened it into the frame and put the picture next to her bed.

"May I come in?' I asked from the doorway. Sam nodded. I sat on the bed and gave her a hug. "It's beautiful," I said.

"Did Jaime really need to go to the hospital for two days? And I can't believe you're taking her straight from there to a drug rehab! Daniel looked so sad when you told us that my heart hurt for him. I can't believe I'm saying this... but I just miss her so much already! I know she was mean to me at times, but I love her and don't want her to be away from home." She wept uncontrollably.

"I know. My heart aches already too. The doctor suggested we take her right from Children's to Teens Helping Teens Rehab. So unless the doctor has a better solution when we pick Jaime up, it's the best way to help your sister," I emphasized.

"When will we get to see her? How long will she be gone?"

"We won't be able to see her or even talk to her for the first two weeks." My voice cracked, and tears crept down my cheeks.

I wiped away the tears and elaborated, "The director at Teens Helping Teens told us that it will be up to Jaime. She has to follow the rules and learn the twelve-step program, then she will be able to come home with other girls who are further along."

"It just sounds awful, Mom!" Samantha moaned.

"Honey, it's a matter of tough love. Your sister could have died in that drug flop house! We don't even know what other risky decisions she's made. And the next one could take her life. At least being at Teens Helping Teens will keep her safe. Believe me, this is a huge financial decision, a thousand dollars a month! But we have decided to make the sacrifice for your sister's well-being."

"I know. I mean, I understand. But it's still just so sad!" Samantha groaned.

"The collage shows the deep love you have for each other. It will be a comfort to you while Jaime is away."

The principal of All Saints had recommended Teens Helping Teens for Jaime, so we prayed that God would lead us in this decision. When we admitted Jaime to the hospital, a nurse who knew nothing about our circumstances, stopped us and told us that Teens Helping Teens was the best rehab for Jaime. God seemed to be confirming at every turn that Jaime needed to be in that rehab. I had so much hope that completing a drug rehab would give us our Jaime back, but I was overcome with grief. *How can I send my fourteen-year-old daughter away?* The thought was more than I could bear. I couldn't stop accusing myself: *If I had gotten her more help, if I had spent more time with her, if I knew every one of her friends and parents none of this would have happened!* The "what if's" went on and on and kept peaceful sleep at bay.

I heard Chris in the shower and scrambled out of bed. We had overslept and had to be at the hospital in an hour to meet with Jaime's doctor.

"Why didn't you wake me?" I asked, irritated.

"I wanted you to sleep as long as possible. You tossed and turned all night, mumbling about something," he informed me.

"I had nightmares about leaving Jaime at Teens Helping Teens," I moaned.

We walked into the hospital ten minutes late and found the waiting room. Chris took my hand, his eyes full of compassion. "It's going to be OK. This is the best thing we can do for Jaime."

I patted his hand. "At least I have you to lean on, but you got yourself into this mess... your dad tried to warn you about dating me and so did I! You could have married the 'good Catholic girl' and been spared from all of this craziness but nooo... you wouldn't listen," I teased.

"There is no place I would rather be," he crooned and pierced my heart with his bedroom eyes.

A nurse took us back to a small, tan room with a plaid love-seat and two blue chairs. A few minutes later a doctor came in and shook our hands. "Hi, I'm Dr. Smyth, the child psychologist here." He sat down in one of the chairs and opened a file.

"I have looked at Jaime's history and the assessments we have done with her. She has been through a lot. It is my opinion that she has situational depression and anxiety and has been using drugs to self-medicate. I could give her a prescription that might help. But with her behavior and drug use, I don't think it would be a long-term solution. A drug rehab with intensive talk therapy, in my opinion, would benefit her the most."

I looked at Chris with teary eyes. This was the third time we had received the same advice from a professional. It was God's confirmation that we needed to take Jaime to Teens Helping Teens.

"We will complete her paperwork and she will be discharged in an hour. She's an intelligent, sweet girl," Dr. Smyth acknowledged. "I hope she gets the help she needs."

"Thank you. We are actually taking her straight to Teens Helping Teens Rehab from here," Chris informed Dr. Smyth, who nodded approvingly.

Jaime was dressed and ready to go when we reached her room. She sat on the edge of the bed. Her face was drawn, it was evident she hadn't slept. Jaime gave me a weak hug and said, "It was so noisy I haven't slept in two days, and the food was awful. I'm starving!" She was angry when we brought her to the hospital. Now she seemed drained, like she had no fight left in her.

"Where would you like to go to get something to eat?" I plastered on a smile. *What kind of parents are we? Our daughter will be locked up with total strangers and we won't even be able to talk to her or see her for two weeks! She didn't know what was about to happen to her and I'm asking her where she wants to eat as if everything was perfectly normal.* I grabbed her overnight bag and I held her hand as we walked to the exit where Chris was waiting with the car.

Jaime had chosen lunch at her favorite fast food place. Chris and I were conspicuously quiet, and Jaime felt the awkwardness. Her eyes darted back and forth between Chris' face and mine, looking for a hint. "Jaime, honey," I began, and I could see her bristle.

"Mom, what's wrong?"

She looked at me and then at Chris. "What is it?"

"The doctors and other professionals feel you need to go to a long-term drug rehab in order to get the help you really need, and we've made an appointment to check one out after lunch."

She nodded her head in agreement while scarfing down her fries. We continued eating in silence. This felt like our "last meal" together before we led her to the gas chamber! Life was about to change in ways we could not comprehend.

The one-story brick building was non-descript. It sat on four acres of land that was in serious need of landscaping. I wrapped my arm around Jaime's shoulder as she walked between Chris and me toward the front of the building. We were buzzed into the front door and the Teens Helping Teens director, Pam Owens, greeted us and led us to her office. Jaime sat quietly absorbing her surroundings. I saw surrender in her eyes and got the feeling she wanted help. *Or was it just my imagination because I didn't want her to hate us?* With all the introductions out of the way, Pam asked Jaime a few questions about her hobbies. Then she asked what drugs Jaime had been using. A jovial staff person and an energetic, well-kept teenager popped their heads into the office. Pam signaled for them to come in and introduced them. "This is Sarah Jones, one of our counselors and Jenny Murphy. Jenny has been here for six months and would like to take you on a tour, Jaime." A shadow of confusion crossed her face. She shot a puzzled look at me.

"Go on. We will wait right here. The tour will show you what the program is like," I assured. Jaime hesitated, then slowly stood.

"Jaime, I love your jeans! I heard you like art. I just finished a painting I'm really proud of and would love to show it to you," Jenny boasted.

Jenny was short with sparkling green eyes and long, brunet hair. Her cheerful demeanor put me at ease. It would be wonderful to see Jaime happy again. We all stood and stepped into the lobby. Jaime walked beside Jenny and they disappeared down the hall.

Sarah put her hand on my shoulder. "Jenny will take good care of Jaime. She's doing great in the program and will be by Jaime's side to reassure her and explain how it all works. In two weeks, when you come to family night, Jaime will be content to be here. It is best for Jaime if you leave without saying good bye. Long good-byes are hard on new teens that come into the program. I know this will be difficult for your whole family, but it works best this way," Sarah advised and led us to the door.

A huge knot had formed in my throat. I hurried to the car in front of Chris. He caught up and opened the door.

"She is going to hate us! I can't imagine how scared and angry she will be when she realizes we left her here, and with only the bare necessities and one bag of clothes. She will feel so abandoned!" I croaked out. Chris held me tight, not saying a word.

When my rant ended, Chris consoled me. "I know this is tough on you, but we are out of options. She's safe here and for a little while, we can relax and stop worrying."

I leaned into him and buried my face in his chest, sniffling. I tried to catch my breath. I knew he was right. Somehow, I had to look at the positive side of Jaime being in rehab.

*"The best way to show my gratitude to God
is to accept everything, even my problems, with joy."*

~ Mother Teresa

CHAPTER 28

"**A**re you kidding? Seriously, I can't have my friends over when Jaime comes home with other kids from rehab? Mooommm, this is so unfair! I feel like I'm being punished because Jaime used drugs!" Samantha declared.

"I get it," I acknowledged. "I'm sorry, but we all have to make sacrifices to support your sister and I know this is a big concession on your part."

Her part? The Good Kid, good grades, mission trips to Mexico to volunteer in orphanages and build homes, creating a play time for preschoolers to give neighborhood moms a break. Concessions shouldn't have to be part of the deal. Of course, Samantha felt neglected. All our attention had been focused on Jaime and the drama she caused. We weren't focused on Samantha, was the 'good girl' who deserved all our attention, as did Daniel. Recently, I made a conscious effort to spend more time with Samantha -- we'd go out shopping or to see the latest movie. But life had been unreasonable and cheated her out of what was normal. It seemed impossible to make up for all the attention her sister had sucked away from her. Her moody resentment at the change in our family and the change rehab was demanding from us was understandable.

"Chris, we still have to set up a time for THT staff to come out and approve our house, so Jaime and the girls can sleep here at night. When did you plan to take off the door knobs and latches to install the keyed locks on the doors and windows?"

"I will start this weekend. They said we had several weeks to get that done," he reminded me.

"What? Now we have to be locked up like criminals in jail when Jaime's home!" Samantha stomped upstairs.

I looked helplessly at Chris. "I've never seen Samantha this upset! Usually she rolls with the punches. I'm surprised she doesn't have more compassion for Jaime's situation. But I understand and can't blame her for being angry that Jaime's drug use has pushed us all into this situation. I'll take her to have coffee after school and talk to her while you're at ball practice with Daniel. Don't forget Friday night will be our first family meeting. I'm so glad Jaime has to stay with girls who are further along in the program. I hope she learns the structure and rules quickly, so she can come home!"

Chris hugged me. "You know she has to reach the third phase of the program to come home. Just be patient and enjoy our peace! You know how hectic it's going to be around here when she's home with three or four other girls?"

"You're right. It will be controlled chaos!" I joked. "I'm going upstairs to see how Samantha is."

"Samantha, Honey. Can I come in?" I asked.

"Go ahead. You'll come in whether I want you to or not!" she bellowed.

I pushed the door open with caution and peeked in. Samantha was sitting in her beanbag chair in the corner, reading a book. She glared at me from across the room. "Are there any other THT rules I should know about?"

"To tell you the truth I really don't know. I guess we'll find out together. I want you to know I appreciate you! You are honest, kind and caring, always smiling and thinking the best of others." I looked behind me, for dramatic effect and to make sure no one else could hear me. "Don't tell anyone I said this, but you're my perfect child!"

A smile grew across her face. I continued, "You are the one I never had to worry about. I'm sorry I haven't told you that more often. I didn't realize how hard rehab would be on you, and believe me, I hate all of the required meetings and rules as much as you do. But what choice do we have? Your sister needs to be there, and we have to participate in the program if we want to help your sister."

Her eyes soften. She got up, came across the room, threw her arms around me and started to cry. "I'm just so scared I'll never get my sister back!" Then she backed up a step and added, "Being the one in the middle stinks. Daniel's the cute, adorable baby in the family and with everything Jaime pulled, there is no time left for me! At least now I only have to share you with Daniel, and I don't have to listen to Jaime give you an attitude!"

"Awe, yes, there is always a positive side to everything!" I grinned, "I love you sooo much!"

Watching grass grow was quicker than waiting for two long, agonizing weeks to pass. The day we were scheduled for our first visit, I couldn't concentrate. I would go upstairs and forget what I went for, clomp back downstairs, only to remember and have to ascend the stairs once more to retrieve it. I was about to scale the stairs again when the phone rang, interrupting my unplanned exercise. I answered with a breathy "Hello."

"Hi, Denise. This is Ann Murphy, Jenny's mom. Teens Helping Teens gave me your number. I wanted to invite you to dinner at The Front Porch, with my husband, Bill, and some of the other rehab parents. The restaurant is across the street from the meeting. If you can join us tonight, it will be one of the highlights of your evening!" she assured.

"We would love to! I've looked forward to meeting all of you. And I have a million questions!"

"I'm sure you do; we all did. Believe me, it's normal. There will be a group of six of us seated at a table in the corner. Denise, I just want you to know you're not going to go through this alone," she added sincerely.

Chris, the kids and I walked in The Front Porch, which was decorated with red and white checkered table cloths and steer horns hanging on the walls. Laughter from the table in the corner of the restaurant caught our attention. "That must be the THT parents. Sounds like they have fun. That's a good sign!" I said to Chris and the kids.

Ann stood as we approached the table. "You must be Denise and Chris," she said and instead of offering a hand, she came around the table and hugged us. "And who are these young people?"

"This is our daughter and son, Samantha and Daniel," I pointed out. Ann smiled at them and then introduced us to everyone else at the table.

"I think you will find these dinners extremely therapeutic because, literally, we are the only ones on planet Earth who understand what goes on in THT Country." Everyone agreed and chuckled. "Jaime has stayed at our house for the last several nights. Jenny and Jaime have become close. Your daughter is a sweetheart, and we have really enjoyed getting to know her," Ann added.

My eyes filled with tears. *My daughter...a sweetheart?* She had been so hateful to us when we took her to Children's Hospital, spewing cuss words all over the place. She'd said she never wanted to see us again. Ann noticed I was on the verge of full-blown waterworks.

She leaned over and said, "The first family meeting is always the hardest. I want to warn you. Jaime is supposed to make amends with you when you meet with her one-on-one. You may find out she lied to you about a lot of things. If you can remember the drugs influenced her to do those things, it will help. These kids become different people when they do drugs."

I noticed Samantha shift back and forth in her seat and look away while Ann was talking. *Why was she squirming? Did she know something we didn't?* Quizzing her would have to wait. We'd finished our meal just in time to get across the street. Daniel was too young to attend, so he went to kids' club with the other siblings his age. The families were ushered into an auditorium. I was amazed at the large number of teenagers on stage and searched the faces to find Jaime. There she sat, next to Jenny. Gratitude filled my heart for this spunky gal who had taken Jaime under her wing! The meeting was called to order and the kids got up, one by one, and introduced themselves. They had to say what drugs they had done in the past and what they had accomplished in the program that week. Everyone stood and clapped for each teen who had been promoted to a higher program phase. They also had to announce in front of the whole group if they had been put back a phase for lying or not complying with the program. I was humbled by their honesty and their gratefulness to be at THT.

Then we went into a room where we would meet with Jaime for twenty minutes and she could make amends with us. Chris and Samantha sat down on two chairs arranged in a circle. I was too anxious to sit and paced back and forth. Finally, a staff person I had not met brought Jaime in, holding the back of her jeans. I wanted to yell, "Take your hands off my daughter! How dare you treat her like a prisoner!" But I controlled myself and focused on Jaime.

I gave her a bear hug and weak smile. "Hi, Honey. We have missed you so much!" I gushed.

Jaime's expression brightened. "I have missed you guys, too! And I am so sorry for everything I have done," she croaked out. Then she glanced towards the staff person, who nodded approval for her to continue.

Jaime stared at the floor, shifted her weight from one foot to the other and began, "I need to tell you I'm sorry. I paid Daniel off with quarters, so he wouldn't tell you I went down the street to get drugs." She looked up to see our response. I sat there in silence, and hid the shock on my face, surprised that she would do such a thing. The staff nudged her to continue. "Another time I took Samantha to the same house where I met a guy, used drugs and had sex while I left her downstairs," she confessed. She nonchalantly stated these facts, then waited for our reaction.

I tried to process what I had heard. I didn't know how to respond, so I bolted from the room. I stormed out to the parking lot and a deep wail escaped my lungs. Then I felt Chris, who had run out behind me, wrap me in his arms.

I screamed, "How could she? *How could she*...drag Samantha and Daniel into her hideous reality? She has poisoned their innocent world! They will never get that innocence back! I was actually dumb enough to think we had protected them from everything she was doing." Chris held me and let me continue until I was drained. Samantha had gotten Daniel and joined us at the car.

"I am sorry, Mom. I should have told you. I just didn't want you to be mad at me. And honestly, I never went down the street again with Jaime. I was so mad at her for dragging me down there, and I have never done any drugs! You have to believe me!" Samantha's eyes pleaded.

I hugged her. "I am so angry that Jaime involved both of you in her lies! Is there anything else I need to know?" I coaxed. Samantha shook her head no. Then I added, "I can't imagine other kids in our neighborhood doing drugs! I should be telling their parents what I have found out. What house did Jaime take you to?"

"The ranch, four houses down from us. I don't know what else Jaime has lied about, but that was the only time she took me with her," Samantha confessed.

We pulled out of the parking lot. I laid my head back on the car seat and closed my eyes. I took a deep breath, then said, "Thank you for telling me the truth. I believe you, Samantha."

Our life started to revolve around the rehab and the meetings we were required to attend. We became one big THT family, going through a tough time together. The midweek mandatory classes were intended to educate us on how we related to our children, so we could help them once they came home. Five days later, we attended our first session.

Sarah, the counselor, led the class, "If you are an enabler, it means you bail your teen out of harmful situations and rescue them from their own natural consequences. On the other hand, if you are codependent, your life revolves solely around your teen and you struggle to set limits. In this scenario, you can easily lose your identity because of this one-sided relationship. It is not good to be either. We will help you identify which of these categories you fall into and how to better relate to your teen," she explained.

I leaned over to Chris and said, "Wow, these classes could really help us get to a better place with Jaime." He nodded in agreement.

Six weeks later, after the same information was given over and over, the classes seemed like an attack on the parents. It appeared the counselors deemed the parents as the "real problem" in their children's lives. This aggravated my feelings of self-hate and blame for Jaime's choices and made my fury at the whole situation hard to control.

I excused myself from the class one night and my rage boiled over when I walked down the hall towards the bathroom. I spied colorful posters on the wall titled: *Come to the Teens Helping Teens Bowl-A-Thon to Raise Funds for the Mid-Week Classes.* Without thinking, I reached up and ripped it off the wall. I went on a rampage down the hall, ripping down another poster, then kicking over a plant. The pent-up anger I'd carried for months, for years, exploded in that hallway. I realized it wasn't just Jaime and the drugs. It was Doyle, my parents, and my own abuse as well as my sense of helplessness in protecting my children. And I must admit, the release was gratifying, if only for a few minutes.

I leaned up against the wall, folded over and cried. It was all so much. I loved my daughter with my whole heart and I desperately wanted to help her. But the controlled structure of THT that ruled our lives was suffocating me and harming my other children. God was the only one who understood all we had been through for so long. He understood why I had just lost control after years of trying to hold it all together.

Another Friday night had rolled around. I'd had an ominous feeling all day that only increased in intensity while I got ready for the THT meeting.

"Come on. We're going to be late! Remember, we have to drop off Daniel at my dad's house, so he doesn't have to endure five hours of meetings," Chris prompted.

"OK! I just can't get my earrings in and dropped one on the floor! My nerves are on edge and I can't figure out why," I snapped.

"I understand. After all, it's our first meeting with Jaime's counselor and we don't know what to expect."

"I think it's more than that. Lucky Samantha, she's going to dinner and a movie with her friends. Oh, how I dream of having a date night again! Go ahead and get in the car with Daniel and I will be right down," I sighed.

"I will make sure we have plenty of date nights, when this is all over." Chris gave me a quick kiss and disappeared down the hall.

We made it across town forty-five minutes later and walked into Sarah's office on time. "I'm so glad you were able to meet with me. I would like to talk to you for a few minutes before I have Jaime join us. Jaime's father called today and ask to come to the family meeting tonight," Sarah explained.

I was stunned. I had convinced myself that Doyle wouldn't fill out all the sensitive paperwork the program demanded so he could attend meetings. Maybe it was just wishful thinking. It had been years since Samantha and Jaime had gone to visit Doyle, unless it was a major holiday and gifts were expected. And THT Country was hard enough without an invasion from Doyle.

Sarah continued, "So, unfortunately, your time with Jaime after the family meeting will be cut in half so Mr. Boese can meet with Jaime for ten minutes."

"Really? Sarah, did you take the time to read all the paperwork we filled out? You do know her father sexually abused her when she was a toddler...*that is why she did drugs!* Certainly, you can understand why this is a really lousy idea!" I protested.

Sarah was dumbfounded. "I had no idea. I am so sorry. I must have missed that in the paperwork. But, you know, seeing her father may be a good thing. If memories surface, then I can help Jaime deal with them during our counseling sessions."

I was about to say more when Jaime walked in the door. She barely looked my way and gave me a stiff one shoulder hug. "Jaime, I just told your parents that your dad is coming to the meeting tonight."

A smile lit up Jaime's face, "Really? Will I get to talk to him?"

"Yes, your dad will have ten minutes to meet with you after your parents' time is up," Sarah confirmed.

Ugh, of course she's excited to see him and treats me like the enemy!

Sarah asked, "So, Jaime, do you like being in phase three? Are you ready to bring girls home and mentor them?"

"Yes, I think so. I really want to sleep in my own bed," Jaime eagerly responded. After Sarah asked a few more questions to explore Jaime's feelings around her homecoming, she excused Jaime to join the other kids. We went into the family meeting and found a seat by Ann and Bill. I dreaded seeing Doyle. I scanned the room for any sign of him, so I could avoid him after the meeting. I reminded myself I had a lot of friends and support in THT Country. That calmed my nerves.

The lengthy meeting ended, and we walked out into the lobby. Immediately I spied Doyle, standing in the small waiting area across from us. He was talking to one of the other fathers. He smiled and laughed like he was at a reunion. Doyle moved closer to a woman who stood next to him and put his arm around her. All at once he boomed, "This is my beautiful blushing bride!" Then he glanced our way.

My heart sank. *She's a stranger to Jaime! The ink on Doyle's divorce decree from his second wife is barely dry and now he has a third wife? Why would he bring a woman that Jaime has never met to rehab when his focus should be on Jaime alone!*

Sarah walked up. "Mr. Boese has asked if he can meet with Jaime first. I told him I would ask you."

"Do I really get to say no? Maybe it would be better. Sure," I sassed, then conceded.

Chris put his arm around me and pulled me close. From across the room, I could see Jaime's forced smiled and disappointment when Doyle introduced his new wife. He took up the whole twenty minutes, while I watched the wall clock and fumed. I overheard him tell Jaime how they'd met. Three months later they won a contest and got married on the radio show, *Glendale Today*. The DJ for the show had performed their ceremony on air last Saturday. By the time we sat down with Jaime, my stomach was churning. Her hurt and disappointment turned quickly to anger, which exploded during our five-minute meeting.

"If you had not put me in this place, I would have known my father got married! You are the reason I did drugs! This is all your fault!" she screamed. A counselor monitoring the room overheard Jaime's heated words and saw our discomfort. She came over and ended our time with Jaime.

I knew I was an easy target for Jaime's fury, and I tried not to take her lashing out personally. Compassion for everything she had been through consumed me and became a shield from her misplaced rage. How I longed to take all her hurt and pain away! I mourned for the joyful, vibrant Jaime, I'd lost eleven years earlier. I wasn't sure if we would ever get her back.

"Don't ask God to move mountains
if you aren't willing to pick up a shovel."

~ Billy Cox

CHAPTER 29

*J*could hear laughter coming from the landing on the stairs and then I saw Chris. He looked drained from the long drive home. Chris meandered in front of Jaime, who ran past him, almost knocking me down as she flew up the flight of steps behind me. In typical fashion, there was no hug or hello from my first born. For the last several weeks Jaime had been coming home at night from THT. I came down and saw Jenny, who stood there with three other girls in our front hall.

"Jenny, what's going on? Why is Jaime upstairs?" I asked.

Jenny smirked and pointed her finger my way. "Talking Behind Backs. You know the rules!" she reminded.

Oh brother, here we go again. This is going to be a long night of rules with the spirit of legalism thrown in for good measure!

"OK, OK. I get it. I can't ask you any questions about anything Jaime is doing, has done, or wants to do. I have to ask her directly. Can you at least call her down for dinner?"

She retorted, "TBB, Talking Behind Backs!"

Oh, for crying out loud! I will talk behind your back, her back and anyone else's back that I want to! I turned, trudged back up the stairs. I secretly hoped that the dinner I was in the middle of cooking would burn.

The girls had to do the required 12-step program each night, which made the evening routine fly by. They'd already had a full day of activities at rehab, so exhaustion set in like a rapidly deflating hot air balloon crash landing by bedtime. They all slept in the bonus room above the garage. All I had to do was lock the door behind them and I was off duty.

I climbed into bed and looked forward to a deep, restorative sleep, but was awakened a short time later by an unusual commotion from the bonus room. It was strange, because once the girls fell asleep I never heard one peep out them until morning. I reached for the keys on the nightstand, walked down the dark hallway, flipped the light switch and unlocked the door. When I peeked in, the girls were all huddled on the bed in the dormer window. As soon as the five trembling girls saw me, they broke huddle and scurried around me like chicks to a mother hen and clung to me. They all jabbered incoherently at once.

"Please, I can't listen to all of you at the same time. Jaime, what happened?"

She stammered, "We were all asleep when Lori felt something hit her bed. It woke her up, and then it sat on her bed! She screamed and jumped in bed with me. A minute later, we felt something breeze by us, then bump into our bed!"

Irritated, I muttered, "Seriously? I'm sure it was your imagination. Just go back to sleep."

They held onto me even more tightly, refusing to let me go. They pleaded, "Please, don't leave us alone with that 'thing'!"

Lori wailed, "It will attack us again and we won't be alive by morning!"

I searched those five pair of eyes. They were genuinely afraid. This was not the case of scary stories around the proverbial campfire that now caused them to hear and feel things going bump in the night. Something had spooked them. So, I relented. No one would get any sleep if I went back to my own warm, cozy bed. I had nowhere else to put them that could be locked with a key, and I didn't want to be reported if I broke any rehab rules. I went to the hall closet, got a sleeping bag and my pillow, and asked Chris to lock us in. I wanted to make sure this wasn't an elaborate ploy on their part, so they could sneak off once I fell asleep.

I said a silent prayer and crawled into my sleeping bag. "Girls, relax, quiet down so we can get some sleep," I cajoled. They seemed satisfied that I would keep them safe by bunking with them, and within moments I could hear gentle breathing. They had drifted off to sleep.

I was doing the same, when suddenly my descent into dreamland was interrupted. Lori shot out of bed shrieking, "Something just bounced on my bed and touched me!" This sent the other girls into a screaming frenzy and a shiver down my spine. *This better not be a slumber party turned horror movie,* I thought.

I shimmied out of the sleeping bag and did my best to calm the girls. I sat on the bed and called them to sit with me. I said a prayer, inviting God's peace and presence into the room. The girls finally got quiet and I, curious, began probing them about similar experiences they may have had. Lori was the first to speak up. Her family had lived in a really old house in New England when she was younger. "It was haunted," she said very matter-of-factly. "My whole family saw the ghosts, or something, and they even talked with them!" And now my skin was crawling.

"So, you weren't afraid of the spirits, Lori? Did you talk to them, too?" I asked.

"No. I was only four or five when we lived there, and we moved away right after I turned six. I do remember my aunt standing in the hallway talking to something that I could not see. My mom told us other stories about talking to spirits in that house. But I never saw them or talked to them," Lori insisted.

Another one of the girls laughed. "Do you really believe that stuff? I don't think spirits are real," she chimed.

"They're real," Jaime whispered, eyes focused on the bed-spread. Everyone just stared at her.

"Have you ever heard of familiar spirits?" I asked. Both she and Lori shook their heads.

I continued, "Well, the Bible talks about familiar spirits and tells us not to be involved with them. When your family talked to those spirits in your old house, they opened a door. Some people think the spirits are harmless – even friendly or sent to help them. But they are demons. They seem "familiar" and convince people they can be trusted and believed. But they are under the control of their master, Satan, and they want to control whomever they can."

Lori scrunched up her face in deep thought. The other girls drew closer. After a few seconds, Lori said, "But that was a long time ago. What does that have to do with me now?"

"Your family gave them access to you by talking to them and opened a door to the demonic realm that's never been shut. But another avenue those spirits use to gain entrance into a person's life is through mind-altering drugs. I really believe because of your drug use and the door your family opened you are being harassed by an evil spirit!" I exclaimed.

"I don't want anything to do with an evil spirit! How can I make it go away?" She was terrified at the thought.

"Lori, do you know Jesus?"

"When I was six, after we moved, my family started to go to church and I learned some of the stories in the Bible, so I guess I know who He is."

"Have you ever asked Jesus into your life?"

"No, I haven't, but I want to now! I want this stuff to stop!"

"When Jesus died on the cross, overcame death and rose on the third day, He took away the power of sin and the demonic realm over our lives. All we have to do is accept His gift and tell Him we are turning away from our past sin to walk in a new relationship with Him." Lori nodded her head in agreement to what I shared.

"OK, I will lead you in a prayer to ask Jesus into your life and then we will command the spirit to leave in the name of Jesus and shut the door to the demonic realm."

We looked up scriptures in Deuteronomy and Leviticus. Then I led Lori and the girls in prayer. I read Ephesians 6:12 aloud to show them that God says our struggle is not against flesh and blood, but against the rulers, against the authorities, against the powers of this dark world and against the spiritual forces of evil.

The girls were amazed at what was in the Bible and started to share stories that confirmed they had all seen evil spirits while doing drugs. I was sure the night's event would be shared with the counselors at rehab tomorrow and would make for interesting conversation. But for now, I was rejoicing that God had used an evil entity's aggression to teach the girls about Him!

The best revenge is a life well lived with God.

CHAPTER 30

"Chris, Sarah called today, and you will never believe what she told me!" I exclaimed.

"Jaime is doing terrific and has completed the program. We're free!" he joked.

"I wish. No, better than that. Jaime had a memory surface of her childhood abuse. Sarah's hopeful that now Jaime will be able to talk about it, really deal with the pain and she won't use again! And the news gets better. Sarah called Doyle to confront him about the abuse! Can you believe that?"

"Wow! That is great news! We can hope and pray this helps Jaime. I wonder if Doyle will continue to come to meetings now that the truth is coming out." Chris wondered.

"If Doyle admits he abused Jaime and apologizes, I know it would give her the breakthrough she needs for healing! I'm going to the Living Spirit healing service tonight, so I can pray for Doyle and Jaime."

I always loved going to Living Spirit. There was always such a heightened sense of expectation. Whenever I felt my faith waning, all I had to do was step through Living Spirit's doors and I knew that Jaime would be completely healed and set free. I knew that our family would be whole, no matter what was happening in our lives.

One of the spirit-filled intercessors I had never met, Mary Therese, looked in my direction, then walked, with a slight limp, over to where I sat with a friend. She was a plump, short, gray-haired woman, and as she got closer a grin appeared on her face. Mary Therese laid her hand on my shoulder, looked me squarely in the eyes and boldly declared, "The Lord impressed upon me that you recently received the gift of tongues. It is a powerful prayer language that the Holy Spirit uses to speak through us. Think about it. No one has ever used this dialect to lie, cuss, or gossip! He has given you an extensive language and God wants you to use it every day!" My friend, who had no clue I spoke in tongues, stared at me in both bewilderment and amazement.

I uttered, "I knew it sounded different from other people, but I didn't understand why. I am humbled and grateful you shared what God showed you. Would you pray with us for my daughter?" This dedicated intercessor sat with us and prayed for Jaime and Doyle. Only God knew how much I would need this gift in the near future.

ॐॐॐॐॐॐॐॐॐॐ

It was a tremendous relief, a few weeks later, when we no longer saw Doyle at the family meetings. But now I would have to see him in court. I had collected letters from Jaime's psychologist, school principal, teachers and her counselor which all stated that it was their opinion Jaime needed to be in a long-term drug rehab. I sent the letters to the insurance company and asked them to pay for the mountain of debt, $20,000 to be exact, but they had denied our appeal.

The divorce decree stated that Doyle was responsible for half of any unpaid medical expenses. My attorney sent Doyle several letters to request he pay half of the rehab bills, but he never responded. Joe assured me that the court would view these expenses as medical, so we decided to take him to court. Doyle walked in without his third wife on his arm. I wondered if she even knew about this court hearing.

Joe greeted him with a handshake. "Will you be represented by an attorney?" Joe questioned.

"I planned to represent myself," Doyle stated.

"OK, very well. How about we go into the courtroom and sit at a table. There is a letter from Jaime's psychologist I would like you to read. It will help you understand why you need to pay for half of the rehab," Joe articulated.

Doyle glanced over his shoulder and shot me a defiant look as Joe handed him the letter and led him into the court room. I stayed in the hallway and the next thing I knew, Doyle breezed past me and tore out of the building.

Joe walked up and handed me a $10,000 check and announced, "There will be no court hearing. I showed Doyle the letter that stated Jaime was being treated for chemical dependency because of childhood incest, and he immediately agreed to pay for half of Teens Helping Teens! My guess is Doyle didn't want the third wife to know anything about the 'Real Doyle' she had married."

On the drive home, I thanked God and rejoiced for the financial help and answered prayer.

*"Keep the faith. The most amazing things
in life tend to happen right at the moment
you're about to give up hope."*

~ Unknown

CHAPTER 31

"What? *No!* You told us that could never happen because the building is always locked!" I screeched into the phone.

"Denise, please calm down and let me explain. The back door they go in automatically locks once the girls are buzzed inside, but they shoved paper into the latch when they walked into the building. It jammed the lock when the door shut and gave them the opportunity to sneak back out when Chris drove away," the director, Pam, explained.

"Why wasn't there a counselor at the back door? I thought there was always someone at the door when the kids came in the morning," I grilled.

"No, the staff monitors the door; we have a camera. When the girls didn't come into the meeting and weren't in the coat room, they examined the door and found the paper wedged in the latch. The staff searched the grounds and they were nowhere to be found. They feel awful about this and so do I," Pam apologized.

"This can't happen! Jaime only had 23 days left to complete the program! Why would she run now?" I pleaded for an answer.

"I agree. It doesn't make sense, but teens can be so impulsive. My guess is with the warm weather, they got bored and decided to take off. Unfortunately, when some kids get close to completing the program, out of fear, they self-sabotage," Pam empathized.

"We were so hopeful that she'd be home for good by her birthday in June." I heaved a sigh. "So, what do we do when we find her?"

"She can certainly come back, but she will be put back into phase one and have to complete the whole program over," Pam explained.

I could feel my blood pressure rise in a wave of heat through my body. "You know what? Jaime has been at THT long enough and will not return! You and the staff are to blame for not making sure that door was monitored by a person, so don't expect a check from us this month! My husband just walked in. I need to go." I slammed the receiver down.

"Jaime and Jenny have run away from THT! Why didn't you stay in the parking lot and watch the door!" I accused. Then I broke down crying. Reality sunk in: Jaime was gone.

"What are you talking about? I watched them go in the building. I always do!" The frustration built in every word Chris uttered.

I sniffled. "Maybe if you had stayed a minute longer this wouldn't have happened. I'm sorry. I know it's not your fault. They shoved paper in the lock and ran back out when you were gone! What are we going to do now? We're back to square one. We can't protect Jaime from herself," I lamented.

Chris walked over and looked down at me and softly he put his hands on my shoulder, "I'm sorry, hon. Really I am." Then he gave me a long hug. Without saying a word, he turned and went outside.

I heard the lawn mower start up. He took the day off to catch up on some things around the house and right now I knew mowing the lawn would be good therapy for him.

Later that afternoon, Ann Murphy called to tell us the girls were gallivanting all over Granite City, the Murphy's hometown. The girls decided to add Jenny's friend, Missy, to their gang and picked her up. Missy's mother had called Ann, frantic that Missy had disappeared with the girls. I vented my anger during my conversation with Ann after I heard about their escapades and blamed THT because they allowed this to happen. Ann didn't seem concerned about their antics and told me she thought the girls would come home in a few days when they got tired and hungry.

When I hung up I was tempted to go after Jaime and find her. I went upstairs instead, closed the door to the bonus room over the garage, collapsed on the floor, kneeling by the side of the couch. "God, please bring her home. Keep her safe... and..." I had no words. What was I to pray? I began to pray in tongues. Several minutes later, I heard: *Let Her Go.*

But, Lord, I know I can find Jaime and bring her back home.

Then the impression became stronger: *Let Her Go.*

OK, God...but please protect them.

I visualized Jaime in my arms and I laid her on the altar in front of God's throne. Then I walked away. Now God was the only one who could protect Jaime. I was so livid with her at that moment, but it became clear I was never able to protect her from her own destructive choices. This time I totally surrendered her. God's altar was the safest place for her to be.

Samantha came through the door from school, tossed her binder on the stairs and headed for the kitchen.

"Hi, honey. How was your day?" I sat down at the table and waited for her to get a snack.

"Fine. I can't go to the family meeting tonight because my friends planned a girl's slumber party at the last minute that should be much more fun than going to THT Country," she smirked.

"Well, there will be no more family meetings at Teens Helping Teens," I declared. Samantha stared at me while my eyes filled with tears.

"What are you talking about, Mom?"

"Your sister ran away from the rehab with Jenny this morning after Chris dropped them off. They are in Granite City right now having a grand old time with another friend of Jenny's! I don't even want to imagine what kind of trouble they are getting into," I fretted.

"I can't believe it! She is so stupid. Mom, I thought she was almost done with the program!" Samantha declared.

"She is now! I am not about to take her back to THT Country when she comes home."

Daniel's ride dropped him off. He walked into the kitchen and started foraging in the pantry for food.

"Hey, little bro, we are off the hook. We never have to attend a family meeting again!" Samantha announced.

He peeked his head out, "Really? But I thought I was going to grandpa's house again."

"OK, Samantha, I will take it from here. Jaime has run away, so now we will need to spend our time in prayer for her," I encouraged.

"Why would she run away, Mom?" Daniel questioned.

"That's the million-dollar question, honey. I'm very sad. We don't know what she will do for shelter, food or without any of her clothes," I choked out.

"God will keep her safe. Can I go to Kerry's tonight and hang out?" Daniel asked.

"Sure, honey, but how about we all go out for dinner first? We haven't gotten to do that in a long time!" I smiled at Samantha and Daniel. "I love you both so much! Thank you both for being so supportive of your sister and the program all these months! I'm so sorry all of our attention has been on your sister." Then I gave them each a long hug. All of our attention had been on one child long enough; now we needed to focus on the two right in front of us.

A day ago, I was optimistic about Jaime's future. Now for my own sanity, I had to believe the rehab program had kept her alive for the last year. I started to connect the dots. God used the demonic activity in Jaime's bedroom to lead her to Jesus before she went to rehab. Now, at least I had the assurance, if Jaime died, she would be in heaven! The declaration I had come to cherish, *He Uses Everything for His Glory and Our Good*, started to resound in my spirit. I knew He wanted me to remember He was in control.

We received a devastating call from Ann two days later. She heard through one of Missy's friends that the girls were on their way to Florida! My heart sank. I chided myself for not going after her when they were in Granite City and wondered if I had heard the Holy Spirit correctly.

I attended church the next day. When Pastor Whit asked for prayer requests, my hand shot up in the air. I looked around the room. "Jaime has run away from drug rehab with two other girls. We believe they are headed to Florida. Please pray for their safety," I urged.

My request was met with blank stares accompanied by silence. Then the pastor called on a couple, who used the time to boast about their child's win at the state baseball tournament. The service continued with no response to my request. I felt so alone, even in church. Apparently, I had not learned what everyone else seemed to know: you weren't supposed to air your dirty laundry in church. I didn't understand. What else was church for, if not to receive support and prayer for serious issues? But I didn't grow up in church, and I was not about to let everyone else's concept of church or God determine my relationship with the Lord. I was free to seek Him and find Him, which allowed me to build a relationship with Him instead of conforming to a group of people.

On Monday I went out to the mail box and found a letter with no return address and recognized Jaime's handwriting. "Chris, look what arrived from Jaime! Please read it...I'm too nervous," I groaned. I handed him the letter and rocked from one foot to the other.

Chris opened it. "Take a deep breath. It says: I love you! I couldn't stand being at THT for one more minute so I made the decision to run. I know I have made my bed, so now I have to lie in it."

"She should have talked to us! We could have helped her make a better decision!" I lamented.

"I'm sure she thought we would never let her leave, but maybe we could have reminded her she only had 23 days left. We have to trust that God's protecting her and will bring her back home to us," Chris said. He hugged me, and we consoled each other, knowing God's grace would carry us through.

I couldn't sleep that night and finally decided to get up around 3 in the morning to pray. I repeated the same requests I had been praying since Jaime had taken off: Lord, keep her safe and bring her back home. Then I prayed in tongues. I was so grateful to have the Holy Spirit pray right through me in this unknown language. I was overwhelmed with a peace that I couldn't explain when the phone on the end table rang. I jumped, and my heart raced, jolting me out of the tranquil state I was in. *Maybe it's Jaime?*

"Hello. Jaime?"

"No. This is Claire, Jaime's friend from school. I just got off the phone with Jaime and she is in Lakewood, Florida. I thought you would want to know."

"Did she sound OK? What else did she tell you? Is there a number I can call her at?" I asked, anxious for more information.

"I'm sorry. She was on a pay phone and her friends were waiting to use it. That was all she said. She sounded OK," she reassured.

Serenity engulfed me after I hung up with Claire and again God impressed upon me not to try and find her. The call from Claire was a gift from Him. Jaime was in the palm of His hand! He was in control. Before I went back to bed, the Holy Spirit reminded me about the events of the night that she'd given her life to the Lord. She was His, no matter what things looked like and His will would be done!

᙭᙭᙭᙭᙭᙭᙭᙭᙭᙭

Three weeks later Tina came over to try some Mary Kay products. I had become a consultant and thought it would be fun to have her do a facial. This part of my life made me feel normal, at least temporarily. We had just finished up when there was a knock on the door. The woman standing there looked familiar, but I couldn't figure out where I knew her from.

"Hi. How are you?" I asked, then quickly made the connection. It was Beth, Scott's mom.

"Scott got a call in the middle of the night from Jaime saying she was in Florida and since it isn't Spring break, it seemed odd. I started to wonder if you knew she was there and thought I should come tell you." That puzzled me. Jaime had broken up with Scott at the end of junior high. *Why would she call him?*

My eyes welled up with tears and I sputtered, "Do you know where in Florida?"

"No, but I wrote down the number she called from. I thought you would want it. Look, I don't know what she said to Scott, but he said she sounded OK. I know I would be heartsick if I didn't know where Scott was... so I had to come tell you. I guess I made the right decision." Beth handed me a piece of paper with a phone number on it.

I shared what I knew with Tina and she prayed with me. Surely, God would let me go after her now! I had to find out where Jaime called from in Florida. My heart pounded while I dialed the number. The phone rang repeatedly. Disappointment set in and I finally hung up. I decided to call the operator and found out it was a number for a pay phone located in Pensacola. She couldn't give me an exact location. I heard the still small voice reassure me: *She will be OK.* Hope sprang up in my heart because I knew there was a reason God had allowed me to know where Jaime was right now.

I decided to call a non-profit group that specialized in runaway teens and ask for their advice. A wonderful, compassionate counselor answered the phone. He listened while I poured out my story, telling him everything we had been through with Jaime.

He explained, "The worst thing you can do is drag her back home. She will most likely run away again. The best thing you can do is convince her to come home on her own, so she can be legally emancipated through the courts. She will then be seen as an adult. This will protect you from her actions; anything she does can't be held against you. Then she will be free to live the way she chooses." That was not the advice I expected, but I was anxious to learn anything I could that might help. But I sure wasn't going to find her and bring her back home just to have her emancipated, so she could live somewhere else! Little did I know how useful this bit of information would prove to be, in the near future.

It was late afternoon and I needed to start on dinner. My thoughts turned to loving the ones that were still with us. I now knew how fleeting these precious moments could be. All the hugs and kisses I couldn't give Jaime, I showered on Samantha, Daniel and Chris. Chris, intrigued by the day's events, encouraged me. "Keep the faith, sweetheart. She's coming home."

"Prayer is not asking. Prayer is putting oneself
in the hands of God,
at His disposition and listening to His voice
in the depth of our hearts."

~ Mother Teresa

CHAPTER 32

Summer had barely started but the days had been unusually warm, and the sun was bright that morning when I got up to pray at the crack of dawn. I knew there was a reason God had allowed me to know where Jaime was, but I wasn't sure what He wanted me to do with the information. I'd promised to take Daniel and Kerry to the pool and was starting to regret making that promise because I wanted to pray all day for answers, but I also wanted to make the summer as normal as possible for Daniel. I shoved my building anger over Jaime's behavior the last several weeks down deep in my subconscious, so I could cope with daily life. The red-hot molten lava was just under the surface waiting to blow, but this lava had no escape route. The path had a "Closed" sign on it. With all the praying I had done, I fooled myself into believing I wasn't angry with Jaime. After all I was distraught about her being gone, so why would I be angry? And I couldn't lose it now. I had to keep it together for everyone else's sake.

After fixing breakfast I went over to discuss the day's plan with Kerry's mom. The pool wouldn't be open for another hour, so I went back upstairs to pray for a little while longer before we had to leave.

I had just settled my thoughts and started to meditate on the scripture, "Be still and know I am God" when I felt a strong impression, an urgency that I had never felt before. The word *"GO"* immediately came into my mind and then it kept repeating *"GO!"* each time with greater intensity. God was telling me to *"GO...FIND HER...NOW."*

I asked, "Where exactly is she? I don't have an address. How am I going to find her?" The only response was *"GO"* even more strongly.

"Am I hearing You correctly, Lord?" I asked.

The urgency increased: ***"GO"***

"OK, I will go, but You have to lead me right to her!"

Fear gripped me, and I had a vision of stepping over bodies passed out in a back alleyway. I would lift each person's head to peer into their eyes to see if one of them was Jaime. As this movie played in my mind, the dreaded thought echoed again and again: *How in the world will I ever find her?*

I called Jenny's mother, Ann, and blurted out, "Jaime and the girls are in the Pensacola area. I am going to Florida to find them. Do you want to go with me?"

"No, I don't feel like I need to go," she calmly conveyed. "But please let me know if we can help in any way. I hope you find them."

"I will call you back when I know my plans," I assured, and then hung up the phone.

I couldn't believe Ann didn't want to come with me and try to find Jenny. It just didn't make any sense. I was wondering how I could get to Pensacola when I remembered my twin cousins on my dad's side were travel agents in Tampa. My cousins, Mark and Matt, grew up in New York State, they were hilarious and easy going. Every summer we'd visit my aunt and uncle's lake house in Michigan. We had so much fun with Mark and Matt who always made life one big adventure. Diane and me. Mark and Matt. Heads always turned to see two sets of identical twins canoeing in the creek and swimming in the lake!

I looked up their number and called.

A cheery voice said, "Hello, Sunshine Travel."

"Hi. This is Denise. Is this Matt or Mark? I can never tell you guys apart on the phone!" I confessed.

In his fast-talking New York accent, he replied, "Well, hi, Denise! This is Mark. So good to hear from you!"

"Hi, Mark. Unfortunately, I'm not calling to catch up or plan that trip we had talked about. I'm calling because I really need your help. Jaime has run away from drug rehab! We're pretty sure she's in Pensacola. I need to get down there as soon as possible to find her, but I don't know how long it will actually take to find her. I guess I need a one-way plane ticket to Pensacola. Can you book one for me?" I blurted out.

"You must be so worried. Sure. No problem. Let me look up the flights while I have you on the line. Um. . . Looks like you can save a little money by flying out of Granite City into Pensacola. It's an early flight tomorrow at 6:00 a.m. Does that work?"

"I will make it work. Book it! Now I just have to get over the fear of searching back alleys to find her. I know Pensacola is several hours from Tampa, but would you be willing to come help me find Jaime?" I pleaded.

"Sure. Anything for a cousin of mine, even if it leads us into dark, dangerous areas!" he joked.

We lived over an hour away from Granite City, and I had no idea how I would make it to the airport at that hour of the morning. I felt sick to my stomach. I had never traveled alone, and I had no plan! This was the most daring, maybe the craziest thing I had ever done.

"Daniel, get your swimsuit on," I called from downstairs. "I have one more call to make and then we'll leave for the pool."

Ann and her family lived in Granite City. I'd never been to their home, but I thought she'd mentioned that they weren't far from the airport. I called her again.

"Hi, Ann. It's Denise again. I booked a flight from Granite City to Florida. It leaves at 6 in the morning. Could I spend the night with you, so I don't miss the flight because of morning traffic?"

"Sure. Bill can take you to the airport. He goes that way for work each morning," she offered. Then she quickly added, "But please don't get here before 8 tonight. There are some things I need to get done."

"OK. Thank you so much! I really appreciate this!" Ann gave me her address and we hung up.

I thought it was odd that she was so specific about the time, but I didn't question it. I was just grateful that fighting the morning rush would not be an issue. I still needed to apprise Chris of my plans. And I wasn't sure how he'd react when I told him that evening that he had to take me to Granite City. *He's going to think I've lost my mind! I can't blame him. Maybe I have? I hope I really heard from God or this was going to be an expensive mistake!*

We left for the pool and the boys played "I Spy" in the backseat, teasing each other, "I spy something red."

"Is it a tree?" the other would joke. Then they would both burst out in laughter.

I tuned out their antics and prayed, "*God, You have to lead me right to her. I can't find her on my own. You've got to make Chris OK with this crazy trip. If he gets upset about it, I can't go. I hope I heard You right! Why now? Why wouldn't you let me go find her when they were in Granite City? Finding her then would have been a piece of cake!* This turbulent whirlpool of thoughts swirled through my mind.

Then all at once I felt warm honey. It started to flow down over my head and gave me peace. I once again heard the word, *"GO"* and felt a deep urgency that commanded me to act.

I begged for more details but started to get the picture. The Holy Spirit had given me all the details I needed and now I had to walk by faith, not by sight. At the pool, I laid in the sun and tried to distract my mind and relax, to no avail. My mind raced to all the unanswered questions. I am a planner. And not having a real plan put me way out of my comfort zone. I hated it. So many questions: *What should I pack? What would I need? Where will I stay?* I couldn't figure out the answers because the bottom line was I didn't know how long I'd be gone! In fact, I didn't know much of anything!

All I did know was I couldn't get to Ann's house before 8:00, my flight left at 6:00 a.m. and my cousins had agreed to meet me in Pensacola to help me search for Jaime. I flung a wave in the air and smiled at the boys as they did cannonballs into the deep end of the pool. I was glad the other moms sitting beside me couldn't read my thoughts!

The pressure from the Holy Spirit didn't let up and the feeling became even more intense. The word *"GO"* nagged at me over and over again. By now I was determined to *"GO"* no matter what Chris said because the feeling became so intense. It felt like I was about to give birth and had to push. You know, when you're ready to push that baby out, you're ready to push and no doctor better tell you to stop! You have no other choice, if you want relief, but to push!

I pretended I was asleep while I sunbathed, but I couldn't relax and decided to give up trying. I asked the boys if they were ready to leave and enticed them with a stop for ice cream on the way home. The bribe worked. They jumped up, grabbed their towels, and raced to the car.

I went to my closet and pictured every scenario I could imagine, trying to figure out what to pack. I knew I only wanted to take a small bag, so I didn't have to haul around a huge suitcase. I was putting a few things in my tote when Samantha came around the corner in her PJs, yawning. She had just gotten back from one of her Mexico mission trips and needed sleep to recover from jet lag and the long trip. She was so soft-hearted when she returned from this trip after seeing people worship in a church with a dirt floor and cardboard walls. Yet the people she met there were so grateful for what they had, and they praised God with a passion Samantha had never seen during worship. Samantha's inner beauty rivaled her outer beauty, and I was proud she was my daughter!

She eyed me with suspicion and said, "Let me guess. You are taking a trip to Tahiti, never to return, flying the coop, right? Can't blame you... but you gotta take me or I'm telling Chris!"

My eyes welled up. "Don't I wish. Actually, I am flying to Florida to get your sister!" I announced.

I didn't believe my own words. It all started to sink in: *I am about to board a plane all by myself and only God knows where I will stay when I get there and how many days it will take to find Jaime.* The thought frightened me.

Samantha, now fourteen, lifted her eyebrows in surprise when I told her the rest of the details. "Well, Mom," she said in a casual tone, "If God directs you --and it sounds like He is-- it will go fine."

That was my girl. She could be very matter-of-fact while encouraging you when it came to the things of God. When Sam decided mission work, was the area of ministry she was interested in, she simply trusted that God would make it possible. She spoke in faith and it happened for her. Sam had developed a very special and sweet relationship with God; she trusted Him in ways I was still learning. Yes, Sam was my special gift from God.

"Sam, please pray that Chris takes the news of my trip well."

"I just heard him come in the front door, so I will have to pray while you are telling him about your plan," she said with a mischievous smile. She winked at me and turned to leave, passing Chris as she went down the hall.

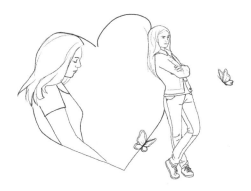

"God is bigger than all your problems,
if you believe."

CHAPTER 33

"What does Sam know that I don't know?" Chris questioned when he came through the bedroom door. "She winked and smiled at me when she passed me a moment ago." He looked into my eyes. "What's up? You look like you are about to skydive into a lightning storm without a parachute!" he teased.

"God has been telling me all day to *"GO"* get Jaime. I called my cousin Mark and he wants to help me find her and he booked a 6 a.m. flight out of Granite City for me to Pensacola, Florida. I told Mark I would call him after my plane landed and I figured out what I needed to do next. I know this sounds crazy, but I must go find Jaime. I called Ann. She said I could stay with them tonight, and Bill will take me to the airport tomorrow morning. For some strange reason, they don't want us to get to their house before 8 tonight," I unloaded without taking a breath.

"Hmmm. Wow... well... umm, OK. That's a lot to absorb. You know I'm nervous about you traveling alone. But I trust the God in you, and if you feel that strongly that He's telling you to go, then you need to go. I'm OK with that. I'm just glad Mark will be there for you. That makes me feel better."

Chris can wear a hole in the carpet when he's worried about something. I looked in his eyes and they told me he really was OK. I knew God had answered my prayer. We decided to eat dinner on the way over to Granite City to kill some time. He loved to go out to eat, and I did not mind the diversion.

By the time we got to the Murphy home, I felt like I was on a date, going to visit old friends rather than a mission to rescue my wayward daughter. It had been fun to spend time with Ann and Bill on Friday nights before the rehab meetings, so I was glad to see them. The men went into the kitchen, and Ann showed me around the first floor. I was impressed by the contemporary and unique design of the house. I almost forgot why we were there and had started to relax as we laughed and reminisced about THT Country. Twenty minutes later the phone rang.

Ann picked up the receiver and I noticed a look of surprise cross her face. "Yes, I'm Ann Murphy," she said. The guys continued to talk, but I wondered what the call was about.

"One of the parents is right here, can you hold on?" She removed the phone from her ear and whispered to me. "The girls have been arrested and they're in jail. Jaime is in the Juvenile Detention Center in Pensacola. Jenny and Missy are in Ft. Walton in the adult jail." Ann handed me the phone. "The officer wants to talk to you."

I was dumbfounded and couldn't believe what I was hearing.

"Hello," I said.

"This is Sergeant McKinney with the Pensacola Police Department. Which one is your daughter?" he asked in a monotone voice.

"Jaime Boese," I mumbled in disbelief.

"She is in our custody at the Juvenile Detention Center. She was not involved in the crime the others have committed, so she is not being charged with anything. We held her because the Murphy girl said she was a runaway. Since she is a juvenile, we can't hold her any longer than twenty-four hours. She will be released to a homeless shelter at 8 tomorrow morning," he explained.

Momma Bear rose up, "NO! She will run again! Don't you dare release her! I have a 6 a.m. flight that gets into Pensacola at 8!" Then I emphasized the words, "YOU WILL NEED TO KEEP HER UNTIL I GET TO THE JUVENILE DETENTION CENTER!" I spelled out.

There was silence on the other end of the phone while Ann, Chris, and Bill stared at me in bewilderment. "How in the world.... did you...know where she was? And that you needed a plane ticket to get here by 8 in the morning?" Sergeant McKinney stammered.

"I only found out yesterday that Jaime was in the Pensacola area after she called from a pay phone. God impressed upon me that now was the time to find her, so I got the plane ticket!" I confessed.

Sergeant McKinney's voice cracked, "I promise, we will not release her...until you get here tomorrow. Can you put Mrs. Murphy back on the phone?"

When Ann got off the phone, she relayed the rest of the story. The girls had been staying in a one-bedroom apartment with six other people doing drugs. Missy and King, a drug dealing thug from New York, had walked by a restaurant and decided to steal a car. They took the car back to the apartment and picked up Jaime, Jenny and King's pregnant sister. They were all high and had been joyriding for a while when the police spotted them in the stolen car and chased them. To get away from the police, they drove 90 miles an hour, jumped curbs, drove on sidewalks and ran red lights. The police finally set up barricades to try and stop them. They eluded the police by busting through two of those barricades, then left the car behind an abandoned building.

Missy and King had talked the whole group into leaving for New York a few days after the chase, so they wouldn't be caught.

Fortunately, the police found the car and five eyewitnesses came forward and gave details of the horrific ordeal. The police found the apartment they were staying in and arrested them the day they'd planned to leave for New York! Now Jenny and Missy would be in jail for a month or so until they could have a court hearing and be released.

God had protected them. They all could have died! The puzzle pieces had fallen into place. It now made sense why the other moms didn't feel led to come to Florida with me to look for their daughters! I thanked God continually that they were alive and OK. I was relieved that Jaime wasn't being charged so she could come home. I didn't want to know any more details. I just wanted my daughter back.

It was all part of God's timing and His plan; finding out Jaime was in Pensacola the day before, the 6:00 a.m. flight I had booked for the next morning, the fact that we couldn't get to the Murphy's until 8:00, then the call from the officer twenty minutes after we arrived. God led me right to her! This was His miracle for my family. No one could deny that! I had gone from feeling like I was about to step off a cliff and plunge into an unknown abyss to soaring like an eagle into the brilliant blue sky! I could see the relief on Chris' face knowing that I wouldn't have to search back alleyways to find Jaime. He reminded me how worried my mom had been when I called her earlier that day to tell her I was flying down to Florida.

"You may want to give her a call," he suggested. He gave me a kiss and walked out the door as I tried to explain all the details of this miracle to my mom. It was too late to call Mark and tell him the good news. I would call him once I was at the detention center in the morning.

I was exhausted from all the excitement and asked Ann to show me where I would be sleeping. I thanked God for providing everything I needed to get Jaime back and started to drift off to sleep when I remembered I was flying by myself the next morning. *"I need one more thing Lord. Could You sit me next to a woman who is friendly on the plane, so I won't feel alone?"* I drifted off in peace and with the assurance MY GOD was with me, and He would get me through the rest of this journey.

Morning came swiftly, and the alarm woke me out of a sound sleep. I rolled over and tried to get my bearings. When I remembered where I was, I bolted out of bed. I could not be late for this flight. I was grateful that I was a morning person; this morning would demand all the energy I had.

I came down the stairs and almost ran into Ann. "Good morning. I can't thank you enough for letting me stay here and for the ride to the airport."

She smiled and replied, "Of course. It's the least we can do! I am so happy that you were here when we got the call from the police officer! I have thought about the timing of things all night and I am just amazed!"

"I am blown away by it too! It is a miracle. The Lord has led me and reassured me the whole time Jaime has been gone. I am so sorry you can't go and get Jenny yet. You must be heartbroken," I gasped.

"I'm just relieved that they were found and are safe. Sitting in jail right now for Jenny is the best thing that could have happened because it will give her time to reflect on her actions and the kind of future she wants," Ann said.

"You have such a great attitude! I'm glad we have gotten to know each other, and you know I will be praying for Jenny." I gave her a hug and got into the car.

The drive to the airport was a quiet one. I silently continued to thank God for this overwhelming display of His love. Bill pulled up to the Delta terminal. I thanked him for everything, grabbed my bag off the backseat and jumped out of the car. When I saw the crowded terminal, my breathing increased, my pulse quickened. I scanned the signs and found the right airline counter. When I got my ticket and found the gate in record time, my anxiety subsided. A cup of coffee hit the spot while I entertained myself by people watching. This worked to distract me from the real mission I was on. I boarded the plane 45 minutes later and found my seat. Then a well-dressed woman sat down next to me.

Smiling, she extended her hand, "I'm Tia Wright. I can't wait to see my family in Pensacola. Why are you traveling there?"

Ugh, that was the last question I want to be asked! I can't end up in a puddle of tears on a crowded airplane with no escape.

"To enjoy the weather," I lied.

"So, what do you do to stay busy?" she inquired.

I should be honest and say I play detective, hunting down my rebellious daughter in my spare time!

"I am a Mary Kay consultant."

"Really? Well, we have a lot in common then. I'm one also!" she crowed. "I've got to tell you about the weirdest experience I had with a client. She demanded that her dog be allowed to experience the facial with her. She felt this would be the only way to know if the products truly worked! I agreed to do it because I needed one more sale to receive the weekly Queen of Sales award. I stood back as the woman lifted the tiny five-pound dog onto the table, thinking it had to be a joke. I just knew the man from Candid Camera would pop up any minute! You should have seen that pooch. Its face became contorted as the dog tried over and over to lick the product off with his long tongue."

We both laughed until it hurt and exclaimed at the same time, "It's a good thing the face scrub is edible!" We were giggling so hard the people in front of us turned around and gawked.

We took the hint and settled down. Tia turned the conversation toward family and shared about her children. Her expression then turned serious as she shared about her son.

"I don't usually talk about him with strangers. I feel like I'm supposed to tell you this, but I don't know why. My sixteen-year-old son, Rob, was so excited about his driving lesson that Friday, but I was concerned. It had been snowing all day and the road conditions were bad. I told the instructor I didn't think they should go out for a lesson. He knew how excited my son was and thought they would be fine driving in the neighborhood. So, I let my son go with him. As they rounded a corner near our house, a snow plow slid out of control and ran over them, instantly killing my son," she explained.

I sat there stupefied and silent, tears streaming down my cheeks. I could not breathe from the huge throbbing lump in my throat. *I never articulated it to anyone, too ashamed to admit it. But there had been so many times I'd wished Jaime would just die to put an end to our family's misery! How could I have ever had that awful thought?*

"I'm going to Florida to get my daughter out of jail. She ran away from a drug rehab. She has been doing drugs and getting into a lot of trouble. There were so many times...I wished she would just die because it has been so painful to watch what she is doing to herself and to our family," I croaked out.

Tia put her arm around me and said, "I would give anything to have just one more second with my son."

I sobbed. I could feel everyone around us staring at me, witnessing this very public meltdown. I felt like a fool, but it felt good to finally admit those hidden, and horrendous, thoughts. Once my weeping subsided and the pain was released, I felt peace. Tia prayed with me and I felt God's presence, which helped me regain my composure before the plane landed. I gave Tia a hug and thanked her again for sharing her story with me.

As I walked down the terminal, my prayer from the night before flashed through my mind. Tia was the answer to that prayer. God had put her there! Later that morning I would truly understand why I needed to hear Tia's story.

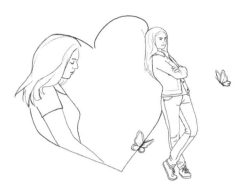

"Commit everything to the Lord,
Trust Him and He will help you."

~ Psalm 37:5 NLT

CHAPTER 34

The reality of it all hit me, when I saw the Hertz sign across the parking lot. I'd never rented a car before, I didn't know how to get to the detention center and I had no way to get us home. Since I hadn't known where she was or how long it would take to find her, I thought I'd only needed a one-way plane ticket. Now, I had a lot to figure out.

I decided that once I got to the detention center I could ask to use a phone to call my cousin. He would help me figure out how to get home with Jaime. A warm breeze ruffled my hair and the sun hit my back as I strode across the parking lot. How I wished I was here on a summer vacation with the whole family to enjoy the beach! *Would that ever happen? Could we ever be a family again?* It was too much to contemplate, so I forced that thought away and

I walked up to the Hertz counter. I told them I needed a compact car for the day.

"How long will you need the car?" the agent asked.

"I am not sure. If I can't bring it back to this location, can I drop it off at one of your other locations?"

"Sure, we have drop off points throughout the area and at the Ft. Walton airport," he explained.

"Good. That will make it easy to get the car back to you. Could you give me a map and directions to get to the *Pensacola Juvenile Detention Center*?" I whispered.

My hands were shaking when I pulled out of the parking lot in the shiny red Mazda. I drove slowly to make sure I didn't miss any turns. I thought I was on the right road but couldn't find the detention center. I pulled over, looked at the map and became frustrated. But I reminded myself that God had already led me to her. When I looked up, I saw a sign *Pensacola Juvenile Detention Center* and smiled. I took a deep breath, found a parking spot and I got out of the car as excitement started to bubble up from some deep place within me. I just wanted to grab Jaime and give her a hug, then plant kisses all over her face to show her how much I loved her! I knew she would be glad to see me!

I approached the woman behind the glass at the counter. "I am Denise Fromm. I have come from Missouri to get Jaime Boese," I stuttered. "Oh, but before you bring her out, may I use your phone? You see, I have to figure out how we're getting home."

I thanked the confused female officer as she led me into a room with a table and a phone. "Hi, Mark," I said when my cousin answered. "Good news! You won't need to help me find Jaime! It's a long story I will have to fill you in on the details later. She's at the juvenile detention center in Pensacola. Now I need your help to figure out how we can get home without spending a fortune!" I grumbled.

"That's great news! You could take a bus home; it's the cheapest but it would take twenty-four hours to get back to St. Louis," he admitted.

"That won't work. I'm afraid Jaime might try to run away again. A bus is out of the question."

The conversation I'd had two days earlier with the counselor that specialized in teen runaways surfaced in my thoughts. *Does she even want to come home? I shouldn't force her. He'd said she had to want to come home.* Either way, I had to have a plan before they brought Jaime out or neither of us would have anywhere to go.

"I found airfare at a reasonable price flying out of Ft. Walton at 8 tonight into St. Louis. Will that work?" Mark asked.

"It will have to. Go ahead and book it. I would have liked a sooner flight, but if that's the cheapest it will do! Thank you so much for all your help."

All I could do was pray that she would not run away from me and that she was ready to come home. I called Chris to fill him in and told him when our flight would arrive in St. Louis.

At the end of the conversation he said, "Denise?"

"Yes?"

He paused for dramatic effect, "I love you."

"I love you, too!"

I waved at the officer and told her I was ready for Jaime to come out. A few minutes later I saw a figure breeze past me that I didn't recognize. I did a double take. I thought they had brought out the wrong girl, but when I looked into her eyes I knew it was my Jaime! My elation burst. She had very heavy makeup on, her hair was dirty and matted and she wore cut off shorts and a halter top. My Jaime didn't dress like that! She had lost at least 30 pounds. I had never seen her so gaunt!

My heart sank as I looked at her. No smile. No hug. No "I missed you" while she ran into my arms. She just sat across from me and rummaged through a big envelope that contained her things. Thoughts gnawed at me, hissing: *"You should just leave her here... she deserves it...look how she's treated you... after all you've done... your family's better off without her."* My rage boiled over and I was about to act on the feelings that bombarded me.

Then, in an instant, I realized who I was being tempted by to act on those feelings—the enemy! It would feel good to get up, walk right out and leave her here! Who would blame me? But my heart swelled and my deep love for her rose to the surface. *I love you too much to leave you here.*

As I stared at her sunken face, I now knew why God wanted me to hear Tia's story about the death of her son. My anger had been building for weeks over her deceit and trickery, and I hadn't even recognized it. But God knew it was there and broke its hold over me on that plane!

It seemed like hours had passed before Jaime said, "Ok, I'm ready to go."

"Do you have any other clothing with you?" I asked.

"No," she snapped.

Dread rolled through the pit of my stomach; this was not going to be easy. We walked to the car in silence. I opened the car door and a scorching blast of air hit my face. The inside of the car was a furnace. Jaime got in and stared straight ahead. I took a deep breath and started the engine. I thought I should explain the travel plan to get home but decided better of it. We had eight hours to kill and that information could wait. At this point, I had no idea if she even wanted to come home. She was still high on something. Maybe if I got some food in her, she would sober up, open up and talk. Then I glanced at her sideways. That outfit. *I can't take her on a plane dressed like that!*

"How about we go to the nearest mall and get some food and new clothes?" I suggested.

"OK."

OK. A one-word answer was better than none. Lord, fill me with your love for her!

I found a mall close by. We went into a store for teens and she started to try on jeans. I felt like I was rewarding her for running away.

Then the still small voice would whisper, *"She's still high and you don't know what she's been through."*

"Yes, You're right. But I know why she's doing the drugs. She will not deal with the pain from the abuse." That was always the bottom line. She was her own worst enemy, and the fact that she was stubborn didn't help matters. I had no answers left.

She found some very nice jeans and a top that looked like a style she would normally pick out, so I wasn't about to complain about the price. I paid the ransom the store required so we could leave. We went to a little coffee shop next door. Hopefully, a strong cup of coffee would sober her up. It was only eleven in the morning and she was still not talking to me. I didn't know how we were going to spend the next nine hours! I sipped my coffee and I asked the Holy Spirit for guidance. I heard, *"Talk about emancipating her."*

That took me by surprise and I shot back, *"What? You've got to be kidding me! I want her to come home, not be encouraged to stay here!"*

"Remember you don't want to drag her home; it needs to be her idea. You are just giving her a reason to go home," the Holy Spirit nudged.

I was beginning to understand. The information from the counselor couldn't have been a coincidence. God knew I would have blown it by now.

"Jaime, I found out some information while you were gone that I would like to share with you. But first I have some questions to ask you. Is that OK?"

She nodded her head and I continued. "It is clear you were unhappy at the rehab, so I will not take you back there. I need to know if you want to come back home?"

She looked puzzled, probably because she expected me to let her have it.

"Well, I really want to stay here. The people I stayed with are my family now. They took care of me and we did everything together."

I took a deep breath, so I would not respond the wrong way. I pretended to play along while I hid my feelings. "Well, I can understand how you feel, which is why I wanted to share some information I have found out. If you come back home with me now, you can be emancipated by the court, and then you can come back here to live, if that's what you really want," I assured her.

My stomach flip-flopped, and I was sure I would throw up. *I can't believe she wants to live with a brunch of druggies!* Then I added, "Do you know what that means and why you need to be emancipated?"

She just shook her head. I started to question whether she would even remember this conversation.

"Emancipated means that legally you are free to be on your own, even though you're underage, and then you can live anywhere you want. Right now, if I left you here, we would be in legal trouble for not taking care of you."

Jaime looked up from her cup of coffee and smiled. I had her attention now. She bought what I just sold her, and I could see the wheels spinning fast. It gave her a way to save face and a reason to come home! Inside a smile spread across my face. *You are good, Holy Spirit! You are good!!*

"Are you hungry?"

"Yes! I haven't eaten since yesterday morning," she lamented.

"Well, why didn't you tell me?"

I held back tears. She must be so hungry! I suggested we walk down the mall to the food court.

A few minutes later she said, "I don't eat much anymore."

That's obvious. If a strong wind came along you would be gone, swept out to sea!

We found a McDonald's at the end of the mall. I watched her pick over her hamburger and fries. Then we walked around a bit. Little by little, Jaime began to open up and share some of the things she had been through. Normally, I would have loved a day out with Jaime, but this day was surreal. We still had a flight to catch and the future that waited for us at home was unpredictable.

I decided we had better leave early for the Ft. Walton airport. It would take us at least 30 minutes, maybe longer with traffic, to get there from the Bayside Mall. I was sure Jaime would want some coffee before we got on the plane. A torrential downpour began the moment we left the mall, and I was glad we had plenty of time to spare. The monsoon created massive puddles that sent water spraying everywhere as we drove through the parking lot. We were drenched by the time we ran into the terminal. We decided to go upstairs for an hour while we waited to board the plane.

We sat down, and Jaime started to tell me more details of her time away--the drugs they'd done, and the trouble they'd gotten into. As she talked, a man sitting catty-corner from us caught my attention. He was sipping coffee and reading a newspaper. He had salt and pepper hair, and he was wearing a plaid shirt and jeans. He seemed to appear out of nowhere and continued to glance sideways at us. He was eavesdropping, listening intently to every word Jaime spoke.

I felt a cloud of serenity envelop me when he leaned over.

"I overheard your conversation," he said softly, "and feel I have to tell you about my daughter. She lived the life you have described – drugs, trouble with the law, you name it. Now she has three children without marrying any of their fathers. She struggles to take care of her children and must live off welfare. At one point we thought they were going to take her children from her. It breaks her mother's heart to see how she lives now. It didn't have to be this way for her. I wished she had thought more about her choices, valued herself and her future when she was young. She has a hard life. You seem like a smart young lady, and it's obvious how much your mother loves you. Please think about your choices before it is too late," he urged.

Jaime just listened and didn't respond. I was amazed that a complete stranger would share such intimate details and I hoped Jaime would take it to heart. I watched as he went down the escalator into the crowd below, then vanished into thin air. It seemed odd how he had just appeared and now had vanished. I couldn't help but think he was an angel sent to warn Jaime about her future.

We boarded the plane to St. Louis and slept most of the way home. Wearily, we trudged through the passenger boarding bridge into the terminal. Chris stood waiting for us at the gate. He smiled when he saw Jaime, grabbed her up in his arms and gave her a bear hug.

"I sure missed you!" he said. Then he loosened his grip, drew me in for a group hug and kissed me on the cheek. Jaime didn't say much on the way home from the airport. And I decided I'd just give her time.

Sam had stayed home with Daniel because it was such a late flight. The twenty-four-hour expedition had exhausted me and all I could think about, as I walked into the house, was diving into bed. On the stairs I overheard Jaime's voice, so full of love.

"Sam, I missed you so much!" she said to her sister. "I wasn't sure I would ever see you again!"

Standing in the hall I peeked into Sam's room and saw her bolt upright out of bed and hug Jaime like she would never let her go. She pelted her with questions. "What happened? Who did you stay with? How did Mom find you?"

Jaime responded sweetly, "Too much happened to tell you now. I just wanted to say I love you and missed you."

They hugged again, then Jaime stood up. I scrambled to get down the hallway, so I didn't ruin their tender moment. Jaime was my funny, delightful, sweet child who changed drastically after she turned three. This exchange showed me sweet Jaime was still there, deep inside. I hoped someday she would feel safe enough to express her "true" self once again. My dream for her is to be full of the joy and peace that only comes through growing in her relationship with Jesus. I want to see her truly restored to that precious three-year-old girl in my memories. She was so full of life and love, before the abuse stole it all from her.

The next morning started like any other day. I fixed breakfast for the kids, and they sat at the table enjoying it while I put away the dishes. Daniel got up from the table and gave Jaime a hug--the third one of the morning. It warmed my heart.

Then he asked, "Can I go to the fort?"

"Sure honey," I answered. Daniel eyed Jaime. "She will be here when you get back. I promise!"

Samantha smiled at him, then reached over and grabbed Jaime's hand. "Glad you're home!" she smiled as she got up and headed upstairs.

I put the plate in my hand down on the counter and walked over behind Jaime and wrapped my arms around her. "I am so thankful God brought you safely back to us."

She turned around and looked into my face with her clear blue eyes. "What do you mean? What did God have to do with me coming home? The police called you and you came and got me."

I came around the table and sat across from Jaime. "Every day I prayed for your safety and for you to come home to us," I paused. *There was no way to explain every detail to her, I hadn't even processed it all yet.*

"God told me to "**Go**" find you in Pensacola, so I got a plane ticket for a 6 a.m. flight the next morning. When the officer called to tell us you were in the detention center and said you were going to be released at 8 the next morning, I told them they couldn't release you. They only kept you because I had that plane ticket."

Her eyes grew wide and she leaned towards me. "Mom, that would have been awful! I didn't know anyone. I would have been all alone with no money or anything."

"I know...God loves you so much, He gave us a miracle!" I reached across the table and grabbed her hand.

She was silent, digesting the information. Then she said, "I'm glad I'm home."

"You have a bright future ahead of you. We are going to the high school tomorrow to find out how far behind you are and get you enrolled. It will all work out. This will be a brand-new start."

"That sounds good, Mom. Thanks. And I don't want to do that emancipated thing you told me about."

I laughed, "Good! A special someone reminded me to fill you in on your options, but I was hoping you would say that!"

No point in trying to explain that detail right now.

She gave me a hug and went upstairs to find Samantha.

Chris came in from cleaning the garage. He gave me a suspicious look and asked, "So how are you doing after your excursion yesterday?"

I stopped wiping down the kitchen counter and looked at him.

How am I feeling?

That question opened the floodgates. I fell into Chris' arms and the tears flowed, tears of relief and tears of joy, all mixed together. Joy bubbled up from deep inside, an unspeakable joy that assured me of God's love and presence. Never again would I doubt what God could do. My heart swelled with love for Him. Chris' comforting embrace dispelled any fear the uncertain future held.

Fear was replaced by a new-found confidence. God heard me, protected Jaime and answered my prayers. God had proven Himself so profoundly at every turn, and now I knew God was the only one that could keep Jaime safe from her own choices.

Would she heed the words from the angel in the airport? Or would she could continue to make devasting decisions?

God would walk beside Jaime no matter what direction her life took, and I had learned to love her unconditionally, the way God loved me. Fear had ruled my life long enough. Now fear was six feet under. The next time fear reared its ugly head; I would remind fear who my Father is, and I'd remind fear of the power my Father has given me, because of who He is!

His whispered truth was what I held on to. It was all I could trust, and for the rest of the journey ahead, it would be my most valued treasure.

Whispered Truth Epilogue

Years later I found out it had been Jaime's idea to run away to Florida, she felt hopeless about not being able to complete the rehab program. She wanted to stay with us and go back to school so there was no need to have her emancipation. I wish I could tell you she had a lovely time at her prom, graduated and went off to college. But that wasn't the story we lived. Months later she went to live with a friend, never finished school and floundered without direction. Jaime went back to using drugs and had two children. With each pregnancy she would start to get her life back together and my hopes would soar. I yearned for our relationship to be restored and it would seem to be right around the corner, so close, within reach. But every time the cold, hard reality from her choices would shatter my hopes.

I kept praying and waiting, praying and waiting for the real Jaime to come back into our lives. It took seventeen years for those prayers to be answered. So never, never, ever give up on your children. When she was thirty, Jaime was arrested for having drug paraphernalia in her car. Halleluiah! I passionately prayed that God would have His way in her life and no matter what it took, she would finally get the help she needed.

After three weeks in the county jail, Jaime was about to be released, because of overcrowding until her court date. I frantically prayed God would keep her there. She was safe in jail and off drugs. Due to State sanctioned Methadone Clinics, Jaime had traded one drug for another, using Methadone instead of Heroin. When she got arrested she had been addicted to Methadone for eight years. This 'legal' addiction sanctioned by the State, cost her hundreds of dollars a month and she didn't have a job!

At one-point my ten-year-old grandson told me, "My mom trades and sells drugs all the time." The reality was Jaime had weaned herself down to a lower dose of Methadone, so she could sell it and do crystal methamphetamine! I called the Methadone clinic to report her activity, trying to save her life because mixing Methadone and other drugs is a recipe for death. The counselor's response was, "Well we can't keep them from doing other drugs." I thought that was why they did drug testing at the clinic! Their clients knew how to 'work the system', the other drugs they consumed were undetectable in 24 to 48 hours. At that time, the statistics showed that 4,000 people died a year from Methadone use and only 1,800 died from Heroin use!

I felt her only chance to be free of the Methadone and to stay sober was to stay in jail. At the next court hearing they would give her the choice to go to rehab and avoid a criminal record or go to jail. I called my father-in-law in desperation and asked him to call his friend, the sheriff of our county. He agreed to call him, and I anxiously awaited by the phone, praying. Jaime was downstairs in a holding tank being processed for release when the deputies got the call from the sheriff telling them to take her back upstairs and hold her until the next court hearing. God answered my prayer!

That was the start of Jaime's new life. She spent two years in court appointed rehab and she's now been clean for seven years! She has a good job, a house, a car and is raising her third child. Yes, the angel in the Florida airport had indeed predicted what Jaime's future could be if she didn't make better choices and that future came to pass. But her third precious child has given her a second chance to be the wonderful mother I always knew she could be. Jaime radiates with joy every time she sees her children and she is grateful to be alive when so many of her friends have died from over doses. And the biggest miracle of all, the loving mother-daughter relationship I waited so long for, has now been restored!

I learned to love my daughter unconditionally; to love her enough to say no, to show her love when she hated me and treated me badly. Through Jaime, God taught me to love wounded hurting women, so I could accomplish His plan for my life as the founder and director of Living Hope Transitional Homes.

There are so many more God stories to be told, so many more times I've heard the whispered truth of God's voice leading me, but those stories will have to wait for another time. God passionately loves us and never leaves us, His miracles envelope our everyday lives. If we pay attention we will find them.

Acknowledgements

Thank you to Deborah Gaston, my editor, who put in countless hours weeding through the mess I e-mailed her while teaching me all over again what I had forgot from English class. You made my story better than I ever thought it could be!

Thank you to Alicia Redmond who created the beautiful cover for *Whispered Truth*. You are a true gift from God.

Thank you to my friends who were brave enough to read my work and give me feedback; Judy Short, Mary Ann Robbe, Mary Beth VonAllmen, Linda Seibel, Barb Steffens, Laurie and Van Cochrane, Diane Lodi, Judie Salyers and to Jane Herms, Director at the Family Nuturing Center.

Thank you to the Honorable Judge Robert Ruehlman for his professional advice and to his wife Tia who read many first drafts and encouraged me out of the 'give up' pit that I was tempted to climb in.

Thank you to the women who endorsed my work; Dianne Leman, Erin Campbell and Dr. Barbara Steffens.

Thank you for the support and endless prayers sent up from the Living Hope for Today prayer and Bible study groups.

Thank you to Kay Worz, an amazing artist who painted the background used on the cover and for the brilliant artwork she created for the headings in chapters 2-19.

Thank you to the gifted illustrator, Cami Bradford, who created the picture for chapter one. Cami also captured Jaime's teen attitude and recreated her junior high artwork, perfectly in her renderings for the headings in chapters 20 – 32.

Thank you to my dear friends and walking buddies, Cindy Lanning and Nancy Shockey, who are editors by trade. I am grateful to Nancy who spent hours proofreading and sending me corrections. They both answered my many, many questions, giving me valuable advice and encouragement, along the way.

Thank you to God for the prophetic words from Zakia McKinney and her team that made me really get to work and finish *Whispered Truth*!

Thank you to Jenn Utech who coached me over the finish line.

Thank you to Donna Amos at Solopreneur Solutions, for the wonderful job she did formatting the *Whispered Truth* manuscript.

Courage Sometimes Skips a Generation

Cindy L. Smith, in her own words

"Write about what disturbs you, particularly
if it bothers no one else."

— from *The Help* by Kathryn Stockett

These are words of advice given to Skeeter Phelan, a character in the novel *The Help*, as she pursues a career in writing. Skeeter courageously takes this advice and writes a book sharing the stories of African-American maids in her 1960s southern community.

One of my favorite lines in the movie, *The Help*, is "Courage sometimes skips a generation. Thank you for bringing it back to our family." Skeeter's mother, Charlotte, didn't have the courage to stand up to her club president when her maid's daughter unexpectedly showed up in the middle of their gathering. Charlotte fires the maid on the spot.

Courage slips from our grasp when we are influenced by our peers and their comfort becomes more important than speaking the truth. My mother's generation didn't dare speak up about such a horrific, uncomfortable topic as abuse, and she couldn't possibly face or fathom the devastation that was happening in our family. She lacked courage to confront my father about the abuse he allowed and perpetrated against my twin sister and me.

I fought paralyzing fear and gathered up an enormous amount of courage to write *Whispered Truth*. I had to write about what disturbed me, hoping my courage would become contagious and stand strong in my family and in other families for generations to come.

I am disturbed by child abuse. I am bothered that real solutions to stop it are not often talked about. I am bothered by the way our court system and child protective services handle the abuse of children. I am disturbed that so many who have been abused are not able to get the help they need to heal and live free of shame and fear.

It's the elephant in the room. Child abuse. No one, and I mean *no one,* wants to talk about this disgusting, obtrusive, enormous thing that is destroying our lives and the lives of our children. We can't talk about it because if we acknowledge that it happens, we have to deal with the shame. The shame that says it is our fault; the shame that tells us we are unlovable. We eat and drink to excess, do drugs, or a more socially acceptable thing, become shop-a-alcoholics to blissfully ignore the elephant in the room.

I fought acknowledging the heartache and pain of my own abuse for years, labeling it as something quite different from what happened to my own daughter. A fierce protectiveness rose up in me because no one had protected me from my abusive father. I was going to protect her if it was the last thing I did. When I couldn't, I had to forgive myself.

There is tremendous pain to work through to change the belief that shame brings. It whispers lies into your soul, hissing at you – *you are worthless or else you wouldn't have been viciously harmed as a child.* It took years of counseling and hours spent in deep prayer with the Lord for the chains of hatred, bitterness and unforgiveness to be broken off me so I could love myself and truly love others.

I spoke out for the first time in my thirties and shared with my husband the only concrete memory of abuse that haunted me since dealing with my daughter's abuse many years before. A funny thing happened. Once I shared about my abuse, the darkness the shame had caused didn't devour me or taunt me any longer. I slowly found my voice to speak the truth and allow God to heal me. Our voices need to be heard. We need to break the silence and tell our stories for all to hear. We need to speak up for ourselves and our children.

When I started to write down what God had done when my teenage daughter ran away, it flew out of my heart on to the page. Then I realized there was so much more God had done that needed to be captured. Those chapters were a struggle. I didn't want to go back down that lonely desert road and relive the nightmare of discovering her abuse, let alone the feelings it brought back. I mourned for my daughter's experiences in childhood that I couldn't change, but writing it revealed a wonderful thing: *I was still free!* Free from the hate that tempted me, free from the unforgiveness that once held me captive, free from the chains that controlled me! Free to share it with others that need freedom from the tight chains of unforgiveness their own abuse has bound them in.

Abuse is often generational in families. I pray you will be the one to bring courage back to this generation by breaking the silence to stop child abuse. Start talking to anyone who will listen about your experiences and the experiences of others and keeping talking so children can be protected. There is a confidential page on my website www.livinghopefortoday.org called "Break the Silence." If you want or need to tell your story for the first time, or maybe the hundredth time, I invite you to visit that page. Know that your voice will be confidentially heard. One thing I have learned, writing is healing.

You are loved. God loves you more than any child, parent or loved one could. He loves you unconditionally and wants to heal your heart from the wounds this world inflicts upon it. Numerous times while writing *Whispered Truth*, I broke down crying, overwhelmed with gratitude for His love and miracles in my life. I pray you, too, find a deep, personal intimate relationship with our Creator. He's waiting with open arms.

If you or someone you know needs help, please call the national phone numbers or visit websites listed below to find a local organization in your area.

Childhelp National Child Abuse Hotline	1-800-4-A-CHILD (422-4453)
Domestic Violence Hotline	1-800-799-SAFE (7233)
Substance Abuse & Mental Health www.samhsa.gov	1-800-662-HELP (4357)
National Runaway Safeline	1-800-RUNAWAY (786-2929)
www.1800runaway.org	
National Suicide Prevention Lifeline	1-800-273-8255

More than Statistics

My curiosity got the best of me when I was writing *Whispered Truth,* so I did some research to understand if things are as bad today in the court system and in child abuse cases as they were in the 1980s. Below are the sad statistics I found:

- **The United States has one of the worst records among industrialized nations** – losing on average between four and seven children every day to child abuse and neglect!
- 1 in 4 girls and 1 in 6 boys are sexually abused by the time they are 18 years old.
- 40 million adult Americans grew up living with domestic violence.
- Domestic violence can cause PTSD in children and the effects on their brain are similar to those experienced by combat veterans!!
- Those who grow up with domestic violence are 6 times more likely to commit suicide and 50% more likely to abuse drugs and alcohol.
- 85% of sexual abuse is perpetrated by someone within the child's social sphere--for example, a relative, a family friend, a teacher, youth worker, religious leader, and neighbor.
- 14% of men and 36% of women in prison in the United States were abused as children.

(The statistics above were reported from; Bureau of Justice Statistics, Department of Justice, U.S. Department of Health and Human Services, Child Help,

Sexual Assault of Young Children As Reported to Law Enforcement, by Howard Snyder, U.S. Department of Health and Human Services)

Research has consistently shown that false allegations of child sexual abuse by children are rare.

Jones and McGraw examined 576 consecutive referrals of child sexual abuse to the Denver Department of Social Services and categorized the reports as either reliable or fictitious. In only 1% of the total cases were children judged to have advanced a fictitious allegation.

(Jones, D. P. H., and J. M. McGraw. "Reliable and Fictitious Accounts of Sexual Abuse to Children" Journal of Interpersonal Violence, 2, 27-45, 1987)

In a more recent study, investigators reviewed case notes of all child sexual abuse reports to the Denver Department of Social Services over 12 months. Of the 551 cases reviewed, there were only 14 (2.5%) instances of erroneous concerns about abuse emanating from children. These consisted of three cases of allegations made in collusion with a parent, three cases where an innocent event was misinterpreted as sexual abuse and eight cases (1.5%) of false allegations of sexual abuse.

(Oates, R. K., D.P. Jones, D. Denson, A. Sirotnak, N. Gary, and R.D. Krugman. "Erroneous Concerns about Child Sexual Abuse." Child Abuse & Neglect: 24:149-57, 2000.)

Research has consistently shown that domestic violence is a major factor in child abuse cases.

A batterer who does file for custody will frequently win, as he has numerous advantages over his partner in custody litigation. These include, 1) his typical ability to afford better representation (often while simultaneously insisting that he has no money with which to pay child support), 2) his marked advantage over his victim in psychological testing, since she is the one who has been traumatized by the abuse, 3) his ability to manipulate custody evaluators to be sympathetic to him, and 4) his ability to manipulate and intimidate the children regarding their statements to the custody evaluator. (p. 5) Because of the effects of trauma, the victim of battering will often seem hostile, disjointed, and agitated, while the abuser appears friendly, articulate, and calm. Evaluators are thus tempted to conclude that the victim is the source of the problems in the relationship. (p. 6)

Bancroft, L. R. (1998). Understanding the batterer in custody and visitation disputes. http://www.thelizlibrary.org/liz/understanding-the-batterer-in-visitation-and-custody-isputes.pdf

"Custody litigation frequently becomes a vehicle whereby batterers attempt to extend or maintain their control and authority over the abused parents after separation... Be aware that many perpetrators of domestic violence are facile manipulators, presenting themselves as caring, cooperative parents and casting the abused parent as a diminished, conflict-inciting, impulsive or over-protective parent."

Goelman, D. M., Lehrman, F. L., & Valente, R. L. (Eds.). (1996). The impact of domestic violence on your legal practice: A lawyer's handbook. Washington D.C.: ABA Commission on Domestic Violence.

Erickson notes: "An adult can fire his/her attorney, but the child may be trapped in a relationship with a law guardian who does not represent the child, and the child's voice may never be heard." I have been involved in cases where I had reason to believe that the law guardian was not doing his/her job or was actively attempting to gain judicial approval for a course of action that would be harmful to the law guardian's client. In some cases, the law guardian communicated with the child so infrequently that it would have been impossible for the law guardian to be familiar enough with the case to be able to represent the child at all. **For example, in**

**one case I am familiar with, a child told his therapist that
he would kill himself if he continued to be forced to visit
— even under supervision — with the father who had sexually abused him and had threatened to kill his mother.
The boy's law guardian had spoken with him only once
and took no action even to seek out the facts, much less
to protect the child.** In fact, he worked closely with the attorney
for the father to make sure that no unfavorable orders were issued
against the father.

*Erickson, Nancy S. (2007, February). Confusion on the Role of Law Guardians.
The Matrimonial Commission's Report and the Need for Change. New York
Family Law Monthly vol. 8 (no. 6), 1-2.*

Problems specific to the fact-finding of child sexual abuse alleged
between divorcing or divorced parents are discussed. Fahn argues
that the legal system's mechanisms for protecting children from
intrafamilial sexual abuse are inadequate. Contrary to the popular assumption that accusers have nothing to lose by raising false
allegations, a mother who fails to meet a stringent standard of
proof faces the risk of losing custody. There is often a judicial bias
against the accusing mother and child. The courts may character-
ize the mother as overprotective, vindictive, or uncooperative and
therefore, transfer custody to the father.

*Fahn, Meredith S. (1991). Allegations of Child Sexual Abuse in Custody Disputes:
Getting to the Truth of the Matter, 25 Family Law Quarterly 193.*

The ACE Study & Test

www.cdc.gov/ace/findings.htm
The CDC's Adverse Childhood Experiences Study (ACE
Study) uncovered a stunning link between childhood trauma and
the chronic diseases people develop as adults, as well as social
and emotional problems. This includes heart disease, lung cancer,

diabetes and many autoimmune diseases, as well as depression, violence, being a victim of violence, and suicide. You can take the test below.

Prior to your 18th birthday:

1. Did a parent or other adult in the household often or very often... Swear at you, insult you, put you down, or humiliate you? or Act in a way that made you afraid that you might be physically hurt?
   If Yes, enter 1

2. Did a parent or other adult in the household often or very often... Push, grab, slap, or throw something at you? or Ever hit you so hard that you had marks or were injured?
   If Yes, enter 1

3. Did an adult or person at least 5 years older than you ever... Touch or fondle you or have you touch their body in a sexual way? or Attempt or have oral, anal, or vaginal inter-course with you?
   If Yes, enter 1

4. Did you often or very often feel that ... No one in your family loved you or thought you were important or special? or Your family didn't look out for each other, feel close to each other, or support each other?
   If Yes, enter 1

5. Did you often or very often feel that ... You didn't have enough to eat, had to wear dirty clothes, and had no one to protect you? or Your parents were too drunk or high to take care of you or take you to the doctor if you needed it?
   If Yes, enter 1

6. Were your parents ever separated or divorced?
   If Yes, enter 1

7. Was your mother or stepmother:
   Often or very often pushed, grabbed, slapped, or had

something thrown at her? or Sometimes, often, or very often kicked, bitten, hit with a fist, or hit with something hard? or Ever repeatedly hit over at least a few minutes or threatened with a gun or knife?
If Yes, enter 1

8. Did you live with anyone who was a problem drinker or alcoholic, or who used street drugs?
If Yes, enter 1

9. Was a household member depressed or mentally ill, or did a household member attempt suicide?
If Yes, enter 1

10. Did a household member go to prison?
If Yes, enter 1

Now add up your "Yes" answers: ____ This is your ACE Score

As your ACE score increases, so does the risk of disease, social and emotional problems. With an ACE score of 4 or more, things start getting serious. The likelihood of chronic pulmonary lung disease increases 390 percent; hepatitis, 240 percent; depression 460 percent; suicide, 1,220 percent.

CPSIA information can be obtained
at www.ICGtesting.com
Printed in the USA
FFHW020840100919
54844252-60555FF